Chemical and Biological Weapons

International Humanitarian Law Series

VOLUME 76

The International Humanitarian Law Series is a series of monographs and edited volumes which aims to promote scholarly analysis and discussion of both the theory and practice of the international legal regulation of armed conflict.

The series explores substantive issues of International Humanitarian Law, including:

- Protection for victims of armed conflict and regulation of the means and method of warfare
- Questions of application of the various legal regimes for the conduct of armed conflict
- Issues relating to the implementation of International Humanitarian Law obligations
- National and international approaches to the enforcement of the law and
- The interactions between International Humanitarian Law and other related areas of international law such as Human Rights, Refugee Law, Arms Control and Disarmament Law, and International Criminal Law.

The titles published in this series are listed at *brill.com/ihul*

Chemical and Biological Weapons

The Interconnectivity of Norms

Edited by

Barry de Vries

BRILL | NIJHOFF

LEIDEN | BOSTON

Cover illustration: PJR10 – 20030316 – Camp Hammersmith, Kuwait: United Kingdom Army soldiers with the 33 Royal Engineer Regiment Joint Task Force EOD Group talk to each other wearing highly protective chemical suits 16 March 2003 during a EOD demonstration at Camp Hammersmith. The experts on land mines, submunitions, chemicals, and other hazards demonstrated how they would deal with any such hazards encountered in the Kuwaiti or Iraqi desert. EPA photo AFPI/Paul J. Richards.

This work was supported by the German Federal Ministry of Education and Research (Grant Number 01UG2202A).

The Library of Congress Cataloging-in-Publication Data is available online at https://catalog.loc.gov
LC record available at https://lccn.loc.gov/2025035528

Typeface for the Latin, Greek, and Cyrillic scripts: "Brill". See and download: brill.com/brill-typeface.

ISSN 1389-6776
ISBN 978-90-04-73918-5 (hardback)
ISBN 978-90-04-73919-2 (e-book)
DOI 10.1163/9789004739192

Contents

Notes on Contributors

Csilla Bertha
is an IP counsel at a pharma company, EGIS Plc, and a Ph.D. candidate at the Faculty of International Law Eötvös Loránd University, Budapest. Her academic research focuses on the challenges facing the Chemical Weapons Convention.

Kristoffer Burck
is a Ph.D. candidate of international law in the CBWNet project at Justus-Liebig-University Giessen and associate fellow at PRIF. His research focusses on arms control, specifically chemical and biological weapons, at the intersection of law and international relations.

Glenn A. Cross
is the founder of Crossbow Analytics LLC, a firm specializing in analysis of WMD issues. Since the early 1990s, he worked on chemical- and biological-weapons issues for several US government agencies. From September 2008 to October 2010, he was the deputy national intelligence officer for WMD responsible for biological-weapons issues on the director of national intelligence's National Intelligence Council. He is the author of *Dirty War: Rhodesia and Chemical Biological Warfare, 1975–1980* (2017) and several peer-reviewed book chapters and articles in academic journals.

Craig Eggett
is an assistant professor of International Law at Maastricht University. He holds a Ph.D. and LL.M. from Maastricht University and an LL.B. from Durham University. Craig teaches and researches on public international law and international criminal law.

Elisabeth Hoffberger-Pippan
is a senior researcher at the Peace Research Institute Frankfurt (PRIF), specializing in international law, especially humanitarian and human rights law, as well as arms control and emerging military technologies. Her work focuses on compliance with norms against chemical and biological weapons and the implications of artificial intelligence in warfare.

Alexander Kelle
is senior researcher at the Institute for Peace Research and Security Policy at the University of Hamburg (IFSH). He coordinates CBWNet and is assigned to the IFSH Berlin Office. Previously, he was Senior Policy Officer in the Office of Strategy and Policy of the OPCW in The Hague (2013–2019). Prior to this he taught and conducted research at the universities of Bradford, Belfast, and Bath, UK. He received his Ph.D. in political science from J.W. Goethe University Frankfurt.

Robert Lawless
is an associate professor in the Department of Law and Philosophy at the United States Military Academy, West Point. He is also Research Director of the Lieber Institute for Law and Warfare and editor for *Articles of War*, the Lieber Institute's LOAC publication forum.

Detlef Mannig
has been an industrial chemist for more than thirty years in multiple functions in Germany, the USA, and China. Having graduated from Bonn University, Yale University, and Munich University, he has been involved in CWC and BTCW issues for also more than 30 years, including functions at chemical industry associations as well as with OPCW. He is author of around 125 publications and presentations (see www.mannig-consulting.com). For his engagement, he received the German Federal Cross of Merit.

Thilo Marauhn
is professor of Public Law and International Law at Justus Liebig University Giessen, Head of the International Law Research Group at PRIF, and Extraordinary Professor of International Arms Control Law at the University of Amsterdam, affiliated with the Asser Institute.

Sarah Thin
is an assistant professor of International Law at Radboud University Nijmegen. She holds a Ph.D. from Maastricht University, an LL.M. from the University of Nottingham, and an LL.B. from Durham University.

Ralf Trapp
is a consultant on chemical and biological weapons arms control, providing services, amongst others, to the UN, the OPCW and the EU. He participated in the negotiations of the Chemical Weapons Convention and the setting-up of the OPCW.

Barry de Vries
is a postdoctoral research fellow at the Justus-Liebig University Giessen, specializing in public international law and arms control law. He holds a Ph.D. from Justus-Liebig University Giessen, an LL.M. from the Free University Brussel and an M.Sc., LL.M. and LL.B. from the Free University Amsterdam.

CHAPTER 1

Multi-normativity and Multi-level Governance: Fresh Perspectives on the Strengthening of Norms against Chemical and Biological Weapons

Thilo Marauhn

The entry into force of multilateral treaties is not the end but the beginning, at most an intermediate step, of complex international normative processes. More precisely: the entry into force of the Chemical Weapons Convention (CWC)[1] and the Biological Weapons Convention (BWC)[2] is not the culminating but the starting point of CBW arms control.[3] This is not to say that the drafting of such treaties does not pose challenges; indeed, the negotiating process leading to the adoption, signature, ratification and entry into force of the CWC is a telling example of the intricacies of multilateral treaty-making.[4] However, once a treaty has entered into force it must be put into operation, which basically means to ensure national and international implementation. Such "making treaties work"[5] often is a major challenge, and the path towards successful operation of a multilateral agreement is full of pitfalls. National implementation confronts the national legislature, and, as a rule, requires more than just the incorporation, adoption or transformation of the treaty into national law.[6] Giving effect to international obligations at the

1 Convention on the Prohibition of the Development, Production, Stockpiling and Use of Chemical Weapons and on their Destruction of 13 January 1993, 1974 UNTS 45, entered into force 29 April 1997.

2 Convention on the Prohibition of the Development, Production and Stockpiling of Bacteriological (Biological) and Toxin Weapons and on Their Destruction of 10 April 1972, 1015 UNTS 163, entered into force 26 March 1975.

3 Thilo Marauhn, 'Dispute resolution, compliance control and enforcement of international arms control law' in Geir Ulfstein, Andreas Zimmermann and Thilo Marauhn (eds), *Making treaties work: human rights, environment and arms control* (Cambridge 2007), 243–244.

4 Thomas Bernauer, *The projected chemical weapons convention: a guide to the negotiations in the conference on disarmament* (New York 1990), UN Doc UNIDIR/90/7.

5 See the title of the edited volume referred to in note 3.

6 See, generally, David L Sloss, 'Domestic Application of Treaties' in Duncan B Hollis (ed), *The Oxford Guide to Treaties* (New York and Oxford 2nd ed 2020), 355–382.

 | DOI:10.1163/9789004739192_002

national level often requires particular implementing legislation, the adoption of administrative procedures, and the setting-up of executive bodies or agencies at the national level.[7] In Europe, at least as far as the European Union (EU) (operating on the basis of the principle of conferral)[8] and its members states are concerned,[9] this is even more challenging, as we have to bear in mind a complex system of power sharing, with exclusive, shared, and supporting competences,[10] not to forget special competences, among others in the field of the EU's common foreign and security policy.[11]

These introductory remarks are not meant to unfold all the ensuing complexities. Rather, I would like to focus on the conceptual approach to these complexities. My introduction, hence, is an invitation to draw on the established notion of multi-level governance,[12] and to elaborate a bit on the more recent, but very insightful, notion of multi-normativity.[13] Both concepts are helpful in that they do not simply take note of the inherent complexities of multilaterally regulating common concerns of humankind, but that they allow the sharpening of distinctions between various levels of governance and various expressions of normativity without blurring the lines and without ignoring the linkages and entry-points between them. This introduction mirrors the

7 On the National Authority required according to Article VII, para. 4, CWC: Michael Bothe, 'National implementation of the CWC: some legal considerations' in Michael Bothe, Natalino Ronzitti and Alan Rosas (eds), *The New Chemical Weapons Convention: Implementation and Prospects* (The Hague et al 1998), 543, at 552–553 and 556–557; Lisa Tabassi and Anand Dhavle, 'Article VII: National Implementation Measures' in Walter Krutzsch, Eric PJ Myjer and Ralf Trapp (eds), *The Chemical Weapons Convention. A Commentary* (Oxford 2014), 195, at 208–209.

8 Marise Cremona, 'The principle of conferral and express and implied external competences' in Eleftheria Neframi and Mauro Gatti (eds), *Constitutional issues of EU external relations law* (Baden-Baden 2018), 29–62.

9 For an early analysis of the EU's role in implementing the CWC, see Thilo Marauhn, 'Implementing the Chemical Weapons Convention in the EU context' in Bothe, Ronzitti and Rosas, *supra* note 7, 569–590.

10 Articles 2–6 Treaty on the Functioning of the European Union, OJ C 326 (26 October 2012), 47–390.

11 For an interesting perspective see Ramses A Wessel, 'The European Union and international arms control: Assessing legal competences and instruments' in Eric PJ Myjer and Thilo Marauhn (eds), *Research Handbook on International Arms Control Law* (Cheltenham 2022), 89–104.

12 On the notion of multi-level governance in Europe, see, among others, Fritz W Scharpf, 'Notes Toward a Theory of Multilevel Governing Europe' (2001) 24 Scandinavian Political Studies, 1.

13 Thomas Duve, 'Was ist 'Multinormativität'? – Einführende Bemerkungen' [What is ›Multinormativity‹? – Introductory Remarks] 2017 (25) Rechtsgeschichte / Legal History (Journal of the Max Planck Institute for European Legal History), 88.

concern of the work packages assigned to our team at Justus Liebig University in the context of the CBW Network,[14] funded by the German Federal Ministry of Education and Research, and aiming at a comprehensive reinforcement of norms against chemical and biological weapons. Our work packages include both of the above notions, and try to pay tribute to their interrelationship, likewise.

As explained above, the implementation of the CWC and the BWC include complex normative processes. The starting point – at least from the perspective of international law – are the two treaties. Making the CWC and the BWC work requires a complex interplay between international law, regional (including European) law,[15] and national law (in federal states including subnational law), but also with non-legal norms of different origin and of different quality. The object and purpose of such interplay is not a careful analysis of what states parties are required to do, but it is the ambition to ensure effective and meaningful implementation, i.e. an optimum result. Hence, this goes beyond a doctrinal approach in international law, which normally focuses on what must be done, not necessarily on what is the best way to make treaties work.

As multi-level governance systems have long been discussed by international law and international relations scholars, it seems useful to primarily take a look at the more innovative side of this dual approach, namely multinormativity.

Originally, the notion of multi-normativity was developed by colleagues from legal history.[16] The Max Planck Institute for Legal History and Legal Theory[17] has not only pushed the concept but also contributed to a lively dis-

14 <https://cbwnet.org>.

15 Harald Müller, Alexis Below and Simone Wisotzki, 'Beyond the State: Nongovernmental Organizations, the European Union, and the United Nations' in Harald Müller and Carmen Wunderlich (eds), *Norm dynamics in multilateral arms control: interests, conflicts, and justice* (Athens, Georgia 2013), 296, at 309–316.

16 Miloš Vec, 'Multinormativität in der Rechtsgeschichte', (2009) Berlin-Brandenburgische Akademie der Wissenschaften (vormals Preußische Akademie der Wissenschaften). Jahrbuch 2008, 155–166. Duve, *supra* note 13; and Thomas Duve, 'What is global legal history?' (2020) 8 Comparative Legal History 73–115, in particular 111–113. For a more recent application in the context of the prohibition of the use of force, see 'The Multinormative Nineteenth Century on the Legitimacy of War' (Foreword) in Hendrik Simon, A Century of Anarchy? War, Normativity, and the Birth of Modern International Order (Oxford 2024), xi–xiv.

17 See the Department led by Thomas Duve at <https://www.lhlt.mpg.de/3573648/research_department_II>.

course about the notion of multi-normativity. Researchers addressed historical regimes of normativity and carefully analyzed the various expressions[18] of normativity. The starting point is recognition of the fact that rules and norms (in a much broader sense),[19] have different origins. They emerge from different sources of legitimacy.[20] These different sources of legitimacy have to be put into a relationship to each other in order to understand their impact on individuals and society. This is, in other words, part of the question this volume focuses upon: the interconnectivity of norms. But what do these different sources of legitimacy mean?

In the Westphalian system[21] rules originate within the state. The ability of states to adopt rules is what lawyers call the jurisdiction of states[22] – in particular prescriptive but also enforcement jurisdiction. While "ability" is central for jurisdiction, "legitimacy" is likewise crucial for such jurisdiction. As much as "legitimacy" must be distinguished from "legality",[23] legitimacy is important

18 These can, among others, be understood as practices, see Thorsten Keiser, Prozesse vor dem Reichskammergericht als Praktiken in der frühen Neuzeit. Schriftenreihe der Gesellschaft für Reichskammergerichtsforschung, Vol. 48, (Wetzlar 2020).

19 I am referring to a broad understanding of norms as it is applied, among others, by norm research in international relations. For an early approach see Ethan A Nadelmann, 'Global prohibition regimes: The evolution of norms in international society' (1990) 44 International Organization 479–526. For more recent debates see Nicole Deitelhoff and Lisbeth Zimmermann, 'Norms under Challenge: Unpacking the Dynamics of Norm Robustness' (2019) 4 Journal of Global Security Studies 2–17.

20 Apart from popular legitimacy or popular sovereignty (for a critical review of Jürgen Habermas see George Duke, 'Habermas, Popular Sovereignty, and the Legitimacy of Law' (2024) 35 Law and Critique 237–256), we may consider religious legitimacy (see, among others, Stefan Hammer, 'Religion Impacting the Concept of Law' (2021) 7 Interdisciplinary Journal for Religion and Transformation in Contemporary Society 3–12), traditional legitimacy, indigenous legitimacy (this is often linked to the notion of legal pluralism, see Brian Z Tamanaha, 'Understanding Legal Pluralism: Past to Present, Local to Global' (2008) 30 Sidney Law Review 375–411), procedural and / or substantive legitimacy. With enlightenment, popular legitimacy has become central (still worthwhile reading Paschalis Kitromilides, 'Enlightenment and Legitimacy' in Athanasios Moulakis (ed), *Legitimacy / Légitimité* (Berlin 1985), 60–66).

21 Rainer Grote, 'Westphalian System' (last updated June 2006) in Anne Peters (ed), *The Max Planck Encyclopedia of Public International Law* (Oxford) <www.mpepil.com> (accessed 29 November 2024).

22 Bernard H Oxman 'Jurisdiction of States' (last updated November 2007) in Anne Peters (ed), *The Max Planck Encyclopedia of Public International Law* (Oxford) <www.mpepil.com> (accessed 29 November 2024).

23 Thilo Marauhn, 'The International Rule of Law in Light of Legitimacy Claims' in Heike Krieger, Georg Nolte and Andreas Zimmermann (eds), *The International Rule of Law: Rise or Decline?* (Oxford 2019), 277, at 281–282.

for understanding norms. A distinction must be made between the legitimacy of the entity (institutional legitimacy) and the legitimacy of the procedure (procedural legitimacy).[24] In so far as this introduction talks about the legitimacy of the state to set norms, it is the legitimacy of the entity, not the legitimacy of the procedure, that is referred to. In a democracy, the requirements for the legitimacy of norm-setting are far more elaborate[25] – and they are primarily part of the procedure: it is about how the people as the sovereign can set norms (but this focuses more on the internal than on the external dimension of legitimacy). In the Westphalian system, the main question is whether the state (however it may be organized internally) has the legitimacy to set rules. At this point, ability and legitimacy are closely interrelated.

State-authored norms, hence, enjoy (external) legitimacy that can be derived from the state as such. It is noteworthy, here, to pay tribute to distinctions between the Anglo-Saxon / Anglo-American terminology, which will rather focus on the government than on the state, and the Central European (civil law) terminology, which refers to the "nation state" rather than to the government. This should, however, not detract our attention from the fact, that state-authored norms enjoy a distinct degree of legitimacy, largely leading to the notion of "rules" and "law". Today, such legitimacy of state-authored rules – irrespective of whether we can truly speak of a political democracy[26] and of a rule of law-based state[27] – is mostly derived from a constitution, which provides for formal and substantive rules on law-making. At the international level, in the absence of a formally labelled constitutional instrument, similar frameworks can be relied upon, mirrored, among others, in the law of treaties – whether itself treaty-based or customary law-based.[28] The United

24 For a pretty exciting constitutional perspective see John R Hibbing and Elizabeth Theiss-Morse, 'Process Preferences and American Politics: What the People Want Government to Be' (2001) 95 The American Political Science Review 145–153.

25 As an interesting academic-based practical guide, see OSCE, *ODIHR Brief: Guiding Principles of Democratic Lawmaking and Better Laws* (2023), available at <https://www.osce.org/files/f/documents/c/a/552682.pdf> (accessed 29 November 2024).

26 Cf Thilo Marauhn, 'The United Nations and political democracy' in Michael Bäuerle, Philipp Dann and Astrid Wallrabenstein (eds), *Demokratie-Perspektiven: Festschrift für Brun-Otto Bryde zum 70. Geburtstag* (Tübingen 2013), 659–673.

27 Naiade El-Khoury and Rüdiger Wolfrum, 'Rule of Law' (last updated April 2021) in Rainer Grote, Frauke Lachenmann and Rüdiger Wolfrum (eds), *The Max Planck Encyclopedia of Comparative Constitutional Law* (Oxford) <https://oxcon.ouplaw.com/home/mpeccol> (accessed 29 November 2024).

28 Malgosia Fitzmaurice, 'Treaties' (last updated February 2021) in Anne Peters (ed), *The Max Planck Encyclopedia of Public International Law* (Oxford) <www.mpepil.com> (accessed 29 November 2024).

Nations (UN),[29] the Organization for the Prohibition of Chemical Weapons (OPCW),[30] and the BWC regime (albeit institutionally much weaker)[31] are based upon such an understanding of rules.

Treaty law against chemical and biological weapons is based on this Westphalian-style legitimacy. This is embedded in the state, in public law, in public international law, in governance by states. Indeed, the international legal system as it stands today is largely characterized by state structures. The simple formula that states are the primary authors, the primary addressees, and the primary guardians of international law[32] – as traditional as this perspective may be – mirrors the predominant role of states, and the predominant role of (nation) state-authored law.

To return to the work of legal historians on multi-normativity: the Westphalian system with its focus on states is the result of a development whose pre-history is of interest to us. International relations existed long before the 16th and 17th centuries, but their legal structure was not state-centric as today's world. Indeed, the normative framing vested in traditional norms, and in traditional, often religious communities. The very existence of natural law, of customs, of traditions, its religious, metaphysical foundations, not just in Europe, but across many different cultural and geographical environments points to a different source of legitimacy. Norms, rules, entities were not attached to statehood but rather to religious communities and metaphysical reasoning. Multi-normativity, as a concept, comes into play when norms originating from different sources of legitimacy are applicable in parallel, in other words, when the facts trigger the application of religious, communal, and state norms at the same time. Today, however, religious norms and communal or

29 Jochen A Frowein, 'United Nations (UN)' (last updated March 2023) in Anne Peters (ed), *The Max Planck Encyclopedia of Public International Law* (Oxford) <www.mpepil.com> (accessed 29 November 2024).

30 Treasa Dunworth, 'Towards a culture of legality in international organizations: the case of the OPCW' (2008) 5 International organizations law review 119–139. Treasa Dunworth, 'The Organisation for the Prohibition of Chemical Weapons (OPCW)' in Eric PJ Myjer and Thilo Marauhn, *supra* note 11, 530–543.

31 Dominika Švarc, 'Biological Weapons and Warfare' (last updated August 2015) in Anne Peters (ed), *The Max Planck Encyclopedia of Public International Law* (Oxford) <www.mpepil.com> (accessed 29 November 2024), see in particular margin note 17 on the 'Implementation Support Unit'.

32 Cf Thilo Marauhn, 'The State' in Lavanya Rajamani and Jacqueline Peel (eds), *The Oxford Handbook of International Environmental Law* (Oxford 2nd ed 2021), 613, at 614 and 618–622.

indigenous norms do no longer enjoy the same degree of relevance as they used to in the past.[33]

This does not necessarily mean that we escape conflicts between norms originating from different sources of legitimacy. Only the sources of legitimacy have changed, and the question of sources has become intertwined with the form of such norms: legally binding state-authored rules exist in parallel to legally non-binding state-authored or state-approved norms,[34] and in parallel to industry norms, professional norms, ethical standards deriving their legitimacy from academia, and many more. It is not surprising that, against this background, norm research is no longer the exclusive domain of lawyers and theologians. Indeed, there is a growing branch of norm research in international relations, in political science.[35] Taking all this together, there is a broader context of norm research than if we look at it from a strictly speaking legal perspective. In particular, the latter international relations context is very important because it matches to a certain level, research which has been done at the level of legal theory before. International law has long discussed the notion of non-binding norms, of soft law.[36] Thus, there is an overlap; there is space for interdisciplinary work. Addressing the prohibition of chemical and biological weapons, we will have to distinguish between different types of norms: legally binding rules, ethical and moral norms, professional and technical standards, industry norms – this is the bunch of flowers, the bouquet, we will have to look at.

Taking up soft law first, this has become a fairly big topic in international law. The question here has always been how to embed legally non-binding norms into the framework of formally binding legal norms. The primary challenge continues to be the way in which non-binding norms nevertheless influence existing binding rules. This includes a broad range of legally non-binding resolutions by international organizations, but also a variety of technical standards adopted by international organizations or expert bodies. In particu-

33 For an interesting perspective on religion and international law see Reut Y Paz, 'Religion, Secularism, and International Law' in Anne Orford and Florian Hoffman (eds), *The Oxford Handbook of the Theory of International Law* (Oxford 2016), 923–938.

34 Cf Michael Bothe, 'Legal and Non-Legal Norms. A Meaningful Distinction in International Relations' in Thilo Marauhn and Barry de Vries (eds), *Legal Restraints on the Use of Military Force. Collected Essays by Michael Bothe* (Leiden 2021), 15–48.

35 See references *supra* note 19.

36 Cf Daniel Thürer, 'Soft Law' (last updated March 2009) in Anne Peters (ed), *The Max Planck Encyclopedia of Public International Law* (Oxford) <www.mpepil.com> (accessed 29 November 2024).

lar, the ensuing challenges have been taken up in international environmental law,[37] in international economic law,[38] in international health law,[39] and in some other branches. All this, however, has never or hardly ever been discussed from the perspective of multi-normativity because it was largely limited to the question of social or political norms, politically binding norms, and their relationship to legally binding norms.

Our research wants to go beyond this. We want to address the question on how not only social norms or politically binding norms interconnect with legally binding norms, but we want to move into the sphere of industry, into the sphere of ethics, into the sphere of technical standards. This is pretty important because an increasing number of behavior-governing norms emerge out of a different source of legitimacy than the formal rules which apply to the law-making process.

For the purpose of illustration, it seems useful to look a bit more closely at different branches of the law: In the field of international environmental law, increasingly reference is made to standards which were developed either at the national or at the international level. The most prominent example to this end is the International Standardization Organization (ISO),[40] which develops technical standards, and which has moved beyond technicalities and today also addresses governance standards.[41] It is noteworthy that there is more than a formal difference between technical standards ensuring the quality of certain products, detailing production processes, and standards that refer to the notion of good governance. Another interesting interface arises between international environmental law and international economic law. The Agreement on Technical Barriers to Trade,[42] operative within the World

37 Alan Boyle, 'Soft Law' in Lavanya Rajamani and Jacqueline Peel, *supra* note 32, 420–435.

38 For an established, one might say, traditional approach, see already Ignaz Seidl-Hohenveldern, 'International economic "soft law"' (1979) 163 Recueil des cours / Académie de Droit International de La Haye 169–246.

39 Cf Pedro A Villarreal, 'Public international law and human health. Bridging conceptual gaps through governance' (2019) 61.2018 German Yearbook of International Law 45–71.

40 Gerald G Sander, 'International Organization for Standardization (ISO)' (last updated April 2016) in Anne Peters (ed), *The Max Planck Encyclopedia of Public International Law* (Oxford) <www.mpepil.com> (accessed 29 November 2024).

41 ISO 37000:2021 Governance of organizations – Guidance, available at <https://committee.iso.org/ISO_37000_Governance> (accessed 29 November 2024).

42 Agreement on Technical Barriers to Trade of 12 April 1979, 1186 UNTS 276, entered into force 1 January 1980.

Trade Organization,[43] again draw upon norms that have been developed outside the trade-specific expertise, and takes on board health standards or product standards. The source of legitimacy here is different from the source of legitimacy of traditional international law (which would be the agreement between nation states). Rather it originates in the particular expertise of those who are drafting the rules, i.e. professional bodies or expert bodies.[44]

The interesting question (relating to the interconnectivity of norms) always is: where is the entry point for technical, moral, and ethical standards to move into the realm of international law? Looking at the implementation of certain rules, as for example the rules included in the so-called Paris Agreement[45], it is noteworthy that this treaty focus on a particular objective, with very limited content as to how to achieve the objective. The pathway to achieve the objectives of the Paris Agreement, indeed, is left open to some extent. This means that states will have to look at legally non-binding standards, at ethical and moral standards, to implement the treaty in good faith.[46] Interpretation of legally binding rules,[47] hence, is one of the established entry points for other types of norms, norms originating in sources of legitimacy beyond international law, irrespective of whether these are technical, ethical or moral standards. Here, we can build upon the doctrinal and practical insights gained in the context of making soft law operational.

The interconnectivity of such norms is at the heart of this volume. Interconnectivity serves to achieve a common objective. To again refer to international environmental law, the overall objective of the Paris Agreement is to slow down climate change, primarily by limitation, but also by adaptation strategies.[48] It is the common objective, which is laid down in the treaty, and

---

43 Peter-Tobias Stoll, 'World Trade Organization (WTO)' (last updated October 2014) in Anne Peters (ed), *The Max Planck Encyclopedia of Public International Law* (Oxford) <www.mpepil.com> (accessed 29 November 2024).

44 In the context of international environmental law see Sam Johnston, 'The Role of Science' in Lavanya Rajamani and Jacqueline Peel, *supra* note 32, 249–266 and Peter M Haas, 'Epistemic Communities' in Lavanya Rajamani and Jacqueline Peel, *supra* note 32, 698–715.

45 Paris Agreement of 12 December 2015, UN Doc FCCC/CP/2015/10/Add.1, 21, entered into force 4 November 2016.

46 Markus Kotzur, 'Good Faith (Bona fide)' (last updated January 2009) in Anne Peters (ed), *The Max Planck Encyclopedia of Public International Law* (Oxford) <www.mpepil.com> (accessed 29 November 2024).

47 See, in particular, Article 31 of the Vienna Convention on the Law of Treaties (of 23 May 1969, 1155 UNTS 331, entered into force 27 January 1980).

48 Elizabeth C Black, 'Climate change adaptation. Local solutions for a global problem' (2009/10) 22 Georgetown international environmental law review 359–382.

the path to achieving such objective is best developed with the help of additional norms, arising from other sources of legitimacy, but being integrated into the regime by way of interpretation and application.

Looking once again at the insights from legal history, and at the use of multi-normativity by legal historians, one of the primary fields in which they have particularly addressed such multi-normativity is administration, is governance. It could be perceived as governance below the level of law-making, hence, the application of the law. In the process of applying the law the question arose whether or not beyond formal rules, like statutory obligations, there are informal norms which governmental authorities or courts would apply. In legal history these informal norms have been labelled practices.[49] Taking it from here, there is another interrelation between law and social science, more specifically, international relations: this is the analysis of practices at the international level.[50] Traditionally, international law has focused on practices (or rather "practice") in the context of the formation of customary international law, the constitutive elements of which are state practice and *opinio iuris*. This, however, only is a limited perspective as it focuses on the formation or the making of law rather than the application and implementation of the law. This is what needs to be looked at more closely: the impact of practice(s) on "making treaties work". Indeed, this is another aspect of the interconnectivity of norms in the context of implementing international law.

Having sketched out some of the theoretical underpinnings of this volume, including for our work packages "multi-normativity" and "multi-level governance", I would like to finally exemplify this as a starter for the following chapters with regard to biological and chemical weapons.

As to the CW regime, it is beyond question and beyond doubt that we have several levels of or layers of governance. Member states of the European Union, in so far, may serve as a meaningful example as there are more than just two levels: the international, the regional (the EU), the national, and – sometimes even – the sub-national. While the EU largely focuses on law-making, from the perspective of international law, from the perspective of the CWC, this is the application of treaty law and its implementation. Taking Article VII CWC,[51] which requires national implementation of the Convention, as an example, this is indicative of a recognition of multi-level governance: rules at the international, and rules at the national level. Within the EU,

49 See *supra* note 18.

50 Christian Bueger and Frank Gadinger, 'The Play of International Practice' (2015) 59 International Studies Quarterly 449–460.

51 See Lisa Tabassi and Anand Dhavle, *supra* note 7.

appropriate legislation is added at the supranational level. Furthermore, in many federal states, beyond national rules, there are sub-national rules. In the United States, there are rules which originate in state legislature, in Switzerland, in Germany, in Austria, this is similar. Hence, this amounts to at least four different levels of governance in this context.

But there is more to it: as indicated above, the application of the CWC requires more than just substantive or procedural rules. It requires an institutional setting. This institutional setting arises from Article VIII CWC by establishing the OPCW.[52] Institutional settings, likewise, occur at the European, at the national and at the sub-national level.[53] This is – one might say so – traditional public law-based or international law-based multi-level governance.

Moving a step further, there is an important aspect which, in the past, has not so much been addressed from the perspective of (international) law: the role of private actors, in particular of industry norms. We are very grateful in our CBWNet for pertinent research on this conducted by *Ralf Trapp*. Industry has played a major role in the drafting and negotiating process leading to the adoption of the CWC. Now, industry again plays an important role in the implementation of the CWC, importantly after completion of the CW destruction process. Industry does not only provide normative elements to this but it can also be perceived as an additional institutional layer for the implementation of the CWC, thereby also providing for a distinct source of legitimacy. While, obviously, the OPCW, national legislation and institutions, sub-national legislation, and the European Union – all these originate in state legitimacy (public legitimacy), private actors, industry, are rooted in a different kind of legitimacy: professional or business-based legitimacy.

As a [illegible] it is worthwhile in this context to look at so-called industry- and business-driven compliance procedures[54] (not to be confused with non-compliance procedures or compliance control mechanisms at the international level),[55] a set of norms which industry has developed in parallel or alongside state-authored rules (in particular in respect of good governance). Thus, there are distinct performance norms and ethical standards which have

52 See Walter Krutzsch and Treasa Dunworth, 'Article VIII: The Organization' in Walter Krutzsch, Eric PJ Myjer and Ralf Trapp, supra note 7, at 235–296.

53 See *supra* note 7.

54 On corporate compliance see Anna HLP Donovan, *Reconceptualising Corporate Compliance. Responsibility, Freedom and the Law* (Oxford 2020).

55 See already André Nollkaemper, 'Compliance control in international environmental law – traversing the limits of the national legal order' (2002) 13 Yearbook of international environmental law 165–186.

to be applied by people working for a particular industry, and if individuals fail to comply with these rules they may be sanctioned within the more or less closed framework of their respective business. This is different from, but often in parallel to state rules; sometimes, it conflicts with state rules. Hence, there is another aspect that should be better understood in the context of applying norms against chemical and biological weapons.

In the context of the BWC, there is no institutional setting of the same quality and intensity as in the context of the CW regime. It may even be argued that the OPCW provides for a unique setting, which is absent in the BW regime. Therefore, and even more, it is important to analyze the extent to which other actors (beyond the state) fill in this gap and become active in order to enhance the application of the BWC. Unfortunately, the number of individuals and organizations with such a particular expertise is fairly limited. Nevertheless, efforts should be made to invest some time and resources here, and to do more research in this field.

By way of conclusion, I would like to highlight the three perspectives, which I believe are important to better address the interconnectivity of norms against chemical and biological weapons:

The first perspective addresses the source of legitimacy as part of our multi-normativity analysis: Who are the actors actually setting rules, norms, or standards? Who established the rules of the game? Who established the normative framework?

The second perspective is at the other end of the spectrum, namely at the level of the addressees: How do the different addressees (and we have to include non-state actors, including business, here) understand the interconnectivity of norms? How can they ensure that they comply with the various levels and with the various categories of norms? How do they interpret these norms? Is there a common framework for understanding and applying these norms?

Finally, it is important to critically reflect upon the institutional setting. In the context of the OPCW this will become ever more important now as the organization is moving from the period of eliminating existing CW stocks and CW production facilities to the "new" period of the CWC, namely of preventing the renewed production, rise or abuse of chemical substances for chemical weapons purposes. In this context, the institutional framework must go beyond traditional settings of governmental authorities and civil servants; it must include other actors, other institutions, including again non-state actors. This entails an analysis of multi-normativity and multi-level governance which actually is crucial to make the norms against chemical and biological weapons a success.

CHAPTER 2

Normative Interaction in Chemical and Biological Weapons Law

On the Interplay between Treaty Regimes and General International Law

Craig Eggett and Sarah Thin

1 Introduction

The international legal framework for the regulation of chemical and biological weapons (CBW) is normatively heterogeneous. While two widely ratified treaties – the Chemical Weapons Convention[1] (CWC) and the Biological and Toxin Weapons Convention[2] (BWC) – are central to this regime, they do not exist in isolation. Instead, they form part of a complex set of rules and principles emanating from a number of sources and systems, including specific regimes of international law and domestic legal systems. The international law regulating CBW is dynamic, involving significant interactions between its constituent norms and the potential revision of their content. For example, international rules may result in the creation of national rules, treaties are subject to interpretation and revision, and different treaty regimes interact with one another. Of particular interest for both the field of CBW and international law theory more generally is the interplay between treaty law and 'general international law'. The central aim of this paper is to explore the points of interaction in the relationship between treaties and general international law, taking the regimes of the BWC and CWC as examples.

The term 'general international law' has a range of possible meanings,[3] including referring to all norms of general application (including some treat-

1 Convention on the Prohibition of the Development, Production, Stockpiling and Use of Chemical Weapons and on their Destruction (concluded 3 September 1992, entered into force 29 April 1997) 1975 UNTS 45 (hereinafter Chemical Weapons Convention; CWC).

2 Convention on the Prohibition of the Development, Production and Stockpiling of Bacteriological (Biological) and Toxin Weapons and on their Destruction (concluded 10 April 1972, entered into force 26 March 1975) 105 UNTS 163 (hereinafter Biological and Toxin Weapons Convention; BTWC).

3 For a range of views on the meaning of "general international law" see Grigory Tunkin, "Is General International Law Customary International Law Only?" (1993) 4 *European Journal of International Law* 534; Christian Tomuschat, "General International Law: A New Source of

 | DOI:10.1163/9789004739192_003

ies) or as shorthand for customary international law.[4] In this paper, the term is used to refer to non-treaty norms of (typically)[5] general application. This includes customary international law and general principles of law in the sense of Article 38(1)(c) ICJ Statute,[6] as well as principles in the broader sense.[7] This paper focuses on the specific interplay between the CWC and the BWC, on the one hand, and general international law, on the other. The objective is to offer some conceptual insights into the dynamics at play, with a view to contributing to broader theoretical debates in international law.

2 The Operation of the CWC and BWC against the Backdrop of General International Law

The CWC and BWC, like all other treaties, are part of the broader system of international law. As Judge Greenwood explained in the *Diallo* case, "[i]nternational law is not a series of fragmented specialised and self-contained bodies of law, each of which functions in isolation from the others; it is a single, unified system of law."[8] The unity of international law is now widely accepted and, although questions about the interaction between different fields of law remain, it is clear that the discipline has moved on from the fixation on fragmentation.[9] While international law has not been fragmented into distinct and isolated regimes of law, there are significant variations in the normative

International Law?" in Riccardo Pisillo Mazzeschi and Pasquale De Sena, *Global Justice, Human Rights and the Modernization of International Law* (Cham: Springer, 2018).

4 International Law Association, Statement of Principles Applicable to the Formation of General Customary International Law (2000) London Conference of the Committee on the Formation of Customary Law.

5 Bearing in mind the scope for regional or bilateral customary international law, as identified by the International Court of Justice in the *Asylum* (*Colombia v Peru*) (Judgment) [1950] ICJ Rep 266; *Right of Passage over Indian Territory* (*Portugal v India*) (Merits) [1960] ICJ Rep 6.

6 Statute of the International Court of Justice, 18 April 1946, 33 UNTS 993 (hereinafter ICJ Statute) Article 38.

7 For more on this distinction, see Craig Eggett, "The Role of Principles and General Principles in the 'Constitutional Processes' of International Law" (2019) 66(2) *Netherlands International Law Review* 197; Craig Eggett, *General Principles as Systematic Elements of International Law* (2021) PhD Thesis, Maastricht University, Chapter III.

8 Declaration of Judge Greenwood, *Case Concerning Ahmadou Sadio Diallo* (*Republic of Guinea v Democratic Republic of the Congo*) (Compensation) Judgment [2012] ICJ Rep 324 [8].

9 See, for example, Mads Tønnesson Andenæs and Eirik Bjorge, *A Farewell to Fragmentation: Reassertion and Convergence in International Law* (Cambridge: CUP, 2015).

and institutional structures of the different fields of international law. In particular, treaties may have different degrees of comprehensiveness or different institutional structures. Take, for example, the stark institutional differences between the CWC and BWC regimes. The CWC is administered by the Organisation for the Prohibition of Chemical Weapons (OPCW), consisting of the Conference of States Parties (CSP), the Executive Council, and the Technical Secretariat. Broadly speaking, these organs oversee the implementation of the treaty, verify compliance with its norms, monitor the destruction of chemical weapons, investigate alleged uses of such weapons, and play a role in capacity building measures.[10]

The institutional structure of the BWC regime is less sophisticated. Much of the monitoring and development of the regime is done by convening Review Conferences and formal consultative meetings.[11] In addition, the Sixth Review Conference established the Implementation Support Unit (ISU) within the United Nations Office for Disarmament Affairs,[12] which provides assistance to national implementation efforts and confidence-building measures. Nevertheless, it has been argued that there is work to be done in relation to verification and compliance in the BWC regime.[13]

In the language of the fragmentation debate, treaty regimes with higher degrees of institutional sophistication would have been described as 'self-contained' or 'special' regimes.[14] More precisely, though, this term refers to regimes that establish "a special set of secondary rules claims priority over the secondary rules in the general law of [s]tate responsibility."[15] This definition is a reflection of Article 55 of the International Law Commission's

10 See, generally, Article VIII CWC.

11 Article XII BTWC envisaged an initial review conference five years after the entry into force of the BTWC, yet this practice has continued, with the Ninth Review Conference taking place in 2022. Article V BTWC is the basis for formal consultative meetings, with procedures for such Meetings adopted in the Second and Third Review Conferences of 1986 and 1991, respectively.

12 *Final Document of the Sixth Review Conference of the States Parties to the Convention on the Prohibition of the Development, Production and Stockpiling of Bacteriological (Biological) and Toxin Weapons and on Their Destruction* (Geneva, 20 November - 8 December 2006), UN Doc BWC/CONF.VI/6, [36].

13 Kristoffer Burck, Sannimari Veini, and Barry de Vries, "The Legal Effect of the BWC Review Conferences" (2022) *CBWNet Working Paper* No. 2, 10.

14 International Law Commission, Conclusions of the work of the Study Group on the Fragmentation of International Law: Difficulties arising from the Diversification and Expansion of International Law, UN Doc. A/61/10 (2006) [123]–[194].

15 Ibid., [124].

Articles on the Responsibility of States for Internationally Wrongful Acts (ARSIWA),[16] which states:

> These articles do not apply where and to the extent that the conditions for the existence of an internationally wrongful act or the content or implementation of the international responsibility of a state are governed by special rules of international law.

Of course, it is a core feature of treaties that they establish a set of rules that typically apply only between their parties,[17] and so it understandable to consider the conclusion of a treaty as a way for states to contract out of the norms of general international law that would otherwise be applicable. Indeed, the CWC and BWC establish a comprehensive set of norms that differ from those that apply in general international law and, in the case of the CWC, there are elaborate procedures to monitor implementation and ensure compliance that go beyond what exists in general international law. However, the situation is far more complex as norms of general international law continue to play a role in the operation of these treaties. This section considers the influence of general international law on the CWC and BWC by examining the general secondary rules that are at play. This is done in two main parts: (A) a sketch of the position of secondary rules of the law of treaties and the law of state responsibility in relation to the CBW treaties and (B) a more focused examination of the question of interpretation of the CWC and BWC in light of general international law.

2.1 *Secondary Rules: The Law of State Responsibility and the Law of Treaties*

In international law, the term 'secondary rule' is used primarily in the context of the law of state responsibility and, as such, it is sometimes overlooked that there are different kinds of secondary rules that perform different functions in the international legal system.[18] While primary rules are those that

---

16 International Law Commission, Articles on Responsibility of States for Internationally Wrongful Acts (2001) 2 *Yearbook of the International Law Commission* 26 (hereinafter ARSIWA).

17 Vienna Convention on the Law of Treaties (adopted 23 May 1969, entered into force 27 January 1980) 1155 UNTS 331, 8 ILM 679 (hereinafter VCLT 1969) Article 34.

18 See, generally, Herbert Lionel Adolphus Hart and Leslie Green, *The Concept of Law* (Oxford: OUP, 3rd edn., 2012) Chapter V. For a discussion in the context of international law, see Eggett (2021) (n 7) 49–64.

create rights and obligations,[19] secondary rules regulate the operation of these primary rules. On the Hartian understanding of these categories, it is the presence of such secondary rules and the unity of primary and secondary rules that is constitutive of a legal system.[20] In addition to providing the framework for the invocation of responsibility, secondary rules govern the creation, termination, modification, and interpretation of other rules. While individual treaty regimes may indeed establish some special rules to perform these functions, many secondary rules form part of general international law as basic building blocks of the international legal system. The presence of such generally applicable secondary rules is a central component of the unity of international law.[21]

The two main areas of general international law that are most relevant in this regard are the law of treaties and the law of state responsibility. The general law of state responsibility is part of customary international law, but is widely considered to be reflected in the ARSIWA.[22] The determination of breaches of the CWC is largely within the purview of the OPCW, yet there are key rules of state responsibility that still play a role in the application of the obligations contained in the core CBW treaties. As a first example, pursuant to Article 48(1)(a) all States Parties to theses treaties will be able to invoke the responsibility of a violating state on the basis of the notion of obligations *erga omnes partes*.[23] This allows for states that are not directly injured by an internationally wrongful act to invoke responsibility if the obligation violated is owed to a group of states – as is the case in a treaty – and is "established for the protection of a collective interest" of that group of states.[24] The require-

19 Hart (n 18) Chapter v; Ulf Linderfalk, "State Responsibility and the Primary-Secondary Rules Terminology – The Role of Language for an Understanding of the International Legal System" (2009) 78 *Nordic Journal of International Law* 53, 59.

20 Hart (n 18) Chapter 5. See also Chapter x, where Hart made the observation that the lack of sufficient secondary rules led to the conclusion that international law could not be considered a legal system.

21 See, for example, Bruno Simma, and Dirk Pulkowski, "Of Planets and the Universe: Self-contained Regimes in International Law" (2006) 17 *European Journal of International Law*, 483.

22 *Application of the Convention on the Prevention and Punishment of the Crime of Genocide* (*Bosnia and Herzegovina v Serbia and Montenegro*) (Judgment) [2007] ICJ Rep 43 [401].

23 For an overview of standing as an injured state in the context of non-proliferation treaties more generally, see Matthew Happold, "The 'Injured State' in the Case of Breach of a Non-Proliferation Treaty and the Legal Consequences of such a Breach" in Daniel H Joyner and Marco Roscini, *Non-Proliferation law as a Special Regime* (Cambridge: CUP, 2012) 175–190.

24 Article 48(1)(a) ARSIWA.

ment of protecting a common interest will be fulfilled when an obligation aims to "transcend the sphere of bilateral relations of the States parties",[25] and to "foster a common interest, over and above any interests of the States concerned individually".[26] Attempts to establish "general standards of protection for a group or people" could be indicative of actions in the common interest.[27] It would seem clear that the core CBW treaties would contain such obligations, as disarmament regimes are indeed established for such purposes.

A second example of the relevance of the law of state responsibility to the CWC and BWC is the regime applicable to violations of *jus cogens* norms. Under Part Two, Chapter III of the ARSIWA, "serious breaches" of *jus cogens* norms give rise to additional consequences for other states. These include obligations to cooperate to bring about an end to such violations, not to recognise them as lawful, and not to render assistance so as to maintain the unlawful situation.[28] If any of the rules on CBWs are *jus cogens*, then these additional consequences would take effect in cases of their violation. The recent work of the ILC on this topic has greatly contributed to the debate on the nature and potential of the concept of *jus cogens* in the modern international legal system.[29] The final entry in the ILC's "non-exhaustive list of peremptory norms of general international law (*jus cogens*)" is "the basic rules of international humanitarian law".[30] There is some practice to suggest that certain core rules of the law of armed conflict could reach the level of *jus cogens*. This much was suggested by the ICJ in the *Nuclear Weapons Advisory Opinion*, where it referred to the basic rules of humanitarian law as "intransgressible".[31] As the Court did not expressly rule on the existence of *jus cogens* norms, it is not possible to precisely demarcate which

---

25 ILC, ARSIWA with commentaries (2001) *Yearbook of the International Law Commission* Vol. II Part 2, 126.

26 Ibid; *SS Wimbledon* (*United Kingdom, France, Italy, and Japan v Germany*) (Judgment) [1923] PCIJ Ser A, No 1, 23. For further discussion on the definition of such common interests, see Sarah Thin, 'In Search of Community: Towards a Definition of Community Interest' in Gentian Zyberi (ed) *Protecting Community Interests through International Law* (Intersentia 2021).

27 ARSIWA commentaries (n 25), 127.

28 Article 41(1) and (2) ARSIWA.

29 For an overview, see the ILC's Analytical Guide: <https://legal.un.org/Ilc/guide/1_14.shtml> (last accessed 15 February 2024).

30 ILC, Fourth Report on Peremptory Norms of General International Law (*jus cogens*) Seventy-First Session, 29 April–7 June and 8 July–9 August 2019, A/CN.4/727 [116]–[127], [137].

31 *Legality of the Threat or Use of Nuclear Weapons* (*Advisory Opinion*) [1996] ICJ Rep 226 [79].

parts of humanitarian law may qualify for such status. Other courts and tribunals have attempted to shed more light on this question. For example, the Trial Chamber in *Kupreškić* concluded that rules "prohibiting war crimes ... are also peremptory norms of international law or jus cogens, i.e., of a non-derogable and overriding character".[32] There are also decisions of domestic courts that have recognised that the prohibition of war crimes is of a *jus cogens* character.[33] The use of "microbial or other biological agents, or toxins" has recently been added to the Rome Statute as a war crime.[34] Further, the use of such weapons may fall within the scope of other war crimes, such as those related to "poison or poisonous weapons"[35] or prohibit the use of weapons that "are of a nature to cause superfluous injury or unnecessary suffering or which are inherently indiscriminate".[36] If this is the case,[37] the general rules of state responsibility would take effect when there are violations of these rules.

The general international law of treaties is largely contained in the Vienna Convention on the Law of Treaties (VCLT) 1969, which is broadly considered to be reflective of customary law. The VCLT 1969 contains all the basic rules for the creation,[38] interpretation,[39] and termination[40] of treaties. Some of the provisions of the core CBW treaties depart from the general rules of the law of treaties in a significant way, as is the case with all treaties, albeit in different ways. For example, both Article XVI CWC and Article XIII BWC impose more stringent requirements for withdrawal of a State Party than are set out in the

32 See, for example, *Prosecutor v Kupreškić* et al. (Judgment) IT-95-16-T (14 January 2000) [520].

33 *Arancibia Clavel, Enrique Lautaro s/ Homicidio Calificado y Asociación Ilícita y Otros*, Case No. 259, Judgment, Supreme Court of Arg[illegible] *Product Liability Litigation*, Judgment, District Court of the United States, Easter District of New York, 28 March 2005.

34 See Assembly of State Parties to the Rome Statute of the International Criminal Court, Resolution ICC-ASP/16/Res.4, which amends the Rome Statute so as to insert this prohibition into Article 8(2)(b)(xxvii) and (e)(xvi).

35 Rome Statute of the International Criminal Court (adopted 17 July 1998, entered into force 1 July 2002) 2187 UNTS 3 (hereinafter Rome Statute) Articles 8(2)(b)(xvii) and 8(2)(e)(xiii).

36 Articles 8(2)(b)(xx) Rome Statute.

37 As evidence of this, see also Amendment to Article 8 of the Rome Statute of the International Criminal Court (Weapons which use microbial or other biological agents, or toxins) (concluded 14 December 2017, entered into force 2 April 2020) C.N.116.2018. TREATIES-XVIII.10.

38 Articles 6–18 VCLT 1969.

39 Articles 31 and 32 VCLT 1969.

40 Articles 54–62 VCLT 1969.

VCLT 1969,[41] referring to the need to explain a decision that "extraordinary events, related to the subject matter of the Convention, have jeopardised the supreme interests of [the] country".[42]

Nevertheless, the general law of treaties remains important for the operation of the CWC and BWC. For example, theoretical debates on the identification and function of 'object and purpose' remain relevant.[43] Uncertainties remain as to how the object and purpose of a treaty is to be identified, as well as how the object and purpose of a treaty is to be used in different contexts of the law of treaties. A particularly complex issue arises in relation to treaties with multiple objects and purposes,[44] and how to reconcile this with the operationalisation of 'object and purpose' in different contexts. As will be discussed below, this is central to the question of treaty interpretation. It is also relevant when considering reservations. While Article XXII CWC prohibits the reservations to the articles of the Convention themselves, it permits reservations to the Annexes to the Convention, provided that such reservations are not incompatible with the object and purpose of the CWC.[45] There are currently twenty-one 'declarations and reservations' to the CWC.[46] In order to assess the impact of these statements, it would be necessary first to consider the general law of treaties. An initial question is whether the statements made constitute reservations or mere declarations of interpretation. According to the VCLT 1969, the definition of a reservation is:

---

41 Article 24 (1) VCLT 1969.

42 Article XVI CWC and Article XIII BTWC.

43 See, for example, Isabelle Buffard and Karl Zemanek, "The 'Object and Purpose' of a Treaty: An Enigma?" (1998) 3 *Austrian Review of International and European Law* 311; David S Jonas and Thomas N Saunders, "The Object and Purpose of a Treaty: Three Interpretive Method" (2010) 43(3) *Vanderbilt Journal of Transnational Law* 565, 578 et seq.; Dino Kritsiotis, "The Object and Purpose of a Treaty's Object and Purpose", in Micheal J Bowman and Dino Kristiotis (eds) *Conceptual and Contextual Perspectives on the Modern Law of Treaties* (Cambridge: CUP, 2018).

44 That a treaty can have multiple objects and purposes has been recognised by the Appellate Body of the World Trade Organisation in *United States – Import Prohibition of Certain Shrimp and Shrimp Products* WT/DS58/AB/R 12 October 1998 [17]. See, also, O Dörr "Article 31: General Rule of Interpretation" in Oliver Dörr and Kirsten Schmalenbach (eds), *Vienna Convention on the Law of Treaties: A Commentary* (London: Springer, 2018), 585.

45 This object and purpose test is also part of the general law of treaties, as reflected in Article 19(c) VCLT 1969.

46 See the overview included in the database of the United Nations Treaty Collection: <https://treaties.un.org/pages/ViewDetails.aspx?src=TREATY&mtdsg_no=XXVI-3&chapter=26> (last accessed 17 February 2024).

> a unilateral statement, however phrased or named, made by a State, when signing, ratifying, accepting, approving or acceding to a treaty, whereby it purports to exclude or to modify the legal effect of certain provisions of the treaty in their application to that State.[47]

If a statement does fall within the definition, then it would not be permitted under Article XXII CWC if it relates to the Convention articles and not the Annexes. If, however, the statement relates to the Annexes, it would then be necessary to assess whether the modifications or exclusions sought by the reserving state are contrary to the object(s) and purpose(s) of the CWC. If the statements do not fall within the definition, they will simply be considered as interpretative declarations. Another issue that arises is that many of the most elaborate declarations to the CWC refer to the objects and purposes of the Convention.[48] Even from the texts of these declarations, it is clear that there is acknowledgement of multiple objects and purposes of the CWC,[49] most notably the "complete prohibition and thorough destruction of all chemical weapons and their production facilities"[50] and the "promot[ion] [of] free trade in chemicals as well as international cooperation and exchange of scientific and technical information in the field of chemical activities for purposes not prohibited under the Convention in order to enhance the economic and technological development of all States Parties."[51] The references to "activities for purposes not prohibited under this Convention" seems to preclude any scope for conflict between prohibition efforts and the promotion of free trade in chemicals, yet it is possible that these objects and purposes could be interpreted so as to achieve contrary results.

The subject matter of the preceding paragraphs represents only a snapshot of some of the potential interactions between secondary rules of general international law and the treaty regimes in focus in this article. The application and operation of chemical and biological weapons law takes place within these broader constellations, and not in a vacuum. The following section looks in more detail at a particular aspect of this interaction, namely the interpretation of chemical and biological weapons law and the role played by the general international law of treaty interpretation.

47 Article 2(1)(d) VCLT 1969.

48 See the declarations of China, Cuba, Iran, Pakistan, and Sudan, UNTC database (n 45).

49 These references to objects and purposes reflect what is included in the Preamble to the CWC.

50 See, for example, the declarations of China and Pakistan (n 45).

51 See, for example, the declaration of Cuba and Iran (n 45).

2.2 *Interpreting CBW Treaties*

The question of interpretation is a central part of the general law of treaties. The rules contained in Articles 31 and 32 VCLT 1969 are widely considered to be customary law and have been recognised as the starting point of interpretation in a range of contexts.[52] That the VCLT serves as the basis for the interpretation of the CWC has also been acknowledged by the OPCW's Technical Secretariat in the context of a discussion on the meaning of the word 'transfer' in Article I(1)(a) CWC.[53] Reference here was made both to the basic rule to interpret "in good faith in accordance with the ordinary meaning to be given to the terms of the treaty in their context and in the light of its object and purpose",[54] in addition to the scope to refer to the *travaux préparatoires* of the treaty.[55] Further rules and techniques of interpretation include reference to subsequent agreements and subsequent practices by the parties, as well as reference to any relevant rules of international law.[56] Subsequent agreement and subsequent practice are of particular relevance in relation to the core CBW treaties given the prominent roles played by the Conference of State Parties in the CWC and Review Conferences in the BWC. For example, in the context of the interpretation of Article I BWC it has been suggested that the control lists of biological dual-use technologies and biological agents and toxins provided by the Australia Group could amount to subsequent agreement or practice of states within the meaning of Article 31(3) VCLT 1969.[57] Given the fact that the Australia Group constitutes just a part of the parties to the CWC, there may not be complete agreement of all parties on the content of such lists, but it is sound that the efforts of states to flesh out the rules of the BWC in this way be used to indicate the interpretation of treaty provisions. It has also been suggested that reference to the preparatory works under Article 32 VCLT

---

52 *Application of the Convention on the Prevention and Punishment of the Crime of Genocide* (*Bosnia and Herzegovina v Serbia and Montenegro*) (Judgment) [2007] ICJ Rep 43, [109]–[110]; *Restrictions on Imports of Tuna- United States*, GATT Dispute Settlement Panel Report (1994) 33 ILM 839, 892; *Arbitral Award of 31 July 1989* (*Guinea-Bissau v Senegal*) [1991] ICJ Rep 53 [70]. See, also, Gleider Hernández, *International Law*, (Oxford: OUP, 2nd edn) 196; James Crawford, *Brownlie's Principles of Public International Law* (Cambridge: CUP, 9th edn), 366.

53 OPCW, Note by the Technical Secretariat, "Conference on 'The Chemical Weapons Convention in 2017: What are the Boundaries to its Future Evolution?' " (2017) S/1562/2017 [9].

54 Article 31(1) VCLT 1969.

55 Article 32 VCLT 1969.

56 Article 31(3) VCLT 1969.

57 Daniel Joyner, *International Law and the Proliferation of Weapons of Mass Destruction* (Oxford: OUP, 2009), 92.

1969 could also serve to clarify which agents would be prohibited under Article I(1) BWC.[58]

The rule providing for systemic integration is also of relevance when considering the relationship between treaties and general international law. This rule, as reflected in Article 31(3)(c) VCLT 1969 provides that interpreters are under an obligation to "take into account any relevant rules of international law applicable in the relations between the parties". This rule serves to facilitate coherence in the international legal system by requiring interpreters to consider the meaning ascribed to terms in other international rules.[59] It simultaneously provides a tool by which external rules of international law may be used as interpretive guidance when applying a particular treaty. Article 31 (3)(c) VCLT 1969 operates alongside and in parallel to the general rule of interpretation in Article 31(1) VCLT 1969 and it will therefore not always be necessary for an interpreter to look to such external rules. Nonetheless, it could be particularly useful in the context of the CWC and BWC. McLachlan identifies three situations in which such recourse would be "consistent with the overall approach adopted by the Vienna Convention":[60] (a) where a treaty contains terms which carry an "evolving meaning"; (b) where the treaty itself reflects a commitment by the parties to progressive development; (c) or where obligations are described in general terms, allowing their interpretation to take account of changing circumstances.[61] It is arguably in the very nature of the CWC and BWC as disarmament treaties that they would fall into category (b). As regards the nature of the terms themselves, consider for example the definition of chemical weapons and toxic chemicals in Article II (1) and (2) of the CWC, or the material scope of the BWC as set out in Article I. These are clearly categories that were intended to be adaptable and adaptive in relation to prevailing circumstances, particularly the modern state of technology. They would therefore appear to fall under category (a) as terms with an "evolving meaning", and may also be open textured enough to fit within category (c). Systemic integration via the rule in Article 31(3)(c) VCLT 1969 could therefore

58 Bakhtiyar Tuzmukhamedov, "Convention on the Prohibition of the Development, Production and Stockpiling of Bacteriological (Biological) and Toxin Weapons and on their Destruction" *UN Audiovisual Library of International Law Historic Archives*: <https://legal.un.org/avl/ha/cpdpsbbtwd/cpdpsbbtwd.html> (last accessed 18 February 2024).

59 Campbell McLachlan, "The Principle of Systemic Integration and Article 31(3)(c) of the Vienna Convention" (2005) 54(2) *International and Comparative Law Quarterly* 279, 279; P Merkouris, *Article 31(3)(c) VCLT and the Principle of Systemic Integration: Normative Shadows in Plato's Cave* (Leiden: Brill/Nijhoff, 2015), 2.

60 McLachlan (Ibid), 317.

61 Ibid.

play an important role in shedding light on such terms, for example, by providing a mechanism through which to take into account current standards within international humanitarian law,[62] international environmental law,[63] or international human rights law,[64] to name only some potentially relevant areas.

The rule on systemic integration is closely related to the idea that underlying principles may serve in the interpretation of treaty law. In this case, instead of considering other rules to which the parties have agreed, the interpreter may consider the broader underlying principles that the rule in question seeks to further. The principles will provide reasons in favour of a particular interpretation and it is for the interpreter to assess their relative weight or importance in a given case.[65] For example, the principle of sovereignty may play a role in interpreting a rule relating to CBW.[66] In declarations made when acceding to the CWC, China and Pakistan made explicit references to sovereignty in relation to their interpretations of the Convention's verification procedures.[67] Similar references have been made by states during Conferences of States Parties when interpreting their obligations under the CWC.[68] Of course, the invocation of a principle in such a manner does not definitively influence the interpretation of the rule in question and the interpreter may decide to assign greater weight to another principle, such as the principle of humanity.[69]

---

62 See notably *Oil Platforms (Islamic Republic of Iran v. United States of America), Judgment* [2003] ICJ Reports 161, [41], where the ICJ acknowledged the relevance of international humanitarian law and rules relating to the use of force in the context of interpreting a treaty of friendship between the two parties.

63 International environmental standards have played a particularly interesting role in the interpretation of international trade and investment law. See, e.g., WTO, *Import Prohibition of certain Shrimp and Shrimp Products – Report of the Appellate Body* (12 October 1998) WT/DS58/AB/R [158].

64 E.g. in the interpretation of "permanent harm to humans" in CWC Article II (2).

65 Ronald Dworkin, *Taking Rights Seriously* (Harvard: Harvard University Press, 1977) 43; R Alexy, *A Theory of Constitutional Rights* (Oxford: OUP, 2002), 446.

66 See, for example, James D Fry, "Sovereign Equality under the Chemical Weapons Convention: Doughnuts over Holes" (2010) 15(1) *Journal of Conflict and Security Law* 45; Note by Technical Secretariat 2017 (n 52) [11].

67 United Nations Treaty Collection Database (n 45).

68 Note by the Technical Secretariat 2017 (n 52) [11].

69 This potential role of the principle of humanity is well-known in humanitarian law more generally. See, MN Schmitt, "Military Necessity and Humanity in International Humanitarian Law: Preserving the Delicate Balance" (2010) 50(4) *Virginia Journal of International Law*, 795.

3 The Influence of CBW Treaties in the Development of Customary International Law

This part of the paper turns attention to the other side of the interaction between CBW treaties and general international law: the influence of the CWC and BWC on the development of customary international law rules. In order to focus the discussion, this paper considers only the potential impact on the development of custom and not of other norms of general international law, such as general principles of law in the sense of Article 38(1)(c) ICJ Statute. As such, and before turning to the different modes of influence exerted by the CWC and BWC on customary law, it is first necessary to sketch the nature of custom and some of the theoretical questions that persist in relation to this source. Following this, we will consider three examples of the normative influence of the CWC and BWC on customary international law: the development of identical customary rules, the expansion of the material scope of treaty rules via custom, and the expansion of the personal scope of treaty rules via custom.

3.1 *Conceptualising the Identification of Customary International Law*

The basic test, as set out in the ICJ Statute, is that the existence of a customary rule is evidenced by "general practice accepted as law".[70] As has been elaborated upon in the case law of the ICJ, this test comprises two core elements: the practice of states and a belief that this practice is required by law (*opinio juris*). The content of these twin elements has most famously been elaborated upon by the ICJ in its *North Sea Continental Shelf* cases.[71] In this case, the Court referred to "settled practice",[72] explaining that such practice must be "extensive and virtually uniform", taking into account the practice of states "whose interests are specially affected".[73] The Court has also consistently reaffirmed the subjective requirement of *opinio juris*,[74] rejecting the idea that custom is merely the generalised practice of states.[75] As explained in *North Sea Contin-*

70 Article 38(1)(b) ICJ Statute.

71 *North Sea Continental Shelf Cases* (*Germany v Denmark; Germany v Netherlands*) (Judgment) [1969] ICJ Rep 3.

72 Ibid., [77].

73 Ibid., [74].

74 See, for example, *Continental Shelf* (*Libyan Arab Jamahiriya v Malta*) (Judgment) [1985] ICJ Rep 13 [19]; *Military and Paramilitary Activities In and Against Nicaragua* (*Nicaragua v United States of America*) (Merits) [1986] ICJ Rep 14 [97].

75 Paul Guggenheim, "Les deux éléments de a coutume internationale" in *Law technique et les principes de droit public: Etudes en l'honneur de Georges Scelle* (Paris: Librairie générale de droit et de jurisprudence, 1950) 275.

ental Shelf, state practice "must also be such, or be carried out in a way, as to be evidence of a belief that this practice is rendered obligatory by the existence of a rule of law requiring it".[76] Despite the enduring prominence of these dual criteria, it can be argued that there remains a significant degree of uncertainty surrounding the process of ascertaining customary international law. For example, some scholars contest the view that these elements are cumulative, instead suggesting that the presence of either significant state practice or *opinio juris* is sufficient.[77] Some would even suggest that the ICJ does not actually perform the test it expounds, instead merely asserting the existence of a customary rule without conducting the necessary investigation into practice and the views of states.[78] Indeed, it is clear that both practical and theoretical issues arise when obtaining and assessing evidence for the existence of state practice and *opinio juris*; determining the 'general' or 'virtually uniform' practice of nearly 200 states is a daunting task, as is discerning the clear motivations behind such practice. It is, therefore, understandable why the ILC took the decision to include the identification of customary law in its programme of work, adopting draft articles on the topic in 2018.[79] These commentaries provide far greater detail on the process of the ascertainment of customary rules and they once again confirm the need for state practice and *opinio juris*.[80]

In its recent decision in *Question of the Delimitation of the Continental Shelf* (*Nicaragua v Colombia*),[81] the ICJ cast doubt on the continued relevance of the twin elements of customary international law. In considering whether the submissions to the Commission on the Limits of the Continental Shelf (CLCS) were relevant for the identification of customary rules, the Court appears to blur the line between state practice and *opinio juris*. The Court

76 *North Sea Continental Shelf* (n 70) [77].

77 David Lefkowitz, "(Dis)solving the Chronological Paradox in Customary International Law: A Hartian Approach" (2008) 21 *Canadian Journal of Law and Jurisprudence* 129, 130; Frederice L Kirgis, "Custom on a Sliding Scale" (1987) 81 *American Journal of International Law* 146, 149.

78 Stefan Talmon, "Determining Customary International Law: The ICJ's Methodology between Induction, Deduction and Assertion" (2015) 26(2) *European Journal of International Law* 417; Hans Kelsen, *Principles of International Law* (New York: Rinehart & Company, Inc., 1952) 450–451.

79 ILC, Draft conclusions on identification of customary international law, with commentaries, *Yearbook of the International Law Commission*, 2018, vol. II, Part Two.

80 Ibid., Conclusion, 2.

81 *Question of the Delimitation of the Continental Shelf between Nicaragua and Colombia beyond 200 Nautical Miles from the Nicaraguan Coast* (*Nicaragua v Colombia*) [2023] ICJ Rep 1.

explained that submissions to the CLCS could be indicative of *opinio juris* "even if such practice may have been motivated in part by considerations other than a sense of legal obligation" and that this was particularly the case given the extent of the practice "over a long period of time".[82] It has been argued that this approach departs from the Court's established jurisprudence, including its *North Sea Continental Shelf* decision.[83] At the very least, it seems that this reasoning acknowledges the difficulties inherent in the identification of custom, accepting that one piece of evidence may be used to demonstrate both the existence of state practice and *opinio juris*.

Before turning to the examples of the influence of the CWC and BWC on custom, it is useful to reflect on the nature of this interaction more generally. There is a broadly held assumption in international law that widely ratified treaties give rise to corresponding rules in customary law. A similar approach has been taken by the ILC in its recent work on general principles of law, where it was explained that the ascertainment of a general principle may be grounded in the determination that a principle "is widely recognized in treaties and other international instruments".[84] At first sight, such arguments seem appealing: it is clear that norms in widely ratified treaties enjoy broad support among states. As such, the argument goes, there is sufficient support for the existence of an international norm of general application; a customary rule or general principle. Despite this basic appeal, it is important to consider the assumptions on which such an approach rests and the consequences of its acceptance. This position essentially equates support for a treaty with acceptance of a general international norm. This issue was identified by the Court in *North Sea Continental Shelf*. Here, the Court examined the practice surrounding the Geneva Convention 1958[85] and the impact of

82 Ibid., [77].

83 Hilde Woker, "Preliminary reflections on the ICJ Judgment in Question of the Delimitation of the Continental Shelf between Nicaragua and Colombia beyond 200 nautical miles from the Nicaraguan Coast (Nicaragua v. Colombia) of 13 July 2023" 21 July 2023, EJIL: Talk! <https://www.ejiltalk.org/preliminary-reflections-on-the-icj-judgment-in-question-of-the-delimitation-of-the-continental-shelf-between-nicaragua-and-colombia-beyond-200-nautical-miles-from-the-nicaraguan-coast-nicaragua-v-co/> (last accessed 19 February 2024).

84 ILC, Second Report on General Principles of Law, Seventy-Second Session 2020 (A/CN.4/741), Draft Conclusion 7(a).

85 Convention on the Continental Shelf (concluded 29 April 1958, entered into force on 10 June 1964) 499 UNTS, 311.

this on the creation of a customary equivalent of Article 6's rule on equidistance. The Court noted that:

> [...] over half the States concerned, whether acting unilaterally or conjointly, were or shortly became parties to the Geneva Convention, and were therefore presumably, so far as they were concerned, acting actually or potentially in the application of the Convention. From their action *no inference could legitimately be drawn as to the existence of a rule of customary international law* in favour of the equidistance principle.[86]

This passage recognises that the actions of states within the framework of treaties should not be assumed to be relevant for the determination of a customary international rule. The critical aspect here is that while such states would be motivated by a sense of legal obligation, that sense of legal obligation arises by virtue of their membership of the treaty and not from the belief that there exists a general rule of customary law. In such contexts, then, it may be more appropriate to consider whether non-parties are acting in a similar manner and have expressed motivations for such practice. The consequences of this position should also be considered. Accepting that a widely ratified treaty amounts to evidence of customary law would be an unlawful imposition of treaty rules on non-parties via general international law. This would run contrary to the basic idea of the *pacta tertiis* rule,[87] and raises questions about whether and to what extent non-parties to a treaty would be required to object to practice within a treaty regime so as to ensure that they were persistent objectors to any customary rules that would emanate from the treaty.

All this is not to say that rules found in widely accepted treaties cannot have (near) equivalents in general international law. Indeed, the parallel application of identical treaty and customary rules was explicitly recognised by the ICJ in the *Nicaragua* case[88] and there are numerous uncontroversial examples of multi-sourced equivalent norms in many areas of international law.[89] Yet, the precise dynamics of this interaction are unclear. It is to this issue that the remainder of the paper is dedicated.

---

86 *North Sea Continental Shelf* (n 70) [76] [emphasis added].

87 Article 34 VCLT 1969.

88 *Nicaragua* (n 73) [188].

89 Tomer Broude and Yuval Shany, (eds), *Multi-Sourced Equivalent Norms in International Law* (Oxford: Hart Publishing, 2011).

3.2 *Developing Identical Customary Rules: The Prohibition on the Use of Biological Weapons*

While the Geneva Protocol 1925 explicitly prohibits the use of biological weapons,[90] the text of the BWC contains no such phrasing. Nevertheless, it is uncontroversial that the BWC effectively does ban use, in addition to the other activities referred to in Article I. The Preamble to the BWC expresses commitment to the principles and objectives of the Geneva Protocol and the proposition that use is also banned by the BWC has been accepted by States Parties in Review Conferences.[91] Already in the Geneva Protocol, the Contracting Parties asserted that the prohibition on such weapons "shall be universally accepted as part of International Law",[92] and it indeed seems that this basic prohibition on the use of biological weapons has found its way into the general corpus of customary international law; the prohibition is absolute and unconditional, frequently described as the "taboo" that finds support in an array of normative structures.[93]

Rule 73 of the International Humanitarian Law Database, compiled by the International Committee of the Red Cross (ICRC), simply states: "the use of biological weapons is prohibited".[94] The commentary to this rule provides significant insight into the normative foundations of this customary rule and the prospective influence of treaty law in its development. This commentary begins with a reference to both the Geneva Protocol and the BWC, immediately referring to the "no first use" reservations that were made to the Geneva Protocol and the later practice of withdrawing such reservations.[95] While acknowledging that 20 such reservations remain, the ICRC explains that 18 of these were made by states who later became party to the BWC. Essentially, the argument goes, membership to the BWC precludes a possibility of retaliation with biological weapons due to the prohibition of possession in Article I (5). Noting that only two states have maintained their opposition to "no first use", the ICRC argues the "drive to eliminate biological weapons over the last

90 Protocol for the prohibition of the use in war of asphyxiating, poisonous or other gases, and of bacteriological methods of warfare (concluded 17 June 1925, entered into force 9 May 1926) 94 LNTS, 65.

91 See, for example, 'Final Document – Fourth BWC Review Conference 1996' (BWC/CONF. IV/9), part II, 15.

92 Geneva Protocol 1925 (n 89).

93 See Elisabeth Hoffberger-Pippan in Chapter 8 and Robert Lawless in Chapter 10 of this edited volume.

94 See ICRC International Humanitarian Law Databases, <https://ihl-databases.icrc.org/en/customary-ihl> (last accessed 20 February 2024).

95 There were initially 37 such reservations.

three decades that States believe that these weapons should not exist and therefore must not be used in any circumstances".[96] References are then made to state military manuals and submissions made to international courts as examples of state practice on the issue, with further support found in UN General Assembly Resolutions that reaffirm the basic principles of the BWC.[97] Finally, it is claimed that the assertions of this rule by the ICRC have not been objected to, even in situations involving non-parties to the BWC.[98]

In its elucidation of the international support for the existence of this basic prohibition as part of custom, it is clear that the ICRC sees the widespread support for the BWC and the Geneva Protocol relevant practice for customary law. Indeed, the consistent reiteration of the core rules of these treaties underscores the general practice and views of states, yet at first sight this may seem at odds with the position of the ICJ in *North Sea Continental Shelf* when it warned against using actions of treaty parties as evidence of customary law. However, the ICRC's position is more nuanced than this. The reference to the actions of international organisations and the specific reference to the practice of non-parties to the BWC demonstrate a clear attempt to identify broad support for a rule and not a simply equivocation of treaty support to state practice and *opinio juris*.

3.3 *Expanding the Material Scope of Rules: The Prohibition on the Use of Herbicides*

The prohibitions contained in Article 1 CWC do not extend to cover the use of chemical weapons against plants. The question of herbicides arose during the drafting of the CWC, with efforts made to include their regulation in the text of the treaty due to their use in the Vietnam War.[99] There was no agreement on this and so the CWC's only reference to herbicides is in its Preamble, which "[r]ecogniz[es] the prohibition, embodied in the pertinent agreements and relevant principles of international law, of the use of herbicides as a method of warfare."[100] This reference could suggest either that there is a specific norm prohibiting the use of herbicides as a method of warfare in general international law or that the use of chemical weapons in such a way would

96 ICRC International Humanitarian Law Databases (n 93) commentary to Rule 73.

97 See, e.g., UNGA Res 3256 (XXIX); Res. 32/77; Res 33/59 A.

98 Ibid., reference is made to ICRC, Memorandum on Respect for International Humanitarian Law in Angola.

99 Natalino Ronzitti, "Assessment of the 1993 Chemical Convention: Light and Shadow" in Giovanni Gasparini and Natalino Ronzitti, *The Tenth Anniversary of the CWC's Entry into Force: Achievement and Problems* (Rome: Quaderni IAI, 2007) 40.

100 CWC Preamble.

effectively fall within the scope of other "agreements and relevant principles of international law". The question arises as to whether customary international law could serve to effectively expand the material scope of the basic CWC prohibitions to include the use of herbicides. To explore this further, it is necessary to consider to which norms this preambular paragraph could refer, before considering whether there is a customary rule prohibiting the use of herbicides and, if so, whether the CWC has played a role in this norm's development.

The Convention on the Prohibition of Military or any other Hostile Use of Environmental Modification Techniques (ENMOD Convention)[101] and the rules of international humanitarian law provide the most prominent examples of relevant norms for the regulation of herbicides in international law. Article I ENMOD Convention contains a prohibition on engaging in "military or any other hostile use of environmental modification techniques having widespread, long-lasting, or severe effects as the means of destruction, damage or injury to any other State Party". Similarly, Additional Protocol I to the 1949 Geneva Conventions contains a prohibition on "methods or means of warfare which are intended, or may be expected, to cause widespread, long-term, and severe damage to the natural environment".[102] The need to protect the natural environment is further elaborated in Article 55 Additional Protocol I, which explains that attacks against the environment by way of reprisals are also prohibited.[103] In addition to these rules, the emergence of a specific human right to a healthy environment could also be of relevance to the regulation of herbicides, extending the prohibitions of their use beyond the context of conflict.[104] Even from this overview, there indeed seems to be a broader context of general international law regulating the use of herbicides. Whether or not there is a [illegible]

In 1969, the question of chemical and biological weapons use in relation to plants was discussed in the UN General Assembly and, while the resolution passed, the voting pattern of 80 affirmative votes, 36 objections, and 3 absten-

101 Convention on the Prohibition of Military or any other Hostile Use of Environmental Modification Techniques (concluded 10 December 1976, entered into force 5 October 1978) 1108 UNTS 151 (hereinafter ENMOD Convention).

102 Protocol Additional to the Geneva Conventions of 12 August 1949 and relating to the Protection of Victims of International Armed Conflicts (Additional Protocol I) (concluded 8 June 1977, entered into force 7 December 1978) 1125 UNTS 3, Article 35(3).

103 Article 55(2) Additional Protocol I.

104 See, for example, Human Rights Council Resolution 48/13 (2021); UNGA Resolution A/76/L.75 (2022).

tions suggests significant disagreement on the matter.[105] The United States has been persistent in its position that no treaty includes a ban on the use of herbicides, despite its formal renunciation of their use.[106] Further, while the ICRC's IHL Database does contain a rule on herbicides, its formulation as a conditional prohibition may suggest that the use of herbicides is covered by other agreements and norms of general international law, in the same way as the CWC's Preamble claims. Rule 76 of the ICRC's Database reads:

> The use of herbicides as a method of warfare is prohibited if they: a) are of a nature to be prohibited chemical weapons; b) are of a nature to be prohibited biological weapons; c) are aimed at vegetation that is not a military objective; d) would cause incidental loss of civilian life, injury to civilians, damage to civilian objects, or a combination thereof, which may be expected to be excessive in relation to the concrete and direct military advantage anticipated; or e) would cause widespread, long-term and severe damage to the natural environment.

The first two of these alternative conditions are covered by the general prohibitions of the CWC and BWC, while the remainder fall within the scope of international humanitarian law rules and the ENMOD Convention. That being said, the ICRC's commentary to Rule 97 begins with the claim that "[b]efore the adoption of the Chemical Weapons Convention, there was disagreement as to whether herbicides were prohibited under the Geneva Gas Protocol".[107] This wording suggests that the advent of the CWC has played a role in the development of international law on the question of herbicide use, despite the conscious decision to not include such a rule in the text of the treaty itself. This is, presumably, a nod to the formulation of the CWC's Preamble. Following its reference to the CWC, the ICRC commentary proceeds to discuss "developments in international law" that support the existence of a customary rule, noting discussions in the context of the ENMOD Convention about the use of herbicides.[108] The mention of the CWC and ENMOD Convention here signifies that the ICRC interprets the views and practice of states in relation to treaties as relevant for the ascertainment of customary law. At first sight, the approach of the ICRC seems in contrast with the position of the ICJ in *North Sea Continental Shelf*. However, it is possible to view the statements made here as evi-

---

105 UNGA Resolution 2603A (XXIV).

106 Ronzitti (n 98), 41.

107 ICRC International Humanitarian Law Databases (n 93) commentary to Rule, 76.

108 Ibid.

dence of support for general international law rules, despite the fact that they were made in the context of treaty regimes.

Whether or not there is a specific customary rule prohibiting the use of herbicides may have limited practical effect, as such use is clearly regulated by a number of other international rules. Yet, this example illustrates the normative density in the field of CBW, as well as the scope for interaction between such norms. The CWC's Preamble at least acknowledges these dynamics, but may also be viewed as a catalyst for the crystallisation of customary law on the matter.

3.4 *Expanding the Personal Scope of Rules: The Application of* CBW *Rules to Non-state Actors*

States are the primary addressees of treaties. As such, the rules contained in treaties, generally speaking, apply only to states.[109] In the context of CBW, the basic prohibitions contained in the CWC and BWC are directed only towards states. Yet, it is broadly accepted that the such prohibitions apply also to non-state actors more generally, particularly in the case of terrorism or organised armed groups in conflict situations. The CWC and BWC contain no reference to such groups, but the support enjoyed by the treaties and the consistent reaffirmation of their basic rules may be evidence of the development of parallel customary rules that bind non-state actors. This has the effect of enlarging the material scope of the basic prohibitions on CBW. Two basic trends are at play here: the influence of international humanitarian law and the impact of UN resolutions on the matter.

In its discussion of both chemical and biological weapons, the ICRC asserted that the prohibition on use extends to non-international armed conflicts.[110] Support for these [illegible] from the military manuals of states, domestic and international court cases, and the finding that "no official contrary practice was found".[111] A particularly prominent discussion of this was in the *Tadić* case, where the Appeals Chamber of the ICTY examined state practice on the matter and, referring also to the Geneva Protocol, found that "there undisputedly emerged a general consensus in the international community on the principle that the use of those weapons is also

109 States can, of course, explicitly grants rights and impose obligations on non-state actors. Examples include human rights treaties and investment treaties.

110 ICRC International Humanitarian Law Databases (n 93) commentary Rules 73 and 74.

111 ICRC International Humanitarian Law Databases (n 93) commentary Rule, 74.

prohibited in internal armed conflicts."[112] Such a position seems consonant with the basic idea that non-international armed conflicts, too, are governed by the basic principles of international humanitarian law and that the use of CBW inherently violates these principles. Similarly, and as referred to above, uses of CBW could also constitute international crimes and so entail individual responsibility.

Further, UN organs have tackled the issue of the possession and use of CBW by non-state actors. Most prominently, UN Security Council Resolution 1540 obliges states to refrain from supporting non-state actors in "developing, acquiring, manufacturing, possessing, transporting, transferring or using nuclear, chemical or biological weapons and their means of delivery" and to adopt national legislation prohibiting such activities.[113] This resolution also calls upon states to "renew and fulfil their commitment" to international agreements such as the CWC and BWC, recognising the relevance of treaty obligations to the objective of preventing CBWs from getting in the hands of non-state actors. While resolutions such as this recognise the threat posed by non-state actors, they continue to pose obligations on states to ensure such actors cannot obtain and use CBWs. Once again, it may be that the practical relevance of distinctions drawn here is rather limited; there are numerous rules regulating state behaviour towards non-state actors and CBWs, as well as the basic rules of humanitarian law and international criminal law prohibiting uses. Yet, there is clear recognition of the risks of CBW use by non-state actors, as demonstrated by a 2017 Decision of the OPCW Executive Council,[114] as well as the discussions surrounding the threat of bioterrorism.[115] Although the CWC and BWC do not deal with these issues head-on, the reaffirmation of their core principles and the role of other norms, in particular, the law of armed conflict, can play a role in developing general rules on the topic. The practice around the treaties can be indicative of views on the state of general international law and, in line with the general approach to treaties,[116] states do

112 *Prosecutor v Tadić* (Decision on the Motion for Interlocutory Appeal on Jurisdiction) Case No. IT-94-1-A (2 October 1995) [124].

113 UNSC Resolution 1540 (2004). See also Resolution 1672 (2006).

114 OPCW Decision EC-86/DEC.9 (13 October 2017).

115 See, for example, Alexander Kelle, *Prohibiting Chemical and Biological Weapons: Multilateral Regimes and Their Evolution* (Boulder: Lynne Rienner, 2014) 187–188, 205; James Revill and Malcom Dando, "The Rise of Biosecurity in International Arms Control" in Brain Rappert and Chandré Gould (eds), *Biosecurity. Origins, Transformations, and Practices* (London: Macmillan, 2009) 42–43.

116 See, generally, Erik Bjorge, *The Evolutionary Interpretation of Treaties* (Oxford: OUP, 2014).

not see the CWC and BWC as static instruments but as capable of dynamic and evolutive interpretation and application.

4 Concluding Remarks

The CWC and BWC are hugely significant treaties that form the core of a sophisticated regime regulating CBW. In the case of the CWC, the regime possesses a robust institutional framework to monitor the implementation of the treaty and to review its operation. Nevertheless, these treaties do not exist in a vacuum. They function as part of the international legal system, both influencing and being influenced by the structures and processes of general international law. These treaties provide excellent examples for studying these dynamics. It is clear that the general law of treaties and the rules on state responsibility continue to play a role in how the CWC and BWC are applied, with issues of interpretation highlighting the scope for interaction between an array of international norms. The flip side of this relationship further demonstrates the normative density and degrees of influence between the treaties and general international law. The high levels of support for the CWC and BWC have, in a variety of ways, influenced support for general customary norms on CBW. The treaties serve as a focal point for state practice and discussions on the status of international law on the topic, and there are significant points of interaction with other instruments and regimes, particularly international humanitarian law. These normative forces have the effect of expanding the scope of application of treaty rules via customary international law, and it seems that there is significant support for such effects even among non-parties.

Recognising and conceptualising the ways in which these normative networks intersect and influence each other is an essential part of consolidating international legal protections in this area. The lessons learned here also offer an opportunity for the enhancement of general international law theory on normative interaction, beyond CBW law. No human is an island, just as no treaty nor legal rule exists in isolation. Understanding these norms within the legal system, and their interaction with that system, is essential.

CHAPTER 3

Interconnectivity of CBW Regimes in Light of Recent Developments in Science and Technology

Csilla Bertha

1 Introduction

Scientific and technological development permeates the – peaceful and non-peaceful – uses of chemistry and biology, and, consequently, the Chemical Weapons Convention (the CWC)[1] and the Biological Weapons Convention (the BWC)[2] (the CWC and the BWC hereinafter together referred to as the Conventions). The Conventions set out the obligations of States Parties in connection with chemical and biological disarmament respectively and promote the use of science for peaceful purposes. This study wishes to assess the potential impacts of scientific and technological development on the international chemical and biological weapons (CBW) regimes that are becoming more and more interconnected, in consideration of the fact that the ever-current state of science and technology is closely interrelated with the scope and implementation of the Conventions.

First, the study explains some recent trends in science and technology, which are relevant for the interpretation of the Conventions. Then, the definitions of chemical and biological weapons are discussed demonstrating that the drafters in fact considered the need for the adaptability of the Conventions *vis-á-vis* future developments in science and technology.

The study also elaborates on institutional issues and on the question to what extent the institutions established by the CWC, namely the Organisation for the Prohibition of Chemical Weapons (OPCW), the Scientific Advisory Board (SAB) and verification mechanisms, can serve as an example for sup-

1 Convention on the Prohibition of the Development, Production, Stockpiling and Use of Chemical Weapons and on their Destruction. The CWC opened for signature on 13 January 1993 and entered into force on 29 April 1997.

2 Convention on the Prohibition of the Development, Production and Stockpiling of Bacteriological (Biological) and Toxin Weapons and on their Destruction. The BWC opened for signature on 10 April 1972 and entered into force on 26 March 1975.

 | DOI:10.1163/9789004739192_004

porting the BWC regime based on the fact that the core elements of the two Conventions are closely intertwined with the state of science and technology as a consequence of the material scope of the Conventions.

Science and technology define the capacity of States Parties to respond to a potential CBW attack. Both Conventions prescribe that States Parties shall cooperate in order to enhance peaceful scientific research and provide assistance to each other in case of an attack.[3] It comes naturally that response too requires a chemical or a biological (medicinal) solution, which strongly depends on the material and immaterial resources of States Parties, which drives us back to the state of science and technology.

Finally, the author wishes to mention potential platforms and avenues for cooperation between various stakeholders, emphasising the importance of education and outreach to initiate and maintain an active dialogue in order to prevent the re-emergence of chemical and biological weapons and to promote the peaceful uses of science.

2 Relevant Trends in Science and Technology

Since the entry into force of the Conventions (1975 and 1997 respectively), life sciences have seen remarkably rapid advances with the prospect of benefitting humankind. Due to the dual-use nature of science and technology, advances might pose unforeseen risks for the object and purpose of the Conventions. However, in order to be able to adequately assess such challenges facing the Conventions, first we have to understand the relevant trends in science and technology. These trends are discussed below in light of corresponding literature but without aiming to give an exhaustive list of advances in life sciences.

Globalisation characterises many aspects of the post–Cold War era, including the chemical and biological industry. The globalisation of these industries resulted in thousands of facilities spread all around the world as well as an easier flow of information. Research and development (R&D) increasingly takes place in a new, globalised environment, with the Internet providing a platform for communication and the global distribution of information and knowledge, thereby enabling and encouraging new forms of scientific collaboration, including the emergence of virtual laboratories, shared databases and open-source software.[4] Increasing access and ease of use of communications

---

3 CWC, *supra* note 1, Art. X(1); BWC, *supra* note 2, Art. VIII and X.

4 Peter van Ham, Sico van der Meer, Malik Ellahi, 'Chemical Weapons Challenges Ahead: The Past and Future of the OPCW. With a Case Study on Syria. Clingendael Report' (October 2017)

technologies along with the growing availability of resources to support research, global research capacity expands and diffuses on an international level.[5]

Another notable trend in natural sciences in the 21st century is their prominent convergence. Convergence has been recognised by the OPCW's Scientific Advisory Board[6] and also by a working paper submitted to the Meeting of the States Parties to the BWC,[7] the latter describing convergence as an integrative and collaborative approach in the life sciences, which brings together theoretical concepts, experimental techniques and knowledge of different disciplines at the crossroads of chemistry and biology. The "omics" disciplines are considered as an example of scientific convergence, which are studies of all constituents collectively of a set of data or biomolecules, such as genes (genomics), lipids (lipidomics) or proteins (proteomics).[8]

A logical consequence of the convergence between chemistry and biology on the level of arms control treaties is that it is increasingly becoming the same science base that is underpinning both the CWC and the BWC,[9] which requires a clarification of the relationship between the two treaties. Convergence might result in the invention and application of new synthesis routes to existent toxins and the possibility of new, laboratory designed toxins. While usually discussed in the context of the future biotech revolution, as a result of converging sciences, the biotech revolution could also hold implications for the future of chemical weapons. A demonstrative example is the fact that most drugs that will be a result of advanced biotechnology are likely to be chemical agents, and, as such, future chemical weapons will have the potential to profit from the advanced understanding of the biochemical processes in

<https://www.clingendael.org/sites/default/files/2017-10/Clingendael_Report_Chemical_Weapons_Challenges_Ahead_2017.pdf> (accessed 31 January 2024), p. 20.

5 National Academy of Sciences, 'Report in Brief, Life Sciences and Related Fields: Trends Relevant to the Biological Weapons Convention' (2011), <https://nap.nationalacademies.org/resource/13130/Life-Sciences-Related-Fields-Report-Brief-Final.pdf> (accessed 31 January 2024).

6 Convergence of Chemistry and Biology, 'Report of the Scientific Advisory Board's Temporary Working Group' SAB/REP/1/14 (2014).

7 Review of Developments in Science and Technology: Key Points from the 2012–2015 BTWC Intersessional Programme – Submitted by the United Kingdom of Great Britain and Northern Ireland' (1 November 2016) BWC/CONF.VIII/WP.17.

8 R Trapp, 'CHAPTER 7. Convergence of Chemistry and Biology, and Nanotechnology' in Michael Crowley, Malcolm Dando and Lijun Shang (eds), *Preventing Chemical Weapons* (Royal Society of Chemistry 2018) <http://ebook.rsc.org/?DOI=10.1039/9781788010092-00191>.

9 Robert J Mathews, 'Chemical and Biological Weapons' (26 October 2015) U of Melbourne Legal Studies Research Paper No 723, forthcoming in Rain Liivoja and Tim McCormack (eds), Routledge Handbook of the Law of Armed Conflict (Routledge) <https://ssrn.com/abstract=2679720> (accessed 31.01.2024), p. 22.

the human body. This could then open the possibility to develop advanced chemical weapons (ACWs). A particular interest of state actors to develop a specific class of ACWs concerns the development of non-lethal (advanced) riot control agents or incapacitants that are not banned under the CWC for law enforcement purposes.[10]

Another concern closely related to the convergence of chemistry and biology is the advances of nanotechnology. Nanotechnology and nanoscience are terms that refer to the investigation and use of entities (particles) at the nanoscale, where at least one of the dimensions is somewhere between 1 and 100 nm.[11] Nanotechnology and nanoscience also encompass a range of techniques rather than a single discipline and stretch across the whole spectrum of science, touching medicine, physics, engineering and chemistry[12], which may have potential military applications. Three aspects of chemical and biological arms control can be identified where the advances of nanotechnology could have an impact. These fields are (i) the development of novel agents, (ii) the use of nanotechnology for delivery systems and (iii) applications in protection against CBW. As nanotechnology advances, it is likely to be possible to design materials that act like chemical or biological agents but may be out of the scope of either the CWC or the BWC.[13]

Structural and technological trends in the chemical and biological industries (manufacturing) should also be examined for a better understanding of the operation of the Conventions. The structural changes in industry emerge from globalisation – as discussed above – resulting in new production locations, and changes in trade patterns and market conditions, which cause a shift from industry's product-driven approach to a solution-oriented one. New production locations are being established in developing countries, where national implementation of the Conventions is less advanced.[14]

10 Tim Sweijs and Jaakko Kooroshy, The Future of CBRN (The Hague Centre for Strategic Studies, 2010) <https://hcss.nl/report/the-future-of-cbrn/> (accessed 31 January 2024), 14–15.

11 Trapp, *supra* note 8, p. 206.

12 Jim Whitman, 'The Arms Control Challenges of Nanotechnology' (2011) 32 Contemporary Security Policy, 99.

13 Wallach, Evan J, 'A Tiny Problem with Huge Implications – Nanotech Agents as Enablers or Substitutes for Banned Chemical Weapons: Is a New Treaty Needed?' (2009) 33(3) Fordham International Law Journal 858, 859.

14 Trapp, Ralf, 'Research, development and production: impact and challenges for future verification under the CWC' in Jean Pascal Zanders (ed), *The Future of the CWC in the Post-destruction Phase* (Report No. 15, European Union Institute for Security Studies 2013) 15, 18–19.

On the technological side, the developments in the use of flow reactors, especially microreactors, need to be monitored as a prominent factor altering chemical industrial practice. The major advantages of microreactors include the safe production of hazardous, corrosive chemicals and certain classes of biologically active chemicals, which are not or hardly possible under batch conditions. In addition, it became easier to perform highly energetic reactions, work with unstable intermediates, employ reactive agents and use catalysts more effectively in microreactors, which could potentially result in novel production processes.[15] A further advantage is that microreactors can be operated in parallel in order to afford an increased throughput. This way, despite their small size, microreactors could produce tons of materials per year if operated in parallel.[16]

In the biotech industry, the space and resources necessary for the production of biologics has decreased and more compact equipment can be used in smaller, lower-cost facilities. The increased use of biosynthesis and bio-based production, scaffolds and "biopharming" accelerates the speed and yield of producing biological agents. In addition, there is an increase in the use of disposable or single-use equipment, which offers possibilities for faster technological breakout, enabling switching from permitted to prohibited technologies.[17]

The use of computers and automation in manufacturing processes has become more widespread. These methods can facilitate production under the most efficient reaction conditions and enhance the safety of plant operators, which advantages could also be applied in the context of production of CBW by minimising operator exposure and limiting the release of toxic vapours into the atmosphere that might be detected by sensitive monitoring equipment.

In connection with the spread of new computer-based techniques in the chemical industry, a new method known as combinatorial chemistry developed. Combinatorial chemistry provides the possibility to synthesise large libraries of chemical compounds that can then be evaluated for useful proper-

15 Katie Smallwood and others, 'Impact of Scientific Developments on the Chemical Weapons Convention (IUPAC Technical Report)' (2013) 85(4) Pure and Applied Chemistry 851, 856.

16 Parshall, George W, 'Scientific and Technological Developments and the CWC' in Jonathan B Tucker (ed), *The Chemical Weapons Convention: Implementation Challenges and Solutions* (Monterey Institute of International Studies, April 2001) 53, 54.

17 InterAcademy Partnership Conference Report, The Biological and Toxin Weapons Convention: Implications of Advances in Science and Technology (June 2016) 12, 16 <https://www.interacademies.org/publication/biological-and-toxin-weapons-convention-implications-advances-science-and-technology> (accessed 31 January 2024).

ties. Generally speaking, the procedure involves mixing reactive chemicals in multiple combinations to generate hundreds or thousands of compounds. In correspondence with the high productivity enabled by computation, automation and combinatorial chemistry, an equally effective method for screening large numbers of compounds became necessary. From a non-proliferation perspective, the risks posed by combinatorial chemistry as a new development method are its potential abuse to develop new lethal or toxic chemical weapons for military or terrorist purposes.[18]

Computation, the interplay of biotechnologies with artificial intelligence, machine learning and a high degree of automation are accelerating the development of biomedical products, too. Synthetic biology, the scientific disciple encompassing all aspects of the engineering of biosystems, is rapidly developing and tools that lower the education, training, cost, time and equipment threshold required to modify and employ pathogenic organisms as biological weapons advance.[19] A particularly powerful development in biotechnology has been the creation and subsequent widespreading of genome editing methods, notably the CRISPR/Cas9, which allows the selective cutting and modification of DNA sequences.[20]

3 The Definition of Chemical and Biological Weapons

3.1 *The General Purpose Criterion*

The central concepts of the BWC and the CWC are the definition of biological weapons[21] and chemical weapons[22] respectively.

---

18 Parshall, *supra* note 16, p. 54–55.

19 Wickiser, J Kenneth, O'Donovan, Kevin J, Washington, Michael, Hummel, Stephen and Burpo, F John, 'Engineered Pathogens and Unnatural Biological Weapons: The Future Threat of Synthetic Biology' (2020) 13(8) CTC Sentinel 2, <https://ctc.westpoint.edu/engineered-pathogens-and-unnatural-biological-weapons-the-future-threat-of-synthetic-biology/> (accessed 31 January 2024).

20 Reiners, Sophie, and Thränert, Oliver, 'The Biological Weapons Ban and Scientific Progress' (CSS Analyses in Security Policy No. 321, April 2023) 3 <https://css.ethz.ch/en/center/CSS-news/2023/04/the-biological-weapons-ban-and-scientific-progress.html> (accessed 31 January 2024).

21 BWC, *supra* note 2, Art. I [...](*i*) *microbial or other biological agents, or toxins whatever their origin or method of production, of types and quantities that have no justification for prophylactic, protective or other peaceful purposes;* (2) *weapons, equipment or means of delivery designed to use such agents or toxins for hostile purposes or in armed conflict.*

22 CWC, *supra* note 1, Art. II(1) *"Chemical Weapons" means the following, together or separately:* (*a*) *Toxic chemicals and their precursors, except where intended for purposes not*

Article 1 of the BWC defines biological weapons as

> (1) microbial or other biological agents, or toxins whatever their origin or method of production, of types and in quantities that have no justification for prophylactic, protective or other peaceful purposes;
> (2) weapons, equipment or means of delivery designed to use such agents or toxins for hostile purposes or in armed conflict.

The definition operates with a General Purpose Criterion (GPC) by defining the material scope of the BWC to microbial or other biological agents and toxins that *have no justification for prophylactic, protective or other peaceful purposes* and related weapons, equipment or means of delivery *used for hostile purposes*. The definition is open in a sense that it covers biological agents *regardless of their origin or method of production* to avoid that the BWC could be considered outdated by future scientific developments, although the General Purpose Criterion itself is not explained further in the text of the BWC. The General Purpose Criterion is therefore manifested in the requirement that States Parties may never produce biological agents or toxins of types and quantities that are not justified for purposes defined in the BWC, so it is in fact the vagueness of the General Purpose Criterion that ensures that the BWC is future proof.[23] The BWC, however, being a much older treaty, differs from the CWC in a sense that no schedules or lists have been agreed by the States Parties on the types and quantities of agents and toxins, which are most likely being used as biological weapons, providing less demarcation as to the borders of prohibited and legitimate activities.

As the CWC was drafted two decades after the BWC, the drafters of the CWC enjoyed the benefit of the experiences of the BWC. The CWC was prepared right after the end of the Cold War, when ambitions of the future States Parties allowed for a wide consensus for chemical weapons disarmament, which resulted an effective and comprehensive disarmament treaty. Such progress is also reflected in the definition of chemical weapons compared to the definition of biological and toxin weapons. Although the definition of chemical

---

prohibited under this Convention, as long as the types and quantities are consistent with such purposes; (b) Munitions and devices, specifically designed to cause death or other harm through the toxic properties of those toxic chemicals specified in subparagraph (a), which would be released as a result of the employment of such munitions and devices; (c) Any equipment specifically designed for use directly in connection with the employment of munitions and devices specified in subparagraph (b).

23 Reiners; Thränert, *supra* note 20, p. 2.

weapons draws from that of biological weapons by putting the General Purpose Criterion at the heart of the definition, the CWC further clarifies the definition of chemical weapons by providing an explicit definition for toxic chemicals[24] as well as for the term "purposes not prohibited under this Convention. The clause, "purposes not prohibited under this Convention" constitute the General Purpose Criterion under the CWC, which makes the definition of chemical weapons and the CWC itself future proof. According to the definition set forth in Article II(9)

> "Purposes not Prohibited Under this Convention" means: (a) Industrial, agricultural, research, medical, pharmaceutical or other peaceful purposes; (b) Protective purposes, namely those purposes directly related to protection against toxic chemicals and to protection against chemical weapons; (c) Military purposes not connected with the use of chemical weapons and not dependent on the use of the toxic properties of chemicals as a method of warfare; (d) Law enforcement including domestic riot control purposes.

The CWC thus makes it clear that toxic chemicals, their precursors and the delivery equipment and devices designed for their employment are by definition chemical weapons, except when intended for peaceful purposes, provided that the types and quantities are consistent with such purposes. In particular, the CWC contains three Schedules containing lists of chemicals and precursors which provide a framework for verification activities depending on the toxicity and industrial application of the listed chemicals.[25] According to the CWC, the Schedules shall not be understood as a definition or an exhaustive list of chemical weapons,[26] taking into consideration that the advances of science and technology might extend or alter the category of chemical weapons. The Schedules were drafted based on conceptions of utility dating from the Cold War period, which means that the lists of chemicals were prepared based on types of agents that fitted old war requirements. Basically this meant

24 CWC, *supra* note 1, Art. II(2) *Any chemical which through its chemical action on life processes can cause death, temporary incapacitation or permanent harm to humans or animals. This includes all such chemicals, regardless of their origin or of their method of production, and regardless of whether they are produced in facilities, in munitions or elsewhere.*

25 M Sossai, 'Drugs as Weapons: Disarmament Treaties Facing the Advances in Biochemistry and Non-Lethal Weapons Technology' (2010) 15 Journal of Conflict and Security Law, 5, 11–12.

26 CWC, *supra* note 1, Annex on Chemicals, Part B, paragraph 1.

focusing on toxic chemicals with intensely aggressive features; however, a limited number of such toxic chemicals exist[27] practically restricting the scope of the Schedules and determining the main targets of industry verification.

3.2 *The Impacts of Scientific and Technological Advances on the Definition of CBW*

Recent trends in science and technology – discussed above in Chapter 2 – pose new challenges for the interpretation and application of the definition of chemical and biological weapons, and, more closely, the General Purpose Criterion. Although in both cases it is theoretically clear that the GPC provides protection against yet unknown chemical and biological weapons that could be invented as a result of new technologies and the application of advanced biological and chemical processes, the ultimate success of the GPC in practice lies on its implementation. Both Conventions set out obligations for their respective States Parties; however, national implementation of the General Purpose Criterion of the CWC and the BWC alike need to be improved.[28] There could be multiple reasons behind the inaccurate and incomplete implementation of the GPC, which are, *inter alia,* the difficulty of executing effective policies as a matter of practical administration on the basis of a flexible definition[29], or the fact that certain elements of the GPC, such as the definition of 'toxic chemicals' or 'life processes' can be interpreted differently not only by lawyers and policymakers but scientists too.[30] Apart from ensuring that States Parties themselves comply with their obligations, they must also implement national legislation preventing private actors to abuse chemical and biological agents on their territory, under their jurisdiction or control.[31] An important challenge for both regimes arises from the fact that scientific and techno-

27 JP Perry Robinson, 'Difficulties Facing the Chemical Weapons Convention' (2008) 84(2) International Affairs 223, 226.

28 Graham S. Pearson, Implementation of the General Purpose Criterion of the Chemical Weapons Convention (Bradford Disarmament Research Centre, Department of Peace Studies, University of Bradford, 2003) CWC Review Conference Papers: First Review Conference, No. 3 <https://bradscholars.brad.ac.uk/handle/10454/876> (accessed 31 January 2024); M Sossai, 'Contribution of National Implementation Approaches to Enhance Compliance with the Biological Weapons Convention' [2014] SSRN Electronic Journal <http://www.ssrn.com/abstract=2690326> (accessed 3 June 2024); Syed Javaid Khurshid, 'Chemical Weapons Convention Implementation and Challenges ISBN-978-969-23235-3-6/2018' <http://rgdoi.net/10.13140/rg.2.2.18204.74884> (accessed 3 June 2024).

29 Robinson, *supra* note 27, p. 238.

30 Sossai, *supra* note 25, p. 12–13.

31 BWC, *supra* note 2, Art. IV; CWC, *supra* note 1, Art. VII, points 1–3.

logical advances provide easier access to materials, equipment, scientific knowledge and technical know-how, and that the convergence of sciences and sectors enable private companies or even individuals to be in a position to produce and use CBW.[32]

Advances in nanotechnology also need to be highlighted in connection with the definition of chemical and biological weapons. As discussed above, the two Conventions ban any existing and future chemical and biological weapons, which include nano-sized particles used as weapons, regardless of the physical form that they take, unless they affect the human body in ways other than through chemical and biological processes. This general ban is underlined by the definitions of the CWC and the BWC, which render the regimes applicable to toxic chemical and biological agents and toxins regardless of their origin or of their method of production. The same absolute ban should also be applied *mutatis mutandis* to nano delivery systems.[33]

The applicability of the CWC, the BWC and the Geneva Protocol[34] to nano-sized mechanical systems (mimics) or nanomimics is a more difficult question. The notion of nanomimics might seem futuristic or could even be considered as something created in science fiction but their application to become reality is approaching.[35] Nanomimics are robots on the nanoscale, which could possibly enter the human body, penetrate cells, and cause them to act in a programmed fashion, so the risk that they could also be used for hostile purposes exists. Accordingly, any attempt to avoid their coverage under the CWC, the BWC and the Geneva Protocol might result in ambiguities and unwanted consequences. There are, in fact, strong arguments for their coverage, such as the drafters' intents, the wordings of the treaties, the fact that all of these weapons cause a chemical and/or biological reaction and the general principle of good faith under international law.

32 Filippa Lentzos, 'How to Protect the World from Ultra-Targeted Biological Weapons' (2020) 76 Bulletin of the Atomic Scientists, 302.

33 Wallach, *supra* note 13, p. 942–943.

34 Protocol for the Prohibition of the Use in War of Asphyxiating, Poisonous or Other Gases, and of Bacteriological Methods of Warfare (the Geneva Protocol) drawn up and signed at the conference which was held in Geneva under the auspices of the League of Nations from 4 May to 17 June 1925, and it entered into force on 8 February 1928. The provisions of the Geneva Protocol are explicitly recognised by the CWC and the BWC.

35 Cf. e.g. Muskan Aggarwal and Sunil Kumar, 'The Use of Nanorobotics in the Treatment Therapy of Cancer and Its Future Aspects: A Review' [2022] Cureus <https://www.cureus.com/articles/108503-the-use-of-nanorobotics-in-the-treatment-therapy-of-cancer-and-its-future-aspects-a-review> (accessed 31 January 2024).

The drafters of the Geneva Protocol were well aware of the problems caused by fine particles that are capable of passing through personal protective equipment and recognised the distinction between processes and devices. This indicates that their decision to include "analogous devices" in the treaty text next to the ban on poisonous and asphyxiating gases was an intentional move to ban the wartime use of weapons analogous to poisonous and asphyxiating gases. Since nanomimics are analogous to poisonous and asphyxiating gases, their involvement under the scope of the Geneva Protocol can strongly be argued. The BWC was negotiated during the Cold War period and as such, its essence came from a two state consensus between the United States and the Soviet Union in the 1970s. The agreed wide scope of the treaty text indicates that the intention of the drafters of the BWC was to ban all new genetic development and manipulation of potential living weapons and their products by banning microbial or other biological agents or toxins, together with their means of delivery. The CWC's negotiations also commenced during the Cold War but were prolonged to the post–Cold War era. The result of such long negotiations and interim steps was a wide and comprehensive coverage, including the prohibition of potential newly developed chemical weapons.[36]

The Geneva Protocol prohibits "the use in war of asphyxiating, poisonous or other gases, and of all analogous liquids, materials or devices" and the "use of bacteriological methods of warfare".[37] The BWC banned the development, production and possession of the entire class of biological and toxin weapons, not limiting the prohibition to uses in war, regardless of the origin or method of production of such weapons.[38] In addition to incorporating the Geneva Protocol, the CWC (i) covers banning the development, production, acquisition, stockpiling and possession of chemical weapons, (ii) defines chemical weapons to include delivery systems and (iii) declares that peaceful development of chemicals is not prohibited.[39] Taken together the texts of the Geneva Protocol, the BWC and the CWC, the coverage of banned nano-sized particles and delivery systems can be established with speculative nanobots falling under the term 'analogous devices'.[40]

From a scientific perspective, it can be argued that although chemical, biological and physical processes are mixed at the nanoscale, nano weapons interact with the human body in a way mimicking chemical and biological

36 Wallach, *supra* note 13, p. 945–949.

37 Geneva Protocol, *supra* note 34, Preamble.

38 BWC, *supra* note 2, Art. I.

39 CWC, *supra* note 1, Art. I(1), Art. II(1) and (9).

40 Wallach, *supra* note 13, p. 949–950.

weapons or toxins. Therefore, their effects are functionally equivalent to chemical and biological weapons, based on which, with good faith, the ban of nanomimics can be established under the Conventions. The good faith requirement in the interpretation of treaties is a general rule of interpretation set forth by Article 31(1) of the Vienna Convention[41]. According to the cited provision of the Vienna Convention, "*a treaty shall be interpreted in good faith in accordance with the ordinary meaning to be given to the terms of the treaty in their context and in the light of its object and purpose*". This provision has particular importance for arguing that the ban on chemical and biological weapons and analogous devices shall cover devices mimicking such agents, including nanomimics.[42]

On the basis of the arguments put forward above, there is no real need to amend either the CWC or the BWC, since the presented arguments overwhelmingly support the interpretation that nanomimics should be covered under the current wording of the CWC and the BWC if used for hostile purposes. However, once the threats posed by nanomimics and other nanobots become closer to reality, it would be sensible to consider the addition of a clarificatory wording to the definitions of chemical weapons and biological weapons, e.g. to include the term 'equivalents' or 'analogous devices' of toxic chemicals in the definition of chemical weapons in the CWC and do the same with the definition of biological and toxin weapons in the BWC.[43]

4 The Adaptability of the Conventions on an Institutional Level

The BWC came into force during the Cold War period and the CWC was drafted and adopted at the end of the Cold War era. Accordingly, the primary focus of the Conventions was demilitarisation through the destruction of CBW stockpiles and the tools envisaged by the drafters were drawn on the basis of the experiences of the Cold War.

The drafters of both the CWC and BWC were conscious of the potential impact scientific and technological development could have on the implementation of the Conventions, which is reflected in the two Conventions as an obligation of States Parties to review the operation of the respective treaties to assess whether their provisions are adequately implemented and to con-

---

41 Vienna Convention on the Law of Treaties, done at Vienna on 23 May 1969, entered into force on 27 January 1980.

42 Wallach, *supra* note 13, p. 951–952.

43 *Ibid.*, p. 954–955.

sider any new scientific and technological developments relevant to the CWC and the BWC.[44] Such reviews are organised in the form of Review Conferences in both cases.

4.1 *The Role of Institutions*

4.1.1 Mechanisms Established under the BWC

To improve the implementation of the BWC, various implementation and consultation mechanisms were established by the treaty itself. Meeting arrangements under the BWC are the Review Conferences, the Meeting of State Parties and the Meeting of Experts.

The Meeting of State Parties and the Meeting of Experts are held annually with the participation of all States Parties and signatory states. The aim of the Meeting of State Parties is to reach consensus on taking effective actions in relation to specific issues relating to the BWC. The Fifth Review Conference held in 2002 decided to give a mandate to the Meeting of Experts, which mandate has been renewed by each Review Conference since then. The Meeting of Experts is held prior to the Meeting of State Parties where factual reports are discussed.[45]

The Implementation Support Unit (ISU), which consists of three full-time staff, was established within the Geneva Branch of the United Nations Office for Disarmament Affairs following the Sixth Review Conference in 2006 to provide administrative support in connection with the implementation and universalisation of the BWC and for the exchange of confidence building measures. The mandate of the ISU has, too, been renewed by the Review Conferences held since then. The main responsibilities of the ISU are to provide support and assistance in connection with administration relating to the meetings of the BWC, national implementation, confidence building measures and obtaining universality for the BWC. The ISU also administers the database for assistance requests and offers and facilitates associated exchanges of information.[46]

---

44 BWC, *supra* note 2, Art. XII; CWC, *supra* note 1, Art. VIII(22).

45 Liang Huigang and others, 'Development of and Prospects for the Biological Weapons Convention' (2022) 4 Journal of Biosafety and Biosecurity 50, 51.

46 See Implementation Support Unit of the Biological Weapons Convention, <https://disarmament.unoda.org/biological-weapons/implementation-support-unit/> (accessed 11 May 2024).

4.2 *The Importance of a Dedicated International Organisation to Support Treaty Implementation and to Monitor Compliance: Channelling Scientific Expertise into Decision-Making*

The CWC establishes the Organisation for the Prohibition of Chemical Weapons (OPCW) as the international organisation to achieve the object and purpose of the CWC, to ensure the implementation of the CWC, including international verification, and to provide a forum for consultation and cooperation among States Parties.[47] This means that – unlike the BWC – the CWC has a designated international organisation to monitor the compliance of States Parties and to provide a platform for international consultations.

In the post-Cold War era, when globalisation became a norm with its own consequences, the need to update the BWC to par with the CWC is increasing.[48] Although the OPCW itself has its own challenges arising from, *inter alia*, scientific and technological development, funding issues or the lack of consensus between its States Parties, it would be a welcome development to establish an international organisation to monitor compliance with the BWC and provide a more developed platform for cooperation between States Parties. The establishment of an international organisation could also support exchanging experience and could open up opportunities to conduct joint technical reviews between the two regimes, which were identified by the OPCW advisory panel as important steps to be taken to tackle the issues arising from the interconnectivity of the Conventions. As many of the national delegates and technical experts sitting at CWC and BWC meetings are already the same,[49] this could also support the potential establishment of an international organisation similar to the OPCW to monitor compliance with the BWC.

The Scientific Advisory Board (SAB) is an advisory body of the OPCW, which enables the channelling of scientific and technological expertise into the decision-making processes of the OPCW. Pursuant to the CWC, the SAB is a subsidiary body to provide specialised advice to the OPCW Director-General and the OPCW policy-making organs, as well as States Parties about areas of

47 CWC, *supra* note 1, Art. VIII(1).

48 Jeanne Guillemin, 'Scientists and the History of Biological Weapons: A Brief Historical Overview of the Development of Biological Weapons in the Twentieth Century' (2006) 7 EMBO reports 48–49 <https://www.embopress.org/doi/10.1038/sj.embor.7400689>.

49 John Hart and Ralf Trapp, 'Science, Technology and the Biological Weapons Convention' (2022) Arms Control Association <https://www.armscontrol.org/act/2012-10/science-technology-biological-weapons-convention> (accessed 31 January 2024).

science and technology relevant to the Convention.[50] The SAB is composed of twenty-five independent experts serving in their individual capacity for up to two consecutive three-year terms. The members of the SAB are chosen based on their professional experience in scientific fields that are relevant to the implementation of the CWC. In the early years of the OPCW, the SAB was working on specific issues the Director-General and the Conference of the States Parties provided it with in order to ensure the SAB's independence and objectivity from political influence. The Director-General also established temporary working groups based on his powers granted by Article VIII(45) of the CWC comprising of scientific experts to involve specialised scientific expertise in the SAB's and the OPCW's work.[51] By way of an example, the Temporary Working Group on Convergence established in 2011 was tasked with the assessment of the impact the convergence of sciences has on the implementation of the Convention.[52]

The BWC, however, has not established a scientific advisory body either. Based on recent literature and research, BWC States Parties indicated support for a mechanism to systematically review science and technology relevant to the BWC.[53] In fact, a recent T20 Policy Brief explicitly proposes the institutionalisation of an independent scientific expert group within the ambit of the BWC – similar to the OPCW SAB – which could provide scientific and technical advice to address the shortcomings of the BWC in light of scientific and technological developments.[54] It is, however, not so evident that a potential future scientific advisory mechanism of the BWC should be exactly like the OPCW SAB. While there seems to be a support for the establishment of a systematic scientific and technical advisory mechanism, BWC States Parties will need to agree on its objectives and operation, and the method of using the outputs of scientific reviews need to be clarified. The UNIDIR study prepared

---

50 CWC, *supra* note 1, Art. VIII(21)(h).

51 R Trapp, 'CHAPTER 3. The Chemical Weapons Convention – Past Success, Current Challenges' in Michael Crowley, Malcolm Dando and Lijun Shang (eds), *Preventing Chemical Weapons* (Royal Society of Chemistry 2018) 27, 35–36, 54 <http://ebook.rsc.org/?DOI=10.1039/9781788010092-00025>.

52 Trapp, *supra* note 51, p. 36.

53 Revill, James; Anand, Alisha; Persi Paoli, Giacomo: Exploring Science and Technology Review Mechanisms Under the Biological Weapons Convention, Geneva, Switzerland: UNIDIR, 2021, https://doi.org/10.37559/SECTEC/2021/SandTreviews/01, https://unidir.org/publication/exploring-science-and-technology-review-mechanisms-under-the-biological-weapons-convention/ (accessed 31 January 2024)

54 Saurabh Todi and Shambhavi Naik, 'BWC Scientific Experts Group to Combat Biological Threats' T20 Policy Briefs, June 2023, pp. 3, 7, 13–14 <https://takshashila.org.in/research/bwc-scientific-experts-group-to-combat-biological-threats> (accessed 31 January 2024).

with the participation of 42 respondents provide a comprehensive review of the benefits and challenges of proposed models for establishing a science and technology mechanism under the BWC, encompassing a limited participation model (such as the OPCW SAB), an open-ended participation model and a hybrid model. The study highlights specific issues which should be considered before the establishment of a scientific and technology mechanism. These questions relate to objectives, participation methods, leadership, way of working, institutional support, outputs and funding.[55]

4.2 *The Importance of Verification*

4.2.1 The CWC's Verification Regime

The verification system established by the CWC is considered as a crucial element for compliance management in connection with the international chemical weapons ban. The main tool of verification is the conduct of on-site inspections performed by the inspectors working for the OPCW Technical Secretariat. The Verification Annex of the CWC provides the detailed rules on verification procedures, with special emphasis put on on-site inspections, which are complemented by the provisions of bilateral facility agreements entered into between the OPCW and States Parties for each State Party respectively.[56]

The verification mechanisms established by the CWC can be categorised as (i) routine inspections and (ii) non-routine inspections (i.e. challenge inspections and investigations of alleged use). Pursuant to the CWC, the purpose of routine inspections is twofold: on the one hand, routine inspections aim to verify the declarations on the destruction of chemical weapons, storage facilities and chemical weapons production facilities performed by possessor States Parties; and on the other hand, inspections are targeted at verifying that the industrial activities of States Parties, primarily those relating to Scheduled chemicals, are conducted for peaceful purposes.[57] Challenge inspections and investigations of alleged use are irregular verification measures, which are intended to detect and clarify States Parties' alleged non-compliance with the provisions of the CWC.

With the chemical weapons destruction phase nearing its end, routine verification measures performed by the OPCW tend to focus more on ensuring

55 Revill *et al*, *supra* note 53.

56 E.g. Ralf Trapp, 'Compliance Management under the Chemical Weapons Convention' (The United Nations Institute for Disarmament Research 2019) <https://www.unidir.org/sites/default/files/2019-12/UNID%20WMD%20CE%20-%20Paper%203%20v3.pdf> (accessed 31 January 2024).

57 See CWC, *supra* note 1, Verification Annex for more details.

that no chemical weapons are being produced. From the perspective of scientific and technological development, routine industry inspections pose greater challenge to the effectiveness of the CWC's routine verification system than monitoring the destruction of chemical weapons. This is due to the fact that the scientific background necessary to review the destruction of chemical weapon stockpiles was clear and available to the OPCW, whereas the scientific and technological competences required for successful industry verification (the selection criteria applied to decide which sites should be inspected and with what frequency, the maintaining institutional knowledge within the OPCW Technical Secretariat, etc.) strongly depend on the OPCW's ability of understanding and applying the advances of science and technology.

Routine industry inspections are based on the three Schedules of the CWC, where chemicals are listed in light of their toxicity and conventional (industrial and/or military) applications. States Parties have to submit declarations regularly to the OPCW about industrial activities conducted on their territory or under their control concerning Scheduled chemicals. Accordingly, the aim of the verification of the chemical industry is to monitor the accuracy of States Parties' declarations.

Schedule 1 chemicals are considered as high risk agents that have little or no use for purposes not prohibited by the CWC and are highly toxic chemicals and their precursors. Pursuant to the CWC, these chemicals may only be used for research, medical, pharmaceutical or chemical weapons defence testing purposes and, if over 100 grams of them are produced per year, the responsible State Party must declare them to the OPCW. Schedule 1 facilities are consequently subject to a high frequency of inspection: on average, these facilities are inspected every two years.[58] Although the intensity of these inspections correlates with the high risk attributed to Schedule 1 chemicals by the CWC, the facilities themselves often only pose a moderate risk to the non-proliferation aim of the CWC.[59] Schedule 2 chemicals do have industry applications; however, they are not produced in large quantities in industry and pose a significant risk to the object and purpose of the CWC. The third category, Schedule 3 chemicals may be produced in large commercial quantities for peaceful purposes but have properties that might enable them to be used

58 C.f. OPCW, Conference of the States Parties, 16th Session, 'Programme and budget of the OPCW for 2012' C-16/DEC.12, 2 Dec. 2011, Annex, p. 35.

59 Mohamed Daoudi, John Hart, Ajey Lele and Ralf Trapp, *The Future of the Chemical Weapons Convention: Policy and Planning Aspects* (Stockholm International Peace Research Institute (Stockholms internationella fredsforskningsinstitut) (SIPRI 2013) 35 (accessed 31 January 2024), 19–20.

as chemical weapons. Chemical facilities which manufacture more than 30 metric tons of Schedule 3 chemicals per year must be declared by States Parties.[60]

Hence, the Schedules of the CWC constitute an important guidance for routine industry inspections. This, however, does not mean that only those chemicals are considered as potential chemical weapons – and shall be subject to routine inspection – that are listed in the Schedules, since it is the General Purpose Criterion that defines chemical weapons. The challenge relating to the Schedules as a basis for industry inspections lies in the fact that the Schedules were drafted in the 1990s and, as such, could only consider the state of scientific knowledge available at that time. With the advance of science and technology, new chemical agents are developed which are not included in the Schedules but might pose similar or greater risks to the object and purpose of the CWC and should be subject to routine verification.

Two solutions for the question which chemicals shall be targeted with industry inspections are provided in the CWC itself. First, a more advanced and coordinated national implementation of the General Purpose Criterion could result in more accurate declarations, in line with the national implementation obligation of States Parties set out by Article VII of the CWC. The OPCW already recognised the need to enhance national implementation and offers technical assistance to States Parties in relation to national implementation.[61] Second, the CWC establishes the simplified amendment procedure providing a mechanism for the amendment of the Schedules more swiftly.[62] Since there are solutions available to respond to the challenges facing industry verification arising from the static nature of the Schedules, keeping industry verification effective and up-to-date ultimately depends on the willingness of States Parties to apply these solutions.

60 Gaetano Carminati, Fabrizio Benigni and Emanuele Farrugia, 'Chemical Challenges, Prevention and Responses, Including Considerations on Industrial Toxic Chemicals for Malevolent Use, CW Precursor Material for IEDs' in Maurizio Martellini and Andrea Malizia (eds), *Cyber and Chemical, Biological, Radiological, Nuclear, Explosives Challenges* (Springer International Publishing 2017) <http://link.springer.com/10.1007/978-3-319-62108-1_5>.

61 van Ham *et al*, *supra* note 4, p. 21.

62 Despite the availability of the simplified amendment procedure, the Schedules were only amended once to include the Novichok family chemical agents and carbamate nerve agents in Schedule 1. For more details, please see the article: Costanzi Research, 'Chemicals Added to CWC Schedule 1' (Costanzi Research) <https://costanziresearch.com/cw-nonproliferation/cw-control-lists/cwc-schedule-1-amendment/> (accessed 31 January 2024).

In addition to the inspection of facilities working with Scheduled chemicals, industry verification in a broad sense involves the inspection of so-called other chemical production facilities (OCPFS). OCPFS are chemical production facilities where more than 200 metric tonnes of unscheduled discrete organic chemicals or more than 30 metric tonnes of unscheduled discrete organic chemicals containing the elements phosphorus, sulphur or fluorine are produced yearly.[63] The inspection of OCPFS is viewed by States Parties as a confidence building regime, since – according to the estimation of the Technical Secretariat – approximately 10 per cent of OCPFS pose a relatively high risk to the peaceful use of chemistry due to their technological features exploiting recent developments in industry, such as the use of multipurpose, corrosion-resistant equipment, and the fact that their manufacturing processes are closely associated with those known from traditional chemical weapons programmes.[64]

The challenge facing the selection of industrial plants for inspection is to constantly update and re-assess the selection process focusing on the potential risks associated with the chemicals and procedures used at a given site. This way, the selection of facilities posing no risk to the object and purpose of the CWC could also be better avoided. Again, the solution lies in the political will of States Parties to consider the steps necessary to keep routine industry verification effective and implement measures reflecting the developments in science and technology.

4.2.2 The Expertise of the OPCW Technical Secretariat

At the heart of the verification procedure lies the effectiveness of the activities performed by the Technical Secretariat, especially with regard to the analytical and chemical forensics techniques applied by inspectors during an – on-site or off-site – inspection. The analytical methods known and applied by the Technical Secretariat are key both in respect of routine industry inspections and to demonstrate the capability of the Technical Secretariat to conduct a challenge inspection or an investigation of alleged use, if requested. It is noted that the latter is yet to be tested, since no request for a challenge inspection or an investigation of alleged use has been requested during the OPCW's existence in the last quarter of a century. The question concerning both routine

63 CWC, *supra* note 1, Verification Annex, Section A, Part IX.

64 Daoudi *et al*, *supra* note 59, p. 21.

and non-routine inspections is the same: would the system actually be capable to detect a violation?[65]

As a guiding principle, the continuous revision of the advance of analytics and the new technologies and features introduced in analytical technology is necessary to ensure the soundness of verification. In this regard, the findings of the 2013 IUPAC Technical Report still have relevance today. The specific considerations in light of the advances of science and technology include the assessment of the versatility of the technologies used in different environments, with traditional and emerging chemicals and/or materials (such as toxins) and also in chemicals embedded in complex matrices. Furthermore, with regard to the developments in the areas of miniaturisation and nanotechnology, complex mixture analysis and increased sensitivity need to be further explored to address the evolving needs of the verification system.[66]

The actual performance of chemical analysis occurs in two settings: on-site and off-site. On-site analysis is conducted at inspection sites, which means that the equipment used for on-site analysis must be transportable and rugged against physical stress (most notably in case of air transport), further, it needs be ensured that the instruments can be established within a short period of time on-site and can function reliably if exposed to a wide array of environmental conditions. It is highlighted that the equipment used on-site shall be capable to analyse as broad as possible a range of different chemicals that might pose the risk of chemical weapons proliferation.[67] By way of an example, the Technical Secretariat made progress to shorten the set-up and calibration time in the field and to reduce the time needed for sample preparation. Still, the question is not closed as the number of samples that an inspection team can analyse on-site during the time window set for the inspection is limited.[68] Another example relates to the promotion of multipurpose methods and equipment that can be used for the detection of a broad range of chemicals. Concerning the advance of miniaturisation, the developments in gas chromatography-mass spectrometry (GC-MS) offer opportunities to improve the portability and robustness of inspection equipment.[69]

Off-site analyses are conducted at OPCW-designated laboratories on samples collected at inspection sites. Laboratory settings have the potential to

---

65 Chemical Weapons Convention: Third Review Conference and beyond. Conference Report. Monday 15 – Wednesday 17 October 2012, Wilton Park, WP1178, point 25.

66 Smallwood *et al*, *supra* note 15, p. 857.

67 Ibid.

68 Daoudi *et al*, *supra* note 59, p. 25.

69 Smallwood *et al*, *supra* note 15, p. 857.

provide a platform for the expansion of the OPCW's analytical capabilities by testing and incorporating emerging technologies, for example, to address the need to analyse biomedical samples increases as chemistry and biology converges.[70]

The main issue concerning challenge inspections and investigations of alleged use – but which may also apply for routine inspections – is that the Technical Secretariat needs to maintain its capacity to detect chemical agents and other relevant chemicals (such as degradation products, impurities or biomarkers) other than those listed in the Schedules of the CWC. The OPCW's decision-making organs only showed interest very recently at the 102nd Session of the Executive Council to allow the inclusion of certain non-scheduled chemicals in the analytical database maintained by the OPCW[71], which is a welcome development since reluctance to keep the analytical database up-to-date poses the risk that certain non-traditional chemical weapons threats remain outside the focus of inspectors, either as a result of simply not paying attention to non-scheduled chemicals or due to the lack of equipment or expertise to identify such agents.[72]

The contribution of the SAB to address the above challenges needs to be highlighted with regard to the advances of science and technology. The SAB has already identified a number of issues and proposed viable solutions for the verification system to remain up-to-date. For example, the SAB had a Temporary Working Group on sampling and analysis protocols, furthermore, the SAB identified various gaps concerning the forensic analysis capacities of the Technical Secretariat, taking into consideration the shifting focus of verification from state chemical weapons programs to chemical weapons proliferation threats posed by state and non-state actors.[73]

4.2.3 Implications for the BWC

As demonstrated above through the example of the CWC, verification is key to the effective implementation of a WMD-treaty. Apart from confidence building measures introduced by the Second Review Conference that encourage States Parties to publish information about biodefense developments, the

70 Ibid.

71 Lists of Newly Validated Data on Non-Scheduled Chemicals Relevant to the Chemical Weapons Convention for Inclusion in the OPCW Central Analytical Database EC-102/DEC.2 (2023), <https://www.opcw.org/sites/default/files/documents/2023/03/ec102deco2%28e%29.pdf> (accessed 28 April 2024).

72 Daoudi *et al, supra* note 59, p. 24.

73 Ibid.

BWC does not provide a verification mechanism, which is often considered one of the main shortcomings of the treaty. During the first decade of the BWC being in force, there were States Parties, especially the former Soviet Union, that failed to comply with the BWC and other States Parties did not pay sufficient attention to the lack of verification measures in the BWC. With the rapid development of biotechnology, right after the end of the Cold War, an *ad hoc* group of experts, VEREX was established at the Third Review Conference of the BWC in 1991 to scientifically and technologically examine and determine possible verification measures. Later, a proposal was put forward on to establish an international organisation such as the OPCW and apply a similar verification mechanism as the CWC does.[74] The idea was to adopt a legally binding Additional Protocol to the BWC. However, the proposal was rejected by the US at the 2001/2002 Review Conference because of political and practical reasons, with Russia's and China's tacit approval. Since then, there has been no substantial progress in the questions of verification for about 20 years, until the Ninth Review Conference held in 2022. During the Ninth Review Conference, States Parties agreed to (i) extend the mandate of the Implementation Support Unit by adding a fourth person; (ii) establish a new working group that is open to all States Parties to prepare a report to be adopted by consensus by the end of 2025 on, international cooperation for peaceful purposes, scientific and technological developments relevant to the BWC, confidence building measures and transparency, compliance and verification, national implementation of the BWC, assistance in preparing for biological attacks, and, organisational, institutional and financials questions. Although there is still a wide divergence of views on how to strengthen the BWC, the renewed effort of States Parties to address more intensively the issue of verification of the BWC is a welcome development.[75]

5 Response Capacities

The Conventions recognise the importance of assistance and protection against CBW and encourage States Parties to cooperate in order to reach the highest protection.[76] As mentioned above, the Ninth Review Conference of the BWC underlined the importance of assistance in preparing for biological attacks by entrusting a working group to assess this question. The OPCW, too,

74 Huigang *et al*, *supra* note 45, p. 52.

75 Reiners, Thränert, *supra* note 20, pp. 3–4.

76 CWC, *supra* note 1, Art. X; BWC, *supra* note 2, Art. VII and X.

has already recognised its role on multiple occasions to contribute to assisting States Parties to strengthen their response capacities by facilitating the exchange of information between States Parties and by increasing transparency. Certain related tasks of the OPCW are defined by the CWC, which are primarily implemented by the Technical Secretariat. Accordingly, the Technical Secretariat maintains a data bank, which contains freely available information on various means of protection against chemical weapons, in addition, the Technical Secretariat needs to be able to provide expert advice and assistance for a requesting State Party with identifying how its programmes for the development and improvement of a protective capacity against chemical weapons could be implemented.[77] The ability of States Parties as well as the OPCW to remain competent to adequately address a potential CBW attack correlates with their ability to remain up-to-date with the new developments in science and technology.

From the scientific and technological trends identified in Chapter 3.2, the convergence of chemistry and biology and the applications of nanotechnology are expected to strengthen the response capacities of States Parties to a CBW attack. The convergence of chemistry and biology could enhance the potential to respond to a CBW attack by more effective diagnosis and treatments. Convergence is also expected to increase the pace of drug discovery and to introduce new delivery methods which could neutralise the effect of certain toxins (such as ricin or botulinum toxin) or lead to a long-term protection against them. For example, the SAB's Temporary Working Group on Convergence directed attention to the emergence of protein and antibody-based drugs as effective medical countermeasures against chemical warfare agents.[78]

The potential applications of nanotechnology in the areas of protection against CBW and decontamination are recognised as important developments interrelated with the convergence of sciences. The development of nanofibers for protective clothing is a tangible example of the practical application of nanotechnology for protection against chemical weapons exposure.[79] As for medical countermeasures, the (future) results of research on nano-based drug delivery mechanisms (such as nanopolymers) could have useful applications for the targeted delivery of antidotes.[80]

---

77 CWC, *supra* note 1, Art. X(4)-(5).

78 Trapp, *supra* note 8, p. 205.

79 Smallwood *et al*, *supra* note 15, p. 859.

80 Trapp, *supra* note 8, p. 208–209.

6 Education and Outreach

Education, outreach and international cooperation play an important role in preventing the re-emergence of CBW. A message that emerges from the interaction between the advances of science and technology and the implementation of the Conventions is that it is a difficult challenge for the CBW regimes to keep in track with scientific and technological developments to address the potential threats facing the Conventions. To surmount this challenge, States Parties should actively engage and cooperate with stakeholders in academia and industry though multiple venues, which issue has already been recognised by States Parties and the OPCW on multiple occasions.

6.1 *Institutional Background in the CWC*

The Third Review Conference of the CWC formally recognised the importance of education and outreach in the implementation of the CWC. Based on the recognition of the Third Review Conference, the Executive Council established the Advisory Board on Education and Outreach (ABEO) in 2015 to support the continuous and sustainable implementation of the CWC, bearing in mind the importance of education and engagement with a range of audiences, such as scientists, industry, students, educators, civil society and policymakers.[81]

The ABEO is a subsidiary advisory body of the OPCW, which provides specialised advice in areas of education and outreach relevant to the OPCW's mandate in consideration of the latest advances in these fields. The ABEO may provide advice to the Director-General, the OPCW's policy-making organs and, upon their request, States Parties. The members of the ABEO are in a position similar to the members of the SAB. Accordingly, the ABEO is a group of fifteen independent experts in subjects including education in science, technology, engineering, mathematics and other relevant disciplines or science communication. The members of the ABEO serve in a personal capacity and not as representatives of their respective governments and their tenure is limited to two three-year terms.[82]

As part of the OPCW's and States Parties' cooperative investment in science and technology, the construction of the Centre for Chemistry and Technology

81 Report on the Role of Education and Outreach in Preventing the Re-emergence of Chemical Weapons, ABEO-5/1 (2018) <https://www.opcw.org/fileadmin/OPCW/EC/83/en/ec83s01_c21s01_e_.pdf> (accessed 31 January 2024).

82 See OPCW, 'Advisory Board on Education and Outreach' (Organisation for the Prohibition of Chemical Weapons) <https://www.opcw.org/about/subsidiary-bodies/advisory-board-education-and-outreach> (accessed 31 January 2024).

or the ChemTech Centre within the OPCW began in 2017 to upgrade the capabilities of the Laboratory and Equipment Store. Initially, the work of the Laboratory and Equipment Store focused primarily on supporting the demilitarisation activities and missions as well as the routine inspections of industrial facilities performed by the OPCW. With the advances of science and technology, the work of the Laboratory and Equipment Store has changed and grown to reflect new requirements, including responding to the emergence of new chemical weapons threats with new and improved verification tools and expanding the capabilities to conduct non-routine missions, and also providing greater support for international cooperation and assistance activities.[83]

6.2 *Knowledge within the OPCW*

The OPCW is well aware that specialist knowledge and expertise are required to remain up-to-date with scientific and technological developments. A key question relates to the retention of knowledge and expertise within the OPCW, with limited resources and a continuous overturn of experts because of the OPCW's tenure policy. This challenge is most clearly manifested in the need that OPCW inspectors must have the ability to continuously monitor the chemical industry and make risk assessments in consideration of new chemical processes and technologies.[84]

To ensure the capacity of the Technical Secretariat to conduct verification activities, a group of highly experienced inspectors who have appropriate experience to lead on-site investigations must be maintained. Apart from scientific and technological expertise, it is desirable that inspectors also have operational, political and legal experience, especially in case of a potential challenge inspection, to deal with the sensitive and complex nature of the investigations. The Technical Secretariat and States Parties should pay delicate attention to examine who is capable of managing large inspection teams and successfully carrying out inspections in the field.[85]

6.3 *Cooperation with the Science Community and Industry*

Achieving an effective CBW security policy requires the active engagement of many stakeholders, including the science community, non-governmental

83 See OPCW, 'ChemTech Centre' (Organisation for the Prohibition of Chemical Weapons) <https://www.opcw.org/media-centre/featured-topics/chemtech-centre> (accessed 31 January 2024).

84 van Ham *et al*, *supra* note 4, p. 61.

85 Daoudi *et al*, *supra* note 59, p. 23–24.

organisations with related agendas and the actors in chemical and biological industry.

Scientific organisations could provide opportunities for scientists to contribute as scientific experts to the effective implementation of the Conventions and other disarmament and non-proliferation efforts. A remarkable example of the OPCW's cooperation with academia is its close relationship with the International Union of Pure and Applied Chemistry (IUPAC). IUPAC is a particularly strong partner for the OPCW as the only independent, non-governmental, international organisation devoted to chemistry and the chemical sciences and their application in research, industry and society. IUPAC first engaged with the OPCW through an independent project on examining options for the destruction of chemical weapons stockpiles, which was the first major challenge of the CWC. Even though the OPCW already had the SAB to advise on scientific issues, it was the SAB itself that recognised the benefits of engaging a wider array of expertise to provide scientific inputs for the work of the SAB and the OPCW. This was the first time when an international disarmament treaty organisation requested independent advice from an international scientific organisation, which could serve as a good example to follow by other disarmament treaty mechanisms. Since then, the IUPAC held workshops with the participation of researchers from academia, industry, the OPCW and also government technical experts and policy experts with scientific backgrounds to discuss scientific and technological developments and their implications for the CWC. These workshops might also become a model for the active involvement of scientists in the implementation of international disarmament treaties, providing a platform for the analysis of scientific trends over time. In fact, the success of the IUPAC workshops inspired a similar effort for the BWC, namely the Biosecurity Working Group of the InterAcademy Partnership (IAP) in cooperation with international scientific partners has organised assessment of scientific and technological trends for the BWC Review Conferences. However, the difficulty of involving all relevant actors of biology and biosecurity lies in the diversity and fragmentation of the field, which is manifested in the fact that there are around a dozen of international unions whose activities are relevant for the operation of the BWC, whereas the IUPAC is clearly the only dominant international union in the chemical field. On the positive side, the Biosecurity Working Group of the IAP has become an informal science advisory system, aiming at filling the gap that no such mechanism is established by the BWC itself.[86]

86 KW Bowman, AWM Hay and JL Husbands, 'CHAPTER 17. Role of the Non-Governmental Chemical Science Community in Combatting the Development, Proliferation, and Use of

In consideration of new scientific and technological developments, the involvement of industry through conferences and other platforms for exchanging information and experience is equally important. The OPCW claims that it is no longer seen as an auditor and regulator but as a partner of the chemical industry for improving the verification regime and ensuring that chemicals are not used for prohibited purposes.[87] In demonstration of the above, in 2015, a coordination mechanism was established between the OPCW and the International Council of Chemical Associations (ICCA), the organisation representing chemical manufacturers and producers around the world[88], through the creation of the OPCW-ICCA Joint Steering Committee and the establishment of the Chemical Industry Cooperation Group (CICG).[89] Further, over the past years, the OPCW and the International Chemical Trade Association (ICTA), the world-wide chemical association representing the chemical distribution industry, have intensified their cooperation following a formal exchange of letters. In 2022, the ICTA had the opportunity to contribute to OPCW policy meetings and events. The ICTA also shared knowledge and best practices in support of the development of the OPCW guidelines for the transportation of hazardous chemicals by road.[90]

Another viable option for industry's contribution to the CBW disarmament and non-proliferation is the promotion of responsible science through self-regulation by the application of codes of conduct. Codes of conduct are self-governance mechanisms that establish a set of common principles, which professional communities agree to abide by. A breach of such professional code that amount to a serious deviation of professional practice could possibly

---

Chemical Weapons' in Michael Crowley, Malcolm Dando and Lijun Shang (eds), *Preventing Chemical Weapons* (Royal Society of Chemistry 2018) <http://ebook.rsc.org/?DOI=10.1039/9781788010092-00515> 517, 518–523.

87 Note by the Director-General: Engaging the Chemical Industry Associations C-20/DG.15 (2015).

88 See ICCA, 'International Council of Chemical Associations' (International Council of Chemical Associations) <https://icca-chem.org> (accessed 31 January 2024).

89 See OPCW, 'Working together for a world free of chemical weapons' (Organisation for the Prohibition of Chemical Weapons) <https://www.opcw.org/about/our-partners> (accessed 31 January 2024).

90 See 'Statement by Willem van Lanschot on behalf of the International Chemical Trade Association at the Fifth Session of the Conference of the States Parties to Review the Operation of the Chemical Weapons Convention presented in The Hague on May 16th, 2023' <https://www.opcw.org/sites/default/files/documents/2023/05/ICTA%20statement%20at%20OPCW%20Review%20Conference%20%28revcon%29%205%20.pdf> (accessed 31 January 2024).

incur severe criticism and may even result in exclusion from the "guild". Hence, codes of conduct have a twofold purpose: they allow professionals a considerable space for self-regulation and self-discipline, while at the same time they protect the integrity of the profession by discouraging professional misconduct.[91] As regards CBRN security, a list of duties has been suggested to be included in codes of conduct for researchers to address the risk of possible hostile misuse of their results, including the duty to prevent (CBRN) terrorism, to engage in response activities, to consider negative implications of research, to keep sensitive information confidential and to oversee and limit access to dangerous materials.[92]

A good example is the Hague Ethical Guidelines (the Guidelines), which is a code of conduct developed by a group of chemical practitioners around the world that was adopted in 2015 by the Conference of the States Parties based on the understanding that achievements in the field of chemistry should be used to benefit humankind and the environment. The document is considered an important step to advance the understanding among chemistry practitioners of the importance of nurturing responsible and ethical norms for scientific research and development. The Guidelines have also been widely disseminated to professional societies and industry organisations, have been endorsed by both the ICCA and the ICTA and received a recognition of a global code of ethics for chemists.[93]

7 Conclusion

This study assessed the interconnectivity of the Chemical Weapons Convention and the Biological and Toxin Weapons Convention in light of the advances of science and technology. An inherent relation exists between the two Conventions as the subject matters of both the CWC and the BWC are based on scientific grounds and both chemical and biological agents have a dual-use nature.

91 C.f. AA King and MJ Lenox, 'Industry Self-Regulation without Sanctions: The Chemical Industry's Responsible Care Program.' (2000) 43(4) Academy of Management Journal 698; Gigi Kwik Grönvall, 'A New Role for Scientists in the Biological Weapons Convention' (2005) 23(10) Nature Biotechnology, 1215.

92 Novossiolova, Tatyana; Martellini, Maurizio: Promoting responsible science and CBRN security through codes of conduct and education. In: *Biosafety and Health*, 1, 2019, 59–64. DOI: 10.1016/j.bsheal.2019.08.001.

93 Bowman *et al, supra* note 86, p. 531.

It comes from the scientific underpinning of the Conventions that advances of science and technology affect the two regimes. Notable trends that arguably have an effect on the interpretation of the CWC and the BWC are (i) the convergence of sciences, including the advances of nanotechnology, and (ii) new practices in industry and technology, such as computation, automation, easier access to science and equipment. The aforementioned trends point at the same direction for both the CWC and the BWC, resulting that similar challenges face the two regimes, with a further consequence of potentially increasing the interconnectedness of CBW norms as outlined above.

The author proposes strengthening the cooperation between the CWC and the BWC on the level of definitions to surmount the challenges posed by scientific and technological developments, most notably the convergence between chemistry and biology, considering that the central concept of the definition of biological weapons and chemical weapons is the General Purpose Criterion. The purpose of increased coordination between the two regimes on the level of definitions would be welcome to ensure the effectiveness of the two treaties and to address cases where an agent could potentially fall under the material scope of the CWC and the BWC at the same time.

It was demonstrated above that the CWC is a more advanced regime as it established a dedicated international organisation, the OPCW, to monitor States Parties' compliance with treaty obligations and also a permanent scientific advisory body, the SAB, to channel scientific and technological expertise into decision-making. Although the BWC also created meeting arrangements with the same purpose, the need for a more formal way of monitoring compliance and keeping track of scientific and technological developments relevant to the implementation of the BWC has already been articulated. The author argues that institutionalisation would be beneficial to future implementation of the BWC and proposes that stakeholders learn from the experiences and good practices of the OPCW and the SAB.

The verification system of the CWC is a key element of the effective implementation of the treaty and to build confidence between States Parties. In other words, it is the verification system that makes the CWC a strong WMD disarmament and non-proliferation treaty, even though the regime faces various challenges ensuring that inspections are effective and inspectors are in fact capable to detect chemical weapons. The BWC, on the other hand, does not provide a verification mechanism, which remains one of the main shortcomings of the treaty. Efforts to address such shortcoming have been unsuccessful so far but the author welcomes the results of the Ninth Review Conference where States Parties agreed to readdress the issue of verification.

Finally, the author wishes to emphasise the importance of education and outreach, and argues that the involvement of stakeholders from academia and industry are fundamental for maintaining the relevance of the CWC and the BWC and strengthening CBW disarmament and non-proliferation in the future.

CHAPTER 4

Norms and State Use of Chemical and Biological Agents in Assassinations since 1946

Glenn Cross

Although relatively rare compared to the use of kinetic means, CBW use in assassination operations has been unbroken from 1946 to the present, and indications are that assassinations, including those involving CBW, likely will rise. This discussion will focus on whether international norms and later international agreements have effectively constrained State CBW use in assassinations since the end of World War II (WWII). Several factors account for this lack of constraint on CBW use in assassinations. First is the collapse of the norm against assassination, although arguably a weak norm. Second is the lack of visibility characteristic of CBW assassinations. Third, the relative lack of serious, lasting repercussions following poisons use in assassinations likely will further incentivize CBW use in assassinations. Lastly, CBW use in assassinations is fundamentally different from military CBW arsenals designed for battlefield use.

State use of chemical or biological agents in assassinations contravenes two important norms: the norm against the use of CBW and the norm against assassination. For most of this period, a striking disconnect between CBW use in assassinations and the CBW norms has existed. Only with the apparent collapse of the assassination norm have CBW norms been applied to CBW assassination use – in fact, CBW assassinations were first deemed violations of the CBW norms with the 2017 poisoning of Kim Jong-nam. The continued use of CBW in these cases raises concerns about the practical scope of the norms and related international agreements. Do the norms – and the relevant international agreements – effectively cover CBW use in killing targeted individuals? Have international responses to CBW use in targeted killing been effective in halting these attacks? What effect have CBW assassinations had on the norms' strength or scope?

This paper will first describe the history of State use of CBW in assassinations since the end of WWII and the rationales behind terminating CBW use in operations. Also examined are the role of secrecy in CBW assassination operations, the effectiveness of CBW norms and institutions in curtailing CBW assassinations, the impact of responses to CBW assassinations, the effects of attacks on the CBW norms and the international order, and the continued

 | DOI:10.1163/9789004739192_005

relevance of CBW norms. The intent is to shed light on the historical record and raise awareness about the likelihood that such CBW use will continue and may increase if concerted international action is not taken.

1 Definitions and Methodology[1]

This paper examines State CBW use in assassination operations from the end of WWII to the present. To date, no single comprehensive study of CBW use in assassinations exists, let alone one that examines the impact of norms, laws, or international institutions on the use of these agents in targeted killing. The period was chosen to cover the period of the current international order. For simplicity, assassinations are the intentional killing of targeted individuals or groups of targeted individuals by a nation-state for political purposes. Purposes include advancing foreign policy objectives and ensuring national security and regime security.[2]

Assassination operations here include actions taken involving the planning, preparations, and attempts (failed or successful) to kill an intended target. In most cases of CBW assassination operations, the motivation has been regime security, including the elimination of regime opponents, opposition leaders, members of opposition or dissident groups, dissidents, defectors, security threats, insurgents, terrorists, religious leaders, and members of minority groups. Chemical and biological weapons (CBW) are defined as chemical poisons, biological toxins, and pathogens used to kill the intended target.

It may be valuable to see State CBW use in assassinations as falling under a different category than military CBW munitions. Efforts to constrain CBW use in assassinations may require a refocusing. Arguably, the negotiators of the BWC and CWC did not reflect during the negotiations on the use of these agents in assassinations, although the CWC's General Provision covers such

1 Disclaimer: The views, conclusions, or positions presented herein are solely those of the author and in no way represent the views, conclusions, or positions of the US government or any of its departments, agencies, or entities. Any errors or omissions are the responsibility of the author and the author alone.

2 This definition expands on the one set forth in Franklin L Ford, *Political Murder: From Tyrannicide to Terrorism* (Harvard University Press, 1987), 2. This expanded definition emphasizes that the goal is to advance foreign policy and national security objectives as well as regime security. National security focuses on external threats, while regime security focuses on internal threats. Also, see Warner R Schilling and Jonathan L Schilling, 'Decision Making in Using Assassinations in International Relations' (2016) 131 Political Science Quarterly, 503.

use. The focus of the CWC negotiators appears to have centered on dismantling States' CW arsenals. Rather than targeting troop concentrations on the battlefield of an intra-state conflict, CBW use in assassinations is quantitatively and qualitatively different.

The paper also uses the definition of international norms, their construction, and evolution as set forth in a large body of international relations theory, chiefly from constructivist theorists.[3] No one denies that international norms exist.[4] As defined here, international norms are socially constructed agreements among nations defining acceptable and unacceptable State behaviors.[5,6] Thus, norms provide a degree of order for States in an otherwise anarchic Hobbesian environment. Norms must evolve and adapt to changes in their environment. Failure to evoke threatens to render a norm or norm cluster irrelevant, possibly to the point of norm replacement or norm death.[7]

The current international order[8] is defined as that set of complex interconnected international political, economic, and security institutions, rules,

3 Although much of her arms-control writings focus on nuclear weapons norms, Carmen Wunderlich's work stands out here, especially her work on norm entrepreneurship.

4 Vaughn P. Shannon, 'Norms Are What States Make of Them: The Political Psychology of Norm Violation' (2000) 44 International Studies Quarterly, 293.

5 Heike Krieger and Andrea Liese, 'Much Attacked, Still Standing: How the International Legal Order is Attacked and Defended' (School of International and Public Affairs, Columbia University, 23 October 2023), <https://multilateralism.sipa.columbia.edu/news/much-attacked-still-standing-how-international-legal-order-attacked-and-defended>.

6 To differentiate international norms from international rules, norms are social constructs that evolve as they adapt to changes in the international political, economic, and security environment. Rules are more formal and explicit and often are established by formal negotiations and agreements. Rules often reflect underlying norms, but not all norms become rules. Vaughn Shannon, 'International Norms and Foreign Policy' in Vaughn Shannon, *Oxford Research Encyclopedia of Politics* (Oxford University Press 2017) <http://politics.oxfordre.com/view/10.1093/acrefore/9780190228637.001.0001/acrefore-9780190228637-e-442> and Stefano Gennarini, 'What is an International Norm? How is It Created and Why Does It Matter? – C-Fam' (C-Fam, August 26, 2020) <https://c-fam.org/definitions/international-norm-created-matter/>.

7 Although norm clusters may be resilient, given layered qualities, these clusters also may be mutually reinforcing. See Jeffrey S. Lantis and Carmen Wunderlich, 'Resiliency Dynamics of Norm Clusters: Norm Contestation and International Cooperation' (2018) 44 Review of International Studies 570; One question remains – how does the collapse of one critical norm (say, the assassination norm) affect other norms in the cluster (say, the CBW norms)?

8 This definition is derived primarily from the works of Robert Gilpin and G. John Ikenberry. See Robert Gilpin, *War And Change in World Politics* (Cambridge University Press 1981) and G. John Ikenberry, *After Victory: Institutions, Strategic Restraint, and the Rebuilding of Order After Major Wars, New Edition* (Princeton University Press 2019).

and regulations that evolved[9] since the end of WWII.[10] According to Ikenberry,

> International order is not just the crystallization of the distribution of power. It exists in the organizing principles, authority relations, functional roles, shared expectations, and settled practices through which states do business. It establishes the terms by which states command, follow, benefit, and suffer.[11]

Examples of international institutions include the United Nations and its bodies, the World Bank, the International Monetary Fund (IMF), the North Atlantic Treaty Organization (NATO), and the European Union. Rules established within the framework of this international order define acceptable and unacceptable State behavior. Compliance is incentivized, and some means to sanction noncompliance are set forth.[12]

The time period, 1946 to the present, was chosen to correspond with the era of the current international order. This choice also highlights the stresses norms undergo whenever an international order experiences serious, daresay essential, challenges.

Using a construct from Martti Koskenniemi's *From Apology to Utopia,* this paper endeavors neither to apologize nor excuse State violations of the CBW norms nor to be entirely divorced from the realities of international power politics or national self-interest.[13] The concept of customary law is more useful in comparing the explanatory power of constructivist international relations

---

9 The term "evolved," as used here, may be problematic in that it implies a natural process. An argument can be made that the prevailing major powers impose and sustain an international order for as long as they can. Eventually, challengers arise, and the old international order is replaced.

10 Chatham House, 'Challenges to the Rules-Based International Order' (The London Conference, 2015) <https://www.chathamhouse.org/sites/default/files/London%20Conference%202015%20-%20Background%20Papers.pdf>.

11 G John Ikenberry, 'The Rise, Character, and Evolution of International Order' in Orfeo Fioretos (ed), *International Politics and Institutions in Time* (Oxford University Press 2017) <https://academic.oup.com/book/8563/chapter/154449998>.

12 Adam Ward 'Adapt or Die' in *Ideas for Modernizing the Rules-Based International Order* (Chatham House, June 2019) 2. Ward also points out that the definition of a rules-based international order is a politically contentious one. Little agreement on a common standardized definition seems reachable, according to Ward.

13 Martti Koskenniemi, *From Apology to Utopia: The Structure of International Legal Argument* (Cambridge University Press 2006).

(IR) theory and international legal theory. Although constructivist IR theorists have explored the concepts of norms' life cycles in the past decade, these concepts have not fully evolved and insufficiently explain State CBW use in assassinations in relation to norms as defined in IR theory.

2 State CBW Use in Assassinations

CBW use in assassinations is rare, compared to kinetic assassinations, for a host of reasons explained elsewhere.[14] Nevertheless, CBW has been used continuously throughout the post-WWII era, and its use continues in a relatively small number of transgressor states. Just as assassinations in general are likely to increase given the loosening of constraints, CBW use in assassinations likely will increase as incidents of transnational repression rise.[15] The number of states engaging in assassinations as part of transnational repression also is increasing.[16] A rise in CBW use may not be readily apparent: the use of advanced technologies,[17] and the development of more sophisticated chemical agents and toxins may further obscure evidence of their use and confound current attribution capabilities.[18]

The use of CBW in assassinations has been continuous throughout the period but has changed as the international security environment has changed. The chief variable has been the political nature of the respective governments and their objectives during specific times. The number of CBW assassination operations has waxed and waned during the period as national interests have changed but never completely disappeared. Notably, among

14 Glenn Cross and Richard Beedham, 'State Use of Chemical and Biological Weapons in Assassination Operations: A Historical Review from 1946 to 2000' in *Killing in the Name of the State: State-Sponsored Assassination in International Politics* (Lynne Reinner Publishers, *forthcoming*).

15 Joshua Kurlantzick, 'Renditions and Extrajudicial Assassinations Increasingly Becoming the Norm in International Relations' (Council on Foreign Relations, 4 December 2023) <https://www.cfr.org/blog/renditions-and-extrajudicial-assassinations-increasingly-becoming-norm-international-relations>.

16 Yana Gorokhovskaia, Nate Schenkkan, Grady Vaughan, *Still Not Safe: Transnational Repression in 2022*, (Freedom House, April 2023).

17 Guerric Poncet, *La Mort Fantôme: L'assassinat Ciblé Comme Arme De Guerre* (Editions du Rocher, 2023).

18 Examples of emerging technical capabilities include generative artificial intelligence (AI), nanotechnology, and genetic engineering which can lead to the development of novel CBW agents and delivery means.

the States employing CBW in assassinations, few arguably abandoned CBW use out of respect for CBW norms or international agreements. The chief factor behind a State's abandonment of CBW use in assassinations has been regime change.

Efforts to determine the number of assassinations from the totality of targeted killings is a feat unto itself and would not get us any closer to the number of cases of CBW use. The secrecy surrounding State CBW use in assassinations ensures that we are only aware of those that have become public either through intentional or unintentional disclosure or through discovery by enterprising academics or journalists. In most cases, these revelations occur because of operational or bureaucratic failures. Operational security was not correctly followed, and operators improvised at the last minute or were careless. Of the known cases of CBW use in assassinations, many revelations were due to poor security. Many, however, came to light after decades of obscurity because of publication in memoirs or governmental investigations.

Table 4.1[19] shows that 16 States engaged in 118 assassination operations since the end of WWII. In categorizing State actors by political system, six were Communist states, six were repressive, non-Communist states, and four were democracies. The problem is that Table 4.1 likely undercounts the number of CBW assassination operations for the reasons described above. Therefore, the numbers shown in Table 4.1 are conservative, counting only operations revealed in authoritative sources, such as government reports, US Congressional investigations, and credible participant accounts. In almost all of the cases shown in Table 4.1, multiple credible sources are referenced for each operation. A similar database details an additional 61 alleged CBW assassinations. Data regarding alleged CBW assassinations often is single-source, and the information's credibility and reliability are in question. This unconfirmed data is not used here, but it demonstrates that the universe of possible CBW assassination operations likely is larger than reported in Table 4.1.

The perpetrators' goal of using CBW in assassinations almost always is for the death to appear natural or accidental, thereby confounding detection and attribution. Clandestine assassinations are complicated, time-consuming, and costly, but they have advantages over kinetic attacks. These advantages include the fact that they are undetectable, that they eliminate the likelihood of attribution and retribution, and that they provide the assassination team with time to escape.

19 The tables in this chapter are based on data collected by the author.

TABLE 4.1 CBW use on assassinations from 1946 to 2023

Country	# of CBW operations	Time period	CBW materials	Route of exposure
Bulgaria	5	1978	Ricin and chemical agents	Injection, ingestion, and dermal
Chile	13	1976–1981	Botulinum toxin, sarin	Injection and ingestion
Czechoslovakia	3	1959–c.1975	Poisoned food, poison	Ingestion
East Germany	1	1981	Food poisoned with thallium	Ingestion
France	3	1957–1960	Thallium, toxins	Ingestion and injection
Iran	6	1994–1998	Potassium	Injection
Iraq	9	1979–1995	Thallium	Ingestion
Israel	10	c. 1955–2000	Poisons and toxins	Ingestion and injection
North Korea	6	1996–2017	Chemical agents	Injection and dermal
Rhodesia	2	1975–1979	Ricin and poisoned food	Injection and ingestion
Russia	14	2000–2020	Poisons, toxins, and pathogen	Ingestion, injection, and dermal
South Africa	27	1980–1995	Poisons and botulinum toxin	Ingestion, injection, and dermal
Soviet Union	13	1947–1979	Chemicals, toxins, and pathogen	Ingestion, injection, and dermal
United Kingdom	1	c. 1955	Chemical agents	Inhalation and injection
United States	4	1960–1963	Chemical agents and botulinum toxin	Ingestion
Yugoslavia	1	1969	Chemical agents	Ingestion

3 Rationales behind Termination of CBW Use in Assassinations

Understanding the reasons behind why decision-makers end CBW use in assassinations almost always is difficult, mainly because these decisions are often made on a case-by-case basis within national intelligence organizations, which are themselves very secretive. Of the sixteen nations judged to have been involved in the use of CBW in operations to assassinate targets, only two, possibly three, did so for reasons likely connected to either norms or subsequent international agreements.

Although CBW use has continued, it has progressed through distinct periods, characterizing its use. In the first period, generally from 1946 to 1980, the Soviet Union and its allies – mainly at Moscow's urging – focused on internal security threats (opposition figures, regime critics, dissidents, and defectors). From 1952 to 1963, western democratic governments focused on emerging ideologically anti-Western foreign leaders. From 1976 to 1990, several pro-Western repressive regimes used CBW to assassinate regime threats. As in the cases of Chile, Iraq, Rhodesia, and South Africa, changes in government ended their CBW use in assassination by 1990.

The UK and US[20] intelligence services almost certainly ended CBW programs for assassinations before entering into the BWC. Based on Oleg Kalugin's comments, the Soviets, by the late 1970s or early 1980s, also may have revised their policy regarding CBW assassinations.[21] Whether the French intelligence service maintains a CBW capability for use in assassinations is unknown, but allegations have surfaced in France.[22]

Norm pressures or accession to either the BWC or the CWC likely did not end any State's CBW use in assassinations based on the available information.[23] From the available data, one can conclude that of the 16 identified States, regime change resulted in termination in seven States (44%), policy changes accounted for two States (12%), reasons are unknown in four States (25%), and three States (19%) have not terminated the use of CBW in assassination operations. An additional observation is that most of the 16 identified

20 The CIA retained stocks of marine toxins until after the US ratification of the BWC but claimed that the retention was inadvertently due to a record-keeping problem.

21 Oleg Kalugin, *Spymaster: My Thirty-two Years in Intelligence and Espionage Against the West* (Hachette UK, 2009) 180. Of course, any qualms the Kremlin may have harbored over CBW use in assassinations soon evaporated with the rise of Vladimir Putin.

22 Vincent Nouzille, *Les Tueurs de la République: Assassinats et Opérations Spéciales des Services Secrets*, (Paris: Favard, 2015).

23 Questions remain about the rationale behind the decisions to terminate the use of CBW in assassinations in a few countries (notably the UK and the US).

TABLE 4.2 State termination of CBW use in assassination operations

State	Active in CBW assassinations	Possible explanation for termination	Accession to 1925 Geneva Protocol	Accession to 1975 BWC	Accession to 1997 CWC
Bulgaria	1979	Unknown; possibly lack of indigenous technical capability or political consequences.	7.3.1934	2.6.1972	10.7.1994
Chile	1976–1980	Regime change	2.7.1935	22.4.1980	12.7.1996
Czechoslovakia	1959–c.1975	Unknown	16.8.1938	30.4.1973	Ceased to be a unified state on 31 December 1992
East Germany	1981	Regime change. Maintained a CBW assassination capability until 1988.	X	28.11.1972	German reunification on 3.10.1990
France	1956–1960	Unknown; interest in CBW use in assassinations persisted through the mid-1960s.	10.5.1926	27.9.1984	2.3.1995
Iran	1990–1998	Unknown; the regime imprisoned most of the assassins.	4.7.1929	22.8.1973	3.11.1997
Iraq	1979–1995	Regime change	18.8.1931	19.6.1991	13.1.2009
Israel	c. 1955–2010	Not terminated	10.2.1969	X	Signed on 13.1.1993 but not ratified
North Korea	1996–2017	Not terminated	22.12.1988	13.3.1987	X
Rhodesia	1975–1979	Regime change	X	X	Transitioned to Zimbabwe on 18 April 1980
Russia	2003–2023	Not terminated	5.4.1928	26.3.1975	5.12.1997
South Africa	1980–1993	Regime change	24.5.1930	3.11.1975	3.7.1995
Soviet Union	1947–1979	Regime change; although the program seems inactive from 1979 to 1991	5.4.1928	26.3.1975	Transitioned to Russia as successor state on 26.12.1991
United Kingdom	1956	Government policy change	9.4.1930	26.3.1975	13.5.1996

TABLE 4.2 State termination of CBW use in assassination operations (*cont.*)

State	Active in CBW assassinations	Possible explanation for termination	Accession to 1925 Geneva Protocol	Accession to 1975 BWC	Accession to 1997 CWC
United States	1960–1963	Government policy change	10.4.1975	26.3.1975	25.4.1997
Yugoslavia	1969	Regime change: only one known CBW assassination attempt, although Yugoslavia maintained a capability.	12.4.1929	25.10.1973	20.4.2000

States are either major powers or allies/client States of major powers, arguably lessening the power of CBW norms in constraining behaviors. The exceptions are North Korea, Rhodesia, and South Africa.[24] These States can be described as rogue states, acting largely outside the normative constraints of the international order.

All but one (North Korea) of the 16 identified States involved in CBW use in assassination operations have signed the CWC.[25] Since the CWC came into force in 1997, 22 instances of State use of CBW in assassination operations have taken place (see Table 4.3), involving four States, two of which have agreed to the CWC.[26] Twenty-two instances in the 28 years since the CWC came into force means that 19 percent of CBW assassination operations have taken place during the [illegible]

24 Rhodesia and South Africa both underwent regime changes which resulted in their reintegration into the international community. In Rhodesia's case, it became Zimbabwe in 1980.

25 Israel signed the CWC but did not ratify the agreement. Israel's general position is "peace first." Israel will not ratify the CWC until it has peace treaties with its Arab neighbors, and no longer is threatened by chemical weapons.

26 Although Israel has not ratified the CWC, the Israeli government supports the goals and values of the OPCW and has taken steps to align itself with international CW norms. Israel Ministry of Foreign Affairs, *Statement to the Fifth Review Conference of the Chemical Weapons Convention by Ambassador Modi Ephraim*, n.d. <https://www.opcw.org/sites/default/files/documents/2023/05/CWC%20REVCON5%20Israel%20National%20Statement%20FINAL.pdf>.

TABLE 4.3 CBW use in assassination since CWC came into force

State	# of CBW uses in assassination operations	Date	CWC accession
Iran	1	1998	1997
Israel	2	2009–2010	1993 (signed); not ratified
North Korea	5	2008–2017	–
Russia	14	2000–2023	1997

From this data, the reasonable conclusion is that the CBW norms and international agreements have had little effect on constraining State use of CBW in assassination operations. The weakness of the norms and international agreements to pressure States to abandon CBW assassinations likely is due to several factors. These factors include (1) the secret nature of CBW assassination operations and the capability to avoid detection, attribution, and accountability for norm violation, (2) the weakness of international responses when CBW assassination operations are detected, (3) repeated violations, here pointing to the continued unconstrained use of CBW in assassination operations, including increasingly brazen attacks (ex: Skripal) and (4) a general weakening of international norms as the consensus buttressing the post-WWII international order erodes.

4 Role of Secrecy in State CBW Use in Assassination Operations

The secrecy surrounding state CBW use in assassination operations complicates the issue of the permissibility or illegitimacy of such acts. In almost, if not all, cases where a State has used CBW in an assassination, the State has acted clandestinely. The secrecy surrounding the act has been a critical characteristic of these activities. Secrecy had hidden acts from the public's gaze, obscured the identity of the perpetrators and their sponsors, and complicated attribution. Of note, the use of covert action, including assassinations, also can free the perpetrating state from some normative constraints, such as sovereignty and human rights obligations.[27] An example in which illegality is normalized can be found in the motto of the French foreign intelligence service, the *Direction Générale de la Sécurité Extérieure* (DGSE). That moto, *Partout où nécessité fait loi* ("Wherever necessity makes law"), claims that necessity justifies action, even if illegal. An ethos involving illegal acts (i.e., violation of foreign laws) is not found only in the DGSE[28] but is common in most foreign intelligence services. The purpose is not to evade responsibility or accountability from their own government's oversight but to allow freedom of action to support the national interest as defined by governmental decision-makers. Does this evasion reflect the importance a violator attaches to the prohibitory norm?

More than a concern over norms, the resort to secrecy (covert operations) generally is employed for operational reasons. The principle of *pas vu, pas pris* (no consequences for undetected crimes) explains the rationale for covert actions.[29] In a 2020 *Institut de Recherche Stratégique de l'École Militaire* (IRSEM) paper, the authors assessed the following:

> … even if covert means do not conceal the state that sponsored an operation, they nevertheless protect the state's policymakers regardless of regime type. In other words, the covert character of these operations shields decision-makers from the political, diplomatic, and even legal ramifications of an assassination. Moreover, most of these costs seem to fade over time, while the benefits seem as immediate (elimination of a target) as they can be subjective (a perception of security or power). We conclude that the use of assassination as a political tool will probably become more widespread in the coming years.[30]

---

27 Yvan Lledo-Ferrer and Damien Van Puyvelde, 'Assassination: An Increasingly Uninhibited Instrument of Power' *Institut de Recherche Strategique de L'Ecole Militaire* Research Paper No. 100 (May 28, 2020) <https://www.irsem.fr/media/5-publications/notes-de-recherche-research-papers/2020/rp-irsem-100.pdf>. The *Institut de recherche stratégique de l'École militaire* (IRSEM) is a research institute within the French Ministry of Defense.

28 'Who Are We ? | DGSE' (n.d.) <https://www.dgse.gouv.fr/en/get-to-know-us/who-are-we>.

29 Lledo-Ferrer and Damien Van Puyvelde, 'Assassination: An Increasingly Uninhibited Instrument of Power' *Institut de Recherche Strategique de L'Ecole Militaire* Research Paper No. 100 (May 28, 2020) <https://www.irsem.fr/media/5-publications/notes-de-recherche-research-papers/2020/rp-irsem-100.pdf>.

30 Ibid., 5.

Few of the perpetrating states have shown concern for the impact that CBW use in assassinations may have on the norm, although almost all have been signatories to the Geneva Protocols and the later BWC and CWC. Such clandestine CBW use likely continues to be often undetected, however. To reiterate a caveat mentioned elsewhere here, the secrecy involved in these assassination operations has obscured the actual number of State uses of CBW in assassinations. Therefore, our knowledge of State use of CBW in assassinations is limited, and our numbers are conservative. A greater number of such assassinations are not only possible but also likely.

Public exposure of State CBW use in assassinations has resulted from intentional or unintentional information releases as well as from operational failures. Intentional releases often are the product of government investigations. A notable example is the Church committee hearings that exposed US operations to assassinate foreign leaders. Unintentional information releases include disclosures in memoirs, unofficial histories, or leaks to journalists. Much information is now publicly available to investigators online, via social media, or through online purchases. Bellingcat's investigative work, especially its exposes of Russian CW assassination operations,[31,32] is a prime example.

The footprint of CBW assassination operations lessens the ability of outside entities to detect, identify, and correctly attribute CBW assassination operations unless an operational failure occurs. These operations are planned and prepared for within the figurative walls of highly secretive intelligence and security organizations. Facilities used would have a very small CBW footprint, indistinguishable from other activities underway. Operational teams, including logistics, communication, and reconnaissance, would be small and discreet, using a variety of covers. The activities of these teams would only span several weeks to a couple of months. Not all teams would necessarily be present in the target location simultaneously. To reiterate, the discovery of these activities almost always is due to operational failures. Examples include the botched assassination in 1960 of Felix Moumie by a French agent, the 1997 attempted Israeli assassination of Hamas official

31 Bellingcat Investigation Team, 'The Dreadful Eight: GRU's Unit 29155 and the 2015 Poisoning of Emilian Gebrev - Bellingcat' (Bellingcat, 25 April 2021) <https://www.bellingcat.com/news/uk-and-europe/2019/11/23/the-dreadful-eight-grus-unit-29155-and-the-2015-poisoning-of-emilian-gebrev/>.

32 Bellingcat Investigation Team, 'Russia's Clandestine Chemical Weapons Programme and the GRU's Unit 29155 – Bellingcat' (Bellingcat, 25 October 2020) <https://www.bellingcat.com/news/uk-and-europe/2020/10/23/russias-clandestine-chemical-weapons-programme-and-the-grus-unit-21955/>.

Khaled Mashaal in Jordan;[33] the clumsy 2018 attempt on Sergei Skripal, and the inept poisoning of Alexei Navalny in 2020.[34]

5 Impact of Anemic International Responses

International reaction to all but a handful of incidents involving State CBW use in assassinations has either been silent or muted.[35] The responses that focused on CBW use almost all took place since the 2017 killing of Kim Jong-nam. Earlier reactions to assassinations involving CBW use expressed outrage over the violation of the assassination norm than CBW. Costs imposed on the violators are non-existent, negligible, or short-lived. The response, therefore, has failed to deter or effectively punish violators. As the likelihood of assassinations as a regular and acceptable form of transnational repression grows, unconstrained by effective international action to prevent it, the possibility of State CBW use in assassinations likewise increases.

Robust international reactions to known violations of the CBW norms and agreements are essential to ensure the strength of the norms. Violators must be held accountable for their actions if the norm is to remain viable and rele-

33 For details on the failure of the operation targeting Mashaal, see Misha Ben-David, 'The Man with the Antidote' *I Spy Podcast* (19 November 2019) <https://foreignpolicy.com/podcasts/ispy>.

34 So inept were the Russian operations in 2018 and 2020 that some academics erroneously claim that discovery was intentional, deliberately staged to message Putin's opponents and possible [illegible] the Kremlin and its security organizations. Claims that the intended purpose of Russian assassination operations is a form of strategic messaging or theatrical murder lack a sound evidentiary base to be credible. See Kevin P Riehle, 'Ignorance, Indifference, or Incompetence: Why Are Russian Covert Actions so Easily Unmasked?' (2024) 39 Intelligence and National Security 864; Karl Dewey, 'Poisonous Affairs: Russia's Evolving Use of Poison in Covert Operations' (2022) 29 The Nonproliferation Review 155; For a discussion of Russian operations as signaling and theater, see David V Gioe, Michael S Goodman and David S Frey, 'Unforgiven: Russian Intelligence Vengeance as Political Theater and Strategic Messaging' (2019) 34 Intelligence and National Security 561. Signaling, however, may have a second-order effect on an assassination operation gone wrong.

35 The lack of meaningful international reaction to many of these assassination operations may be due to delayed discovery. In many cases, the operation was not discovered or revealed for years after the event. For example, the operations to kill Patrice Lumumba (1960) and Fidel Castro (1960–1963) were not known until the Church Committee hearings revealed them in 1975. This delay is due to the secrecy that surrounded the operations, and such secrecy is an intended attribute of all CBW assassination operations.

vant. For most of this period, the international community has paid little attention to CBW use. This pattern first changed in 2017 with Kin Jong-nam and later in the 2018 Skripal attempt and, to a lesser extent, the 2020 Navalny assassination attempt. In March 2018, former Russian military intelligence colonel Sergey Skripal and his daughter Yulia were poisoned in Salisbury, England.[36] Although they became critically ill, both ultimately survived the attack. The UK government charged that Russia was behind the attempted assassination[37] using a Novichok nerve agent. In response, twenty Western governments expelled 153 Russian diplomats in protest over the Skripal poisoning[38,39] Furthermore, the US imposed two rounds of sanctions on Russia for its CW use.[40] Moscow retaliated for the expulsions by expelling 189 Western diplomats[41] and protested the US imposition of sanctions. The Russian government vehemently denied any involvement in the attack.[42]

In August 2020, Russian opposition leader Alexei Navalny became seriously ill during a flight from Tomsk to Moscow; the plane made an emergency landing, and Navalny was taken to a hospital in Omsk.[43] Two days later, he was evacuated to Germany, where an initial German laboratory analysis of Navalny's blood indicated the presence of a nerve agent. On his release from the hospital, Navalny declared that Russian President Putin was behind the

36 Vikram Dodd, Luke Harding, and Ewen MacAskill, 'Sergei Skripal: former Russian spy poisoned with nerve agent, say police' *The Guardian* (8 March 2018) <https://www.theguardian.com/uk-news/2018/mar/07/russian-spy-police-appeal-for-witnesses-as-cobra-meeting-takes-place>.

37 BBC, 'Russian spy: Highly likely Moscow behind attack, says Theresa May' (13 March 2018) <https://www.bbc.com/news/uk-43377856; https://www.opcw.org/sites/default/files/documents/EC/87/en/ec87nat12_e_.pdf>.

38 Julian Borger, Patrick Wintour, and Heather Stewart, 'Western allies expel scores of Russian diplomats over Skripal attack' *The Guardian* (27 March 2018) <https://www.theguardian.com/uk-news/2018/mar/26/four-eu-states-set-to-expel-russian-diplomats-over-skripal-attack> (accessed on 5 June 2023).

39 Alia Chughtai and Mariya Petkova, 'Skripal case diplomatic expulsions in numbers' *Al Jazeera* (3 Apr 2018) <https://www.aljazeera.com/news/2018/4/3/skripal-case-diplomatic-expulsions-in-numbers>.

40 Congressional Research Service, *Russia, the Skripal Poisoning, and US. Sanctions,* IF10962 (14 August 2019) <https://crsreports.congress.gov/product/pdf/IF/IF10962>.

41 Chughtai and Petkova (2018).

42 Kathrin Hille and David Bond, 'Russia denies role in nerve agent attack on former spy Skripal' *Financial Times* (9 March 2018) <https://www.ft.com/content/6a344cf4-2381-11e8-ae48-60d3531b7d11>.

43 BBC, 'Alexei Navalny: Putin critic 'probably poisoned' – doctors' (24 August 2020) <https://www.bbc.com/news/world-europe-53892900>.

attack on his life.[44] The international response against Russia to the Navalny attack was more muted than the British-orchestrated expulsions and sanctions following the Skripal attack. However, at the OPCW's Fifth Review Conference in May 2023, state parties of the CWC,[45] such as Croatia, the Czech Republic, Germany, Italy, Latvia, Lithuania, Norway, Romania, Sweden, Switzerland, the United Kingdom, and the United States, as well as representatives from the European Union, denounced Russia's intransigence to further investigations about the two cases and requested that Russia come clean about its involvement in these attacks. As of the writing of this article, Russia continues to deny any involvement in the Skripal and Navalny attacks.[46,47]

One explanation for the ineffective international response to these violations is "the emergence of great power competition and the resulting absence of unity necessary among great powers for effective compliance action,"[48] according to Amanda and Michael Moodie. They go on to quote Carmen Wunderlich et al, "the lesson is that without great power unity – or at least a useful measure of common resolve – the compliance and enforcement system in the nuclear [nonproliferation] regime does not work."[49] This lack of great power unity is evident in the UN Security Council deadlocks on Syrian CW use since 2018 and in deliberations during CWC and BWC Review Conferences. The Russian accusations of US and Ukrainian BW cooperation further

44 Philip Oltermann and Shaun Walker, 'Alexei Navalny says he believes Vladimir Putin was behind poisoning' *The Guardian* (1 October 2020) <https://www.theguardian.com/world/2020/oct/01/alexei-navalny-says-he-believes-vladimir-putin-was-behind-poisoning>.

45 Also, see '26th session of the OPCW Conference of the States Parties: Joint Statement on Alexey Navalny' (UK Government, 2021) <https://www.gov.uk/government/news/[illegible]-of-the-States-Parties-joint-statement-on-alexey-navalny>.

46 'Statement by the Head of the Russian Delegation, Deputy Minister of Industry and Trade of the Russian Federation Kirill Lysogorskiy at the Fifth Session of the Conference of the States Parties to Review the Operation of the Chemical Weapons Convention' (The Hague, 15–19 May 2023) <https://www.opcw.org/sites/default/files/documents/2023/05/RC-5%20Statement%20RF.pdf>.

47 This article was drafted before Mr. Navalny's death while a prisoner in a Russian Arctic penal compound.

48 Jeffrey A Larsen and Shane Smith (eds), *Arms Control at a Crossroads: Renewal or Demise?* (Lynne Rienner Publishers 2024) 179 <https://www.degruyter.com/document/doi/10.1515/9781685859879/html>.

49 Moodie and Moodie, 'Chemical and Biological Weapons' 179, quoting Carmen Wunderlich, Harald Müller and Una Jakob, *'WMD Compliance and Enforcement in a Changing Global Context'; WMD Compliance and Enforcement Series Paper* 11 (*UNIDIR, 2021*) *10* < https://unidir.org/wp-content/uploads/2023/05/Wunderlich-Muller-Jakob_WMD-Compliance-and-Enforcement-Paper-11_WMD-CE-in-a-Changing-Global-Context_2021-05-18.pdf>.

demonstrate the collapse of great power cooperation involving CBW compliance issues.[50]

6 Norms and Institutions Ineffective in Curtaining CBW Assassination Operations

A review of states assessed as involved in CBW assassination operations and the periods when those states were active shows that the CBW norms likely had little to no effect in constraining CBW use in most cases.[51] More concerning is that three states likely are continuing their CBW use in assassinations; however, of these three (Israel, North Korea, and Russia), only Russia is a party to both the BWC and CWC. Therefore, terminating CBW use in assassinations is more likely due to other factors than the normative prohibitions.

Assuming that sets of related norms are mutually supportive, will the collapse of one weaken the other, given the condition that the assassination norm and the CBW norm are equally relevant to prohibiting CBW use in assassinations? If the assassination norm collapses and the moral revulsion toward assassinations fades or even disappears, are the arguments against CBW use here relevant? The argument that CBW use results in greater suffering hardly stands the test. Suffering is suffering, and making moral judgments based on the degree to which a victim suffers is akin to counting the number of angels fit on the head of a pin. This harkens back to Winston Churchill's observation that death due to CW was no more or less morally objectionable than death by high explosive.[52] The implication is that the collapse of the assassination norm undermines the prohibition against CBW use in assassinations unless the international community acts to reassert the importance of preventing CBW use in assassinations.

50 Eva Siegmann, 'False Russian Claims Hijacked the Biological Weapons Treaty. Here's How to Reclaim It' *Bulletin of the Atomic Scientists* (27 May 2024) <https://thebulletin.org/2024/05/false-russian-claims-hijacked-the-biological-weapons-treaty-heres-how-to-reclaim-it/>. All of the documents from the Formal Consultative meeting can be found at <https://meetings.unoda.org/meeting/65052/documents>.

51 See Table 3 and accompanying text.

52 "Gas is a more merciful weapon than high explosive shell, and compels an enemy to accept a decision with less loss of life than any other agency of war," according to Churchill. See minute from the War Office, 12 May 1919, in Martin Gilbert (ed), *Winston S. Churchill, Document Volume 8: War and Aftermath, December 1916-June 1919* (Hillsdale College Press 2008), 649.

7 Attacks on the International Order and Consequences for the CBW Norms

The existing international order is unraveling at a quickening pace and must either evolve to concede greater political and economic power to emerging blocs or collapse. Collapse will produce a new international order, likely arising out of conflict.[53,54] In the second decade of the 21st century, international institutions and the norms underpinning them are threatened, and multipolar security concerns have replaced the Cold War rivalry.[55] A system based on strategic restraint has given way to great power competition reminiscent of the 19th century. Increasingly, the international order is facing challenges to its legitimacy. Russia, China, Iran, and a coalition of nations in the Global South are challenging the leadership of the US[56] and Western European states.

One delegitimizing factor is the weakening of the capacity for strategic restraint (i.e., to work through international institutions and forego coercive instruments of national power). Arguably, as a hegemon faces mounting challenges, its ability to influence world events through international institutions and focus on international cooperation weakens. With the diminished capacity to operate through international bodies, the hegemon or hegemonic aspirants abandon strategic restraint and operate through the use of force. Evidence of the US failure to exercise strategic restraint can be found in the 1999 intervention in Kosovo, the post-9/11 military interventions in Iraq and Afghanistan, and the Global War on Terror (GWOT). As an aspiring revanchist hegemon, Russia has failed to exercise strategic restraint in the 2014 occupation of Crimea and its 2022 invasion of Ukraine. China's growing assertiveness

53 Adam Ward 'Adapt or Die' in *Ideas for Modernizing the Rules-Based International Order* (Chatham House, June 2019) 3. Ward also commented, "A tolerance of conflicts to correct imbalances was implicit to the scheme" (p. 3).

54 Arguably, the "old international order" is not easily "swept away," according to Ikenberry. Suggesting either that powerful challengers succeed or more likely that any new international order contains institutions, norms, and rules of the old. See G. John Ikenberry, 'The Rise, Character, and Evolution of International Order' in Orfeo Fioretos (ed), *International Politics and Institutions in Time* (Oxford University Press 2017) 59 <https://academic.oup.com/book/8563/chapter/154449998>.

55 David A. Lake, Lisa L. Martin, and Thomas Risse, 'Challenges to the Liberal Order: Reflections on *International Organization*' (2021) 75 International Organization 225, 257.

56 Growing isolationist, populist, and protectionist tendencies are eroding the legitimacy of US leadership in the world. See Rebecca Adler-Nissen and Ayşe Zarakol, 'Struggles for Recognition: The Liberal International Order and the Merger of Its Discontents' (2021) 75 International Organization, 611.

in the South China Sea and bellicose actions towards Taiwan point to a weakening of strategic restraint on Beijing's part.

In an era experiencing a weakening of strategic restraint by the major powers (i.e., declining international cooperation and an increasing resort to military force), the world is increasingly anarchic as institutions and norms prove less and less ability to constrain States from bad acts. In what is for security likely a zero-sum game, Cicero's adage *silent enim leges inter arma* ("In times of war, law falls silent)[57] is pertinent to this discussion of norms. Setting aside that this aphorism commonly excuses acts of dubious morality, the point here is that conflict often leads to norm evolution/adaptation and even norm death. Noncompliance to norms is greatest during conflict. The historical record demonstrates that states are likely to pursue their national security interests with little regard for international norms or agreements, especially if goals can be achieved covertly.

Historically, the failure of one international order begets conflict, spawning a new international order.[58] The impact of these changes on international norms remains uncertain. One possible impact on norms of a fractious international security environment is selective adherence to norms. A March 2022 paper from the US National Intelligence Council (NIC) stated the following:

> Diminishing consensus among the major state powers is likely to make it more difficult to condemn or punish bad behavior. In this fragmented environment, states and nonstate actors are likely to see fewer risks in ignoring certain norms, leading some to opt out entirely to selectively adhere or to offer alternative norms.[59]

The NIC paper went on to assess that arms control and nonproliferation norms likely were among those at the highest risk of weakening compliance over the next decade with contravention by at least one major state.[60]

57 Marcus Tullius Cicero, *Pro Milone*.

58 G John Ikenberry, *After Victory: Institutions, Strategic Restraint, and the Rebuilding of Order after Major Wars, New Edition* (Princeton University Press 2019) <http://www.jstor.org/stable/10.2307/j.ctv3znxov>.

59 US National Intelligence Council, 'US-Backed International Norms Increasingly Contested' *NIC Global Trends*, NIC-2021-02491 (October 2021) <https://www.dni.gov/files/images/globalTrends/GT2040/NIC-2021-02491_GT_Future_of_Int_Norms_22Mar22_UNSOURCED.pdf>.

60 Ibid.

8 Are CBW Norms under Attack?

The eroding international order inevitably stresses norms, including the CBW norms. Although the CBW norms crystallized in the interwar period following the horrors of chemical warfare during World War I, those norms underwent enormous stresses during WWII and neared the breaking point.[61] This historical context was one dominated by the European Great Powers and the emerging global influence of the United States. After WWII, the geopolitical environment was conditioned by post-war international order, related institutions, and the Cold War.

Absent large-scale military conflict, several factors are stressing the CBW norms. These include (1) the use of CW in current conflicts, notably the Russian use of riot control agents (RCAs) in Ukraine and the Syrian use of CW against its civilian population, (2) the use of CW in the 2017 assassination of Kim Jong-nam, the 2018 assassination attempt targeting Sergei Skripal, and the 2020 assassination attempt on Alexei Navalny, (3) CBW terrorism, chiefly efforts by ISIS/Daesh to weaponize CBW agents, (4) the politicization and disinformation relating to claims about Ukrainian BW laboratories, and (5) concerns over the relevance of the CBW norms and institutions in the face of the rapid pace of technological change. Although, in the aggregate, these factors contribute to stressing the CBW norms, efforts to strengthen the relevant institutions and combat politicization and disinformation will sustain both the norms and those international agreements.

9 Origins of the CBW Norms and Continuing Relevance

The norm against CW use stretches its origins back to the historical prohibitions against the use of poisons.[62] Noteworthy and often cited is Hugo Grotius's admonition in Book III of his De Jure Bellis ac Pacis, in which he states, "Nevertheless, from old times the law of nations – if not of all nations, certainly of those of the better sort – has been that it is not permissible to kill an enemy

61 Frederic Joseph Brown, *Chemical Warfare: A Study in Restraints* (Princeton University Press 2015).

62 Richard Price, 'A Genealogy of the Chemical Weapons Taboo' *International Organization* Vol. 49, No. 1 (Winter, 1995) 73–103. The historical origins of the CW norm are well-explored in several publications, most notably in Richard M Price, *The Chemical Weapons Taboo* (1. publ, Cornell Univ Press 1997).

by poison."[63] Grotius argued that the use of poisons was a more significant threat to monarchs than to soldiers, and hence, the prohibition arguably focused on the use of poisons in assassinations. Later, in Book III, he addressed the use of poisoned weapons and water contamination.

The seminal prohibition of poisons is found in the US Army's General Order No. 100, issued on April 24, 1863, and commonly known as the Lieber Code, written by Franz Lieber. The Lieber Code states, "The use of poison in any manner, be it to poison wells, or food, or arms, is wholly excluded from modern warfare. He that uses it puts himself out of the pale of the law and usages of war."[64] The 1899 Hague Convention was the first international agreement banning the use of CBW in wartime. The convention expressly prohibited the use of projectiles with asphyxiating gases.[65] The impact of poison gas use during WWI propelled the codification of laws prohibiting its use in war. The norm prohibiting CBW use[66] was first codified in the 1925 Geneva Protocols, and the prohibition of the development, possession, and use of chemical and bacteriological weapons was further strengthened in both the BWC[67] and CWC.

The issue is whether the CBW norms and the associated international agreements remain relevant. The simple and almost incontrovertible answer is yes. Constraint of CBW development, possession, and use remains an absolute moral imperative. The unquestioned importance of CBW prohibitions is demonstrated by both the near universality of the BWC and CWC and international support for these agreements, especially by the major powers. Looking at discursive support for the norms and institutions supports the validity of the norms, and the lessons of Syria's use of CW against its own population render the question mute.[68] However, the question remains whether the

63 Stephen C. Neff, *Hugo Grotius on the Law of War and Peace: Student Edition* (Cambridge University Press 2012) 353–54.

64 United States. War Department and Francis Lieber, *Instructions for the Government of Armies of the United States in the Field* (1863), 7.

65 'The Avalon Project: Laws of War – Declaration on the Use of Projectiles the Object of Which Is the Diffusion of Asphyxiating or Deleterious Gases; July 29, 1899' (n.d.) <https://avalon.law.yale.edu/19th_century/dec99-02.asp>.

66 The inclusion of the prohibition of BW use in war was an afterthought, first proposed by the Polish delegation.

67 The BWC does not explicitly prohibit BW use, but the prohibition on use is implied by the bans on development, production, and possession. The 1925 Geneva Protocol banned CBW use among parties to the agreement, and many nations registered reservations permitting use in retaliation.

68 The complicating issue is that Syria at the time was not a State Party to the CWC. The OPCW was in effect powerless to compel Syria to conform to the CWC's prohibitions. This situation changed only when Syria agreed to accede to the CWC following a bilateral

norms will remain relevant, given the challenges posed by actors seeking to revise the current international order.

10 Discursive Support for the CBW Norms and Conventions

Discursive support for the norms is essential to their viability, and all state parties to the BWC and CWC discursively support the CBW's prohibitory norms and customary law relating to CBW. Given this discursive support for the CBW norms and the near-universal acceptance of both the BWC and CWC as measured by the number of States Parties, the CBW norms and related international agreements appear strong. These State violators have not sought to create an exception and would likely argue that an exception does not exist. The question, then, is whether the actions of transgressors are significant to the strength of the norms or institutions. As a state party to both the BWC and CWC, Russia's blatant and continuous use of CBW in assassinations demonstrates a consistent State practice in contravention of the norm and the conventions. Nevertheless, Moscow discursively has consistently supported the conventions and denied the alleged violations. Significantly, international reaction to these violations has weakened over time, suggesting that the international community is experiencing "sanctions fatigue." Alternatively, the international community may have exhausted all the significant sanctions available to it, given the multiple rounds of sanctions imposed on Russia following its February 2022 invasion of Ukraine.

11 Are There Exceptions to the CBW Prohibitions

Have the CBW norms had an appreciable effect on constraining state CBW use in assassinations, or has a pattern of state practice, in effect, created an exception to the CBW prohibitory norms? One argument is that state practice drives (or can drive) changes to the norm, including the formation of exceptions (or selective adherence, as described in the NIC paper). Norms evolve in response to conditions, which is necessary for norms to remain relevant. Here, a norm is synonymous with customary law, a universal law defined by a consistent his-

agreement between the US and Russia to resolve this impasse. See Joby Warrick, *Red Line: The Unraveling of Syria and America's Race to Destroy the Most Dangerous Arsenal in the World* (Doubleday 2021).

tory of continuous state practice and *opinio juris*. State practice needs to be sufficiently general, representative, and consistent.[69] It should also be public and accessible, often published. Once state practice is accepted as law, states accept a legal obligation to uphold it as law (*opinio juris*), and customary law is formed.[70]

The question then is whether state CBW use in assassinations over decades and by several states as a form of state practice has created an exception to the CBW norms. Here, state practice requires that the practice be sufficiently general and public. In the cases of CBW use in assassinations, the number of states engaging in CBW assassinations has been relatively small – a total of 16 – and the number has declined to three known or suspected perpetrators. Furthermore, state practice known to only a few government officials arguably does not constitute a basis for forming customary law or exceptions to customary law. This point is essential in the discussion of secrecy and whether state CBW use in assassinations forms an exception to the norm. State CBW use in assassinations by its very character is covert, that is, secret,[71] from external observation. Covert action, in and of itself, is not necessarily illegal under international law.[72] As a general principle, covert state actions do not have precedential value. Alexandra Perina stated in her 2015 article, "A covert event cannot serve as a legitimizing precedent for other states' behavior, and in that respect, it may be less destructive than an overt, acknowledged violation."[73] Perina argues that even known or suspected violations lack precedential value if not acknowledged by the perpetrator.[74] Therefore, state CBW use in assassinations does not affect customary law or the CBW norms, and this state practice does not create an exception to the norms.

---

69 United Nations International Law Commission, *Yearbook of the International Law Commission 2018, Vol.II, Part 2* (United Nations 2018), 91.

70 Ibid., 91.

71 Berkeley La Raza Law Journal, 'Legality of Covert Action under Contemporary International Law' <https://lawcat.berkeley.edu/record/1112136>.

72 "Despite widespread public perception that covert conduct necessarily violates international law, states act covertly for a range of legitimate political, diplomatic, and strategic reasons. Covert behavior may be – though certainly is not always – consistent with international law." See Alexandra H. Perina, 'Black Holes and Open Secrets: The Impact of Covert Action on International Law' *Columbia Journal of Transnational Law* 53, no. 3 (1 January 2015) 507–83 <http://jtl.columbia.edu/wp-content/uploads/sites/4/2015/06/Perina-Article_53-CJTL-507.pdf>.

73 Ibid.

74 Ibid., 574.

However, the US Supreme Court ruled in *Bond v. United States* (2011) that the US statute (18 U.S.C. 229) implementing the CWC does not apply to all cases in which a chemical agent is intentionally used to cause harm.[75] The appellant, Bond, argued before the Court that her conduct (i.e., use of a chemical agent to cause harm to a rival for her husband's affections) did not fall under the provisions of 18 U.S.C 229 and that she should not have been prosecuted under that federal statute. The US Supreme Court found, in essence, that the statute covered chemical weapons and grave uses such as during wartime, in terrorist attacks, or assassinations, but did not reach to use in simple assaults, which remained the purview of local authorities. Therefore, the CWC and the US implementing statute intruded on State police powers.[76] From a reading of the US Supreme Court's opinion, the CWC does not cover all intentional uses of chemical agents to kill or cause harm (chiefly criminal murder and assault, which fall under local jurisdiction). However, the statute covers State uses, including assassination and terrorist possession and use.

12 Conclusion

The fact that CBW use in assassinations has taken place since 1946 is incontrovertible. CBW use in assassinations, as a tool of transnational repression, likely will involve a growing number of states and incidents. The CBW norms have been and likely will be ineffective in constraining CBW assassination operations. Their ineffectiveness primarily is due to the secrecy surrounding these operations,[77] but also because of weak international responses. This ineffectiveness does not invalidate the norms, which continue to garner the support of the major powers as well as almost all UN member states. Stresses, however, may produce evolutionary pressures, bringing about changes needed to preserve the norm's relevance. International normative prohibitions existent before the BWC and CWC came into force essentially were ineffective in preventing or constraining state CBW use in assassinations. The ex-

75 *Bond v. United States*, 564 US. 211 (2011) <https://supreme.justia.com/cases/federal/us/564/211/>.

76 *Bond v United States* (LII/Legal Information Institute, 2 June 20149 <https://www.law.cornell.edu/supremecourt/text/12-158>.

77 Secrecy delays detection and complicates attribution to the point that the actor(s) may be identified years after the fact.

istence of the BWC and CWC probably has had little impact on CBW use in assassination operations.[78]

Since the conventions, notably the CWC, came into force in 1997, fewer states have reported CBW use, and two of these (Israel and North Korea) are not parties to both conventions. Russia, party to both the BWC and CWC, continues to employ CBW in assassinations with apparent indifference to the normative prohibitions. If unrestrained by the international community, Russia's blatant contravention of international agreements may spur other states' covert CBW use in assassinations. Those states willing to use CBW in assassinations likely believe that they are protected by others' inability to detect their actions (*pas vu, pas pris*) or attribute them, and – if detected – the Russia example will translate to weaker and short-lived international reactions.

To be effective in halting future CBW assassination operations, the international community needs to recognize (1) the ongoing and persistent use of CBW in assassinations, (2) that this threat is qualitatively and quantitatively different than that posed by military CBW munitions, and (3) that this strong and timely costs must be imposed on violators. Clearly, the international community needs to act to strengthen the CBW norms and expand and reinforce the tools available to nations and international institutions to respond more effectively to CBW use in assassinations. Tools to quickly detect and attribute CBW use will allow governments to hold violators accountable and possibly deter future CBW assassinations. Enhancing international cooperation and coordination, as well as information sharing, could strengthen the abilities of nations to combat this threat. Interpol, for example, can be useful in coordinating national law enforcement agencies and issuing red notices for the arrest and extradition of those involved in CBW assassinations.[79]

As Amanda and Michael Moodie also mention, the CBW arms control community may need to reconsider the models and paradigms that shape deliberations regarding CBW issues.[80] Given the changes in the geopolitical environ-

78 As noted above, regime change has cut the number of States using CBW in assassinations, thereby reducing the overall number of CBW assassination operations since 1990. This impact is clearly demonstrated in the case of South Africa, which rivaled the Soviet Union/Russia in total CBW assassination operations. With the end of South Africa's apartheid government, the number of subsequent CBW assassination operations dropped.

79 Interpol played just such a role in response to Israel's 2010 assassination of Hamas weapons procurement official Mahmoud al-Mabhouh in Dubai. See '11 'Mabhouh Killers' on Interpol List' *The Jerusalem Post* (18 February 2010) <https://www.jpost.com/international/11-mabhouh-killers-on-interpol-list>.

80 Moodie and Moodie, 'Chemical and Biological Weapons', 181.

ment and growing security challenges around the globe, new structures and mechanisms may be needed to confront CBW noncompliance and to break the political deadlock resulting from political polarization.[81] Institutions and the underlying rules may need to adapt. The impact on the CBW norms so far is unknown.

81 Carmen Wunderlich, Harald Müller, and Una Jakob, "WMD Compliance and Enforcement in a Changing Global Context," WMD Compliance and Enforcement Series Paper 11 (UNIDIR, 2021), https://unidir.org/wp-content/uploads/2023/05/Wunderlich-Muller-Jakob_WMD-Compliance-and-Enforcement-Paper-11_WMD-CE-in-a-Changing-Global-Context_2021-05-18.pdf.

CHAPTER 5

Industry's Role in CBW Norms

Detlef Männig

1 Introduction

In industry, the term "norms" is usually associated with technical standards that industry and other entities have designed to speed up the development and use of products, the optimization of supply chains, and to make life easier for consumers.[1] They are very far-reaching and have widely varying applications, such as USB ports[2] or container sizes,[3] to name just two examples. With regard to organizational performance, there are, among others International Standard Organization (ISO)[4] Standards often used synonymously with "Norms".[5,6] Best known and widely used are ISO 9001 (Quality Management Systems)[7] and ISO 14001 (Environmental Management Systems).[8] Related to the CBW context are Environmental, Social, and Govern-

1 Presented at Workshop "Chemical and Biological Weapons: The Interconnectivity of Norms", Giessen, Germany, October 23–24, 2023.

2 Wikipedia, 'USB' (Wikipedia, The Free Encyclopedia) <https://usb.org/documents>.

3 Wikipedia, 'Intermodal container' (20 June 2024) <https://cdn.standards.iteh.ai/samples/76912/7354663676144f8ab1a7b57cb573b0a6/ISO-668-2020.pdf>.

4 International Organization for Standardization, 'ISO - International Organization for Standardization' <https://www.iso.org/home.html>.

5 The German "Deutsches Institut für Normung e.V. (DIN)" is in English the "German Institute for Standardization": <https://www.din.de/en/about-standards/a-brief-introduction-to-standards>.

6 European Standards, sometimes called Euronorm abbreviated EN, from the German name Europäische Norm, "European Norm": Wikipedia, 'European Standard' (20 June 2024) <https://en.wikipedia.org/wiki/European_Standard>.

7 With more than one million certificates issued to organizations in 189 countries, ISO 9001 is the most widely used quality management standard in the world: International Organization for Standardization, ISO 62085:2021, Plastics – Determination of ultimate anaerobic biodegradation in marine sediment (ISO, 2021) <https://www.iso.org/standard/62085.html>.

8 International Organization for Standardization, ISO 60857:2019, Plastics – Determination of the ultimate anaerobic biodegradation of plastic materials in an aqueous system – Method by measurement of biogas production (ISO, 2019) <https://www.iso.org/standard/60857.html>.

 | DOI:10.1163/9789004739192_006

ance Investing (ESG),[9] the UN Global Compact[10] and Responsible Care® (RC) [11] including the RC Security Code.[12] It is a requirement to join the International Council of Chemical Associations (ICCA) to support the CWC.[13] Along with this, ICCA together with the International Union of Pure and Applied Chemistry (IUPAC)[14] endorsed "The Hague Ethical Guidelines",[15,16] Many companies[17] also endorse the United Nations Sustainable Development Goals (UN SDGs)[18] and have committed themselves to reporting under other standards.[19] All of those exemplary activities are by setup (charters, by-laws, codices, contracts, etc.) voluntary.[20] However, some have gained a quasi-legally-binding status for different reasons. Some institutional investors require reporting on Environmental, Social, and Governance (ESG)

---

9 'What Is ESG Investing?' (Investopedia, 21 March 2024) <https://www.investopedia.com/terms/e/environmental-social-and-governance-esg-criteria.asp>.

10 "The world's largest sustainability initiative": United Nations Global Compact, 'What Is the UN Global Compact?' (United Nations Global Compact) <https://unglobalcompact.org/what-is-gc>.

11 International Council of Chemical Associations (ICCA), 'Responsible Care' (ICCA) <https://icca-chem.org/focus/responsible-care/>.

12 <https://cefic.org/app/uploads/2024/05/ResponsibleCare_SecurityCode.pdf>

13 International Council of Chemical Associations, 'Industry Enhances Cooperation with OPCW' (ICCA 9 May 2017) <https://icca-chem.org/news/industry-enhances-cooperation-with-opcw/>.

14 International Union of Pure and Applied Chemistry, 'IUPAC Endorses the Hague Ethical Guidelines' (IUPAC, 4 May 2016) <https://iupac.org/iupac-endorses-the-hague-ethical-guidelines/>.

15 International Council of Chemical Associations, 'ICCA Statement on the Hague Ethical Guidelines' (ICCA, 27 April 2018) <https://icca-chem.org/news/icca-statement-on-the-hague-ethical-guidelines/>.

16 Organisation for the Prohibition of Chemical Weapons, 'The Hague Ethical Guidelines' (OPCW) <https://www.opcw.org/hague-ethical-guidelines>.

17 e.g. Evonik Industries AG, 'Sustainable Development Goals' (Evonik Industries AG) <https://corporate.evonik.com/en/sustainability/sustainable-development-goals>.

18 United Nations, 'Sustainable Development Goals' (United Nations) <https://sdgs.un.org/goals>.

19 Such as the: Global Reporting Initiative (GRI) <https://www.globalreporting.org/>; Disclosure Insight Action (CDP) <https://www.cdp.net/en>; International Financial Reporting Standards Foundation, 'International Sustainability Standards Board' (IFRS Foundation) <https://www.ifrs.org/groups/international-sustainability-standards-board/>.

20 An exception will be the Corporate Sustainability Reporting Directive (CSRD): European Commission, 'Commission Adopts European Sustainability Reporting Standards' (European Commission, 31 July 2023) <https://finance.ec.europa.eu/news/commission-adopts-european-sustainability-reporting-standards-2023-07-31_en>.

performance,[21,22] sometimes used interchangeably with "Socially Responsible Investment (SRI).[23] The market volume is estimated to be close to USD 3 trillion.[24] Related to "purely" financial aspects are issues of securing the supply chain and quality assurances by suppliers, thus ensuring business operations.[25] Especially in the case of Quality Management, many companies would be out of business if they could not demonstrate compliance. Finally, demonstrating sound responsible performance contributes to being an attractive employer and sustaining social/political acceptance.[26]

2 Trust-Building and Verification

Key issues are certification, verification, and confidence-building, which are also elements of the CWC and the BWC. In industry, keeping up the norms is done basically in three ways. The first is inspections of suppliers by (potential) customers. This can be done with paperwork only or on-site. A special case is the "Know your Customer" principle[27] performed by suppliers in order to prevent chemicals from getting into the wrong hands, but also to ensure payments, and to avoid reputational damage (see below). This is the subject of an OPCW workshop to be published shortly. The second way is to use a network in which audits, which have already been performed by other companies

21 Investopedia, 'FTSE4Good Index' (Investopedia) <https://www.investopedia.com/terms/f/ftse4good-index.asp>.

22 Goldman Sachs, 'Sustainability Reporting' (Goldman Sachs) <https://www.goldmansachs.com/investor-relations/corporate-governance/sustainability-reporting/>.

23 Coryanne Hicks, 'Socially Responsible Investing (SRI)' (*Forbes* magazine, 24 May 2023) <https://www.forbes.com/advisor/investing/sri-socially-responsible-investing/>.

24 Statista, 'Sustainable Funds: Asset Size by Region' <https://www.statista.com/statistics/1296334/sustainable-funds-asset-size-by-region/>.

25 Cefic, 'Safety and Quality for Sustainability' (Cefic) <https://cefic.org/a-solution-provider-for-sustainability/a-journey-to-sustainability/safety-and-quality-for-sustainability/>.

26 Natalie Chladek, 'Business Sustainability Strategies' (Harvard Business School Online 06 November 2019) <https://online.hbs.edu/blog/post/business-sustainability-strategies>.

27 Originally for banking only: European Parliament, 'New EU Rules to Combat Money Laundering Adopted' (European Parliament, 24 April 2024) <https://www.europarl.europa.eu/news/en/press-room/20240419IPR20586/new-eu-rules-to-combat-money-laundering-adopted>.

or institutions, are commonly accepted.[28] The third way is to rely on certificates provided by certifying companies.[29]

In general, all activities should serve to ensure that chemicals are transported, stored, used, and eventually recycled, or safely disposed of in accordance with Responsible Care® and the UN Strategic Approach to Chemicals Management (SAICM), now known as the "Global Framework on Chemicals".[30]

2.1 *The Beginnings*[31]

Since the mid-1970s, individual representatives of the chemical industry participated ad-hoc or by invitation from governments in the negotiations at the UN CCD and later CD to address specific industry issues. At that time, it was not clear yet, whether there would be any enforceable verification mechanisms (lacking with the BWC) and what role the chemical industry would play in a future CWC. Does it only impact diplomacy and military, or would it extend to producers and users of chemicals? To be prepared, several chemical industry associations built up working groups "Against Chemical Weapons" to inform their member companies of ongoing discussions in the UN framework.[32]

A game changer was the Government-Industry Conference in Canberra 1989,[33] where the critical role of the chemical industry in the future shaping of a Convention was recognized by negotiators and industry alike. It more or less coincided with the global rollout of the Responsible Care® program in chemical industry, which among other topics formalized the responsible man-

28 See e.g. The "Together for Sustainability" (TfS) initiative <https://www.tfs-initiative.com>; Safety & Quality Assessment for Sustainability (SQAS) <https://sqas.org/>.

29 Meticulous Research, 'Top 10 Companies in Testing, Inspection, and Certification Market' (Meticulous Research, n.d.) <https://meticulousblog.org/top-10-companies-in-testing-inspection-and-certification-market/>.

30 United Nations Environment Program 'Global Frameworks on Chemicals' <https://www.chemicalsframework.org/>.

31 Some of the statements are based on unpublished reminiscences by the successor to Dr. Schrader, who thus knew of the history of the development of Tabun and Sarin and was an expert in pesticides, especially in P-esters. He was therefore appointed a member of a group of experts to advise the German delegation at the CCD and CD from the early 1970s to the late 1980s. The author was involved in CWC issues only since the mid-1980s.

32 e.g. in India: Indian Chemical Council, 'Chemical Weapons Convention (CWC) Helpdesks Managed by ICC' <https://www.indianchemicalcouncil.com/chemical-weapons-convention-CWC-helpdesks-managed-by-ICC.htm>.

33 *Government-Industry Conference against Chemical Weapons, National Convention Centre, Canberra 18–22 September 1989: Final Record* (Dept of Foreign Affairs and Trade 1989).

agement of chemicals by all those who handle and use them along the product chain.[34,35]

Along with that came a more formalized participation of chemical industry experts in the Geneva negotiations.[36] A key issue was the question, which civil chemical production sites would in the future be subjected to what kinds of verification activities. This is how the Schedules 1, 2 and 3 of the Verification Annex according to Art. VI of the CWC evolved.[37] Various proposals were tabled to reach out beyond listed chemicals (types of synthesis carried out, materials of construction, "super-toxic lethal chemicals", ad-hoc inspections, trial inspections, capability, convertibility), but the chemical industry pointed out that all facilities could potentially be converted given political will, resources and know-how. This is how eventually Part IX of the Verification Annex to the CWC[38] was shaped when chemical industry proposed that unlimited access to all of its plants ("anytime, anywhere, no right of refusal") should be established, not only under Art. IX ("Challenge Inspections") of the CWC.[39]

During the final negotiations and the establishment of the Provisional Technical Secretariat (PTS) of the future OPCW,[40] a host of activities by the chemical industry evolved:

2.2 *Auditing of Future Data Security*

At that time, data security was still in its infancy. However, concerns arose whether data obtained by the future TS would remain confidential according

34 Cefic, 'Responsible Care' <https://cefic.org/responsible-care/>.

35 International Council of Chemical Associations (ICCA), 'Responsible Care' <https://icca-chem.org/focus/responsible-care/>.

36 As an example, the author and other colleagues from chemical industry were officially accredited as members of the German Delegation.

37 Organisation for the Prohibition of Chemical Weapons, 'Chemical Weapons Convention: Annex on Chemicals' (OPCW) <https://www.opcw.org/chemical-weapons-convention/annexes/annex-chemicals/annex-chemicals>.

38 Organisation for the Prohibition of Chemical Weapons, 'Part IX: Regime for Other Chemical Production' (opcw) <https://www.opcw.org/chemical-weapons-convention/annexes/verification-annex/part-ix-regime-other-chemical-production>.

39 Organisation for the Prohibition of Chemical Weapons, 'Article IX: Consultations, Cooperation and Fact-Finding' (OPCW) <https://www.opcw.org/chemical-weapons-convention/articles/article-ix-consultations-cooperation-and-fact-finding>.

40 Organisation for the Prohibition of Chemical Weapons, 'Preparatory Commission' (OPCW) <https://www.opcw.org/resources/documents/preparatory-commission>.

to the Confidentiality Annex of the CWC.[41] An expert of chemical industry was tasked with this and indeed found that data leaks were possible when using external Compact Discs (CDs) or flash drives (USB sticks).[42] That this is still an ongoing issue was exemplified by an alleged breach of confidentiality[43] and Russian attempts to hack into the OPCW.[44]

2.3 *Publications in Trade Journals to Increase Awareness for CWC Issues*

Chemical industry associations traditionally inform their members about developments of relevance to their constituencies through periodic newsletters in printed form. Later, this was mostly replaced by postings on their websites and e-mails. For many companies that is their sole source of information, since only big companies can afford to have staff dedicated to monitoring political and legal developments affecting them directly or indirectly. This holds for today as well and is one of the reasons why chemical industry associations play an important role in communication between the OPCW and National Authorities with chemical industry players.

2.4 *Test Run of Questionnaire for Art. VI Reporting*

Art. VI and the relevant annexes are technically very complex. They needed to be "translated" into workable national implementation legislation and reporting templates. This was done by trial reporting exercises.[45] In the meantime, this process is standardized and done mostly electronically.[46] However, different applications of Product Group Codes in national implementation and es-

41 Annex on the Protection of Confidential Information of the CWC: Organisation for the Prohibition of Chemical Weapons, 'Confidentiality Annex' <https://www.opcw.org/chemical-weapons-convention/annexes/confidentiality-annex>.

42 Personal recollection by author; the results were never publicized.

43 Alex Assad, 'The OPCW Douma Leaks Part 4: The OPCW Investigation' (Bellingcat, 11 February 2020) <https://www.bellingcat.com/news/mena/2020/02/11/the-opcw-douma-leaks-part-4-the-opcw-investigation/>.

44 BBC News, 'Salisbury Novichok Suspects Say They Were Only Visiting Cathedral' (BBC News, 5 October 2018) <https://www.bbc.com/news/world-europe-45747472>.

45 Personal recollection of author: A draft questionnaire designed by the German authority, the German Chemical Industry Association (VCI) and the University of Frankfurt (Prof. Dr. Bothe) was sent to selected companies, and their feedback was evaluated.

46 SIX: Organisation for the Prohibition of Chemical Weapons, 'Note by the Director-General: Request from Iraq for the Removal of Chemical Weapons' (OPCW Document S/1192/2014 1 July 2014) <https://www.opcw.org/sites/default/files/documents/S_series/2014/en/s-1192-2014_e_.pdf>; and EDIS: Organisation for the Prohibition of Chemical Weapons, 'Electronic Declaration Information System (EDIS)' (OPCW) <https://www.opcw.org/resources/declarations/electronic-declaration-information-system-edis>.

pecially import/export data result in a high amount of "transfer discrepancies".[47] So far – despite two workshops organized by the chemical industry –, there has been little or no progress in harmonizing national reporting.

2.5 *Regular Meetings of Chemical Industry Representatives with National Authorities on Practical Issues of Future Implementation and Site Visits*

An international agreement with direct impact on chemical and downstream industries (declarations and inspections) by an international inspectorate was absolutely novel to these industries.[48] Industry was used to declarations and inspections by several national authorities but subjecting these to an international organization had to be implemented legally and organizationally, as well as taking into account confidential data.[49]

2.6 *Repeated Statements That the Chemical Industry Is Categorically Opposed to the Misuse of Chemical Products for CW Production Purposes and Supports OPCW Activities*

It more or less began with a refusal from the private chemical industry to provide chemicals for chemical weapons production.[50] Of particular importance was a public appeal by the US. American chemical industry to the US. government to urge ratifying the CWC.[51] References for this topic are up to this date made on numerous websites of chemical industry associations worldwide.[52]

---

47 1.52 of: Organisation for the Prohibition of Chemical Weapons 'Draft Report of the OPCW on the Implementation of the Convention on the Prohibition of the Development, Production, Stockpiling and Use of Chemical Weapons and on Their Destruction in 2022' (OPCW Document C-28/CRP.1 12 July 2023) <https://www.opcw.org/sites/default/files/documents/2023/07/ec10303%20c28crp01%28e%29_1.pdf>.

48 Except for some companies falling under, e.g., GMP inspections ('Good Manufacturing Practice' (Wikipedia), <https://en.wikipedia.org/wiki/Good_manufacturing_practice)>, but not the majority.

49 John Hart, 'Chemical Industry Inspections Under the Chemical Weapons Convention' (Vertic 2001) <https://www.vertic.org/media/assets/VM01Intro_Hart.pdf>.

50 R Jeffrey Smith, 'Suppliers Reject Poison Gas Program' (1990) The Washington Post <https://www.washingtonpost.com/archive/politics/1990/03/27/suppliers-reject-poison-gas-program/28cf9b57-deb7-4cce-b829-ceb371556047/>; Lois Ember, 'Chemical & Engineering News: Business Suppliers Reject Poison Gas Program' (1990) 68(14) p. 4.

51 Fred Webber, 'To Stop Poison Gas Attacks' (1995) The Washington Post, ProQuest Historical Newspapers: The Washington Post.

52 e.g. ICCA: International Council of Chemical Associations (ICCA), 'ICCA Responds to Recent Tragic Events in Syria Involving the Use of Chemical Weapons' (05 April 2017) <https://icca-chem.org/news/icca-responds-to-recent-tragic-events-in-syria-involving

2.7 *Distribution of "Warning Lists"*

Before entities and individuals were placed on legally enforced and published sanctions lists, there were informal warning lists of varying credibility and from a variety of sources. This made it difficult for companies to implement, giving liability and other legal or reputational issues. They nevertheless became more and more integrated into business processes.

2.8 *Training of Sales and Customer Service Functions to Identify Suspicious Inquiries*

This is all about the "Know Your Customer" process (see above). Simply said, Sales is for gaining new customers and retaining existing ones. Customer Service is to coordinate purchase requests with Production, Quality, Logistics, Accounting, and others to ensure the delivery of the right products with the right quality and quantity at the right time to the right place within contractual agreements. It became apparent that another aspect of these routine transactional processes needed to be considered, namely, to ensure that chemicals do not get into the wrong hands.

Typically, a customer profile will be established (and regularly updated) by checking:

- Is it an existing customer with long-standing relationship?
- Was the new customer visited by a sales or technical service representative?
- Is there a need for a financial background check?
- Is the customer knowledgeable to properly handle the requested chemicals?
- Are types and quantities consistent with the intended purpose?
- Are there unusual requests for shipping such as
  - packaging
  - delivery address
- Are there unusual requests for payments such as
  - cash
  - banking transactions with dubious partners
  - upfront
  - crypto currencies?

-the-use-of-chemical-weapons/>; South Africa: Chemical and Allied Industries' Association (CAIA), 'CAIA Hosts Celebration of South Africa's 20 Years of Membership' <https://www.caia.co.za/news/caia-hosts-celebration-south-africas-20-years-membership/>; Philippines: SPi Global, 'Search Results for "CWC"' <https://spik.com.ph/?s=CWC>.

IT tools such as SAP GTS (Global Trade Services) or others can be helpful in this respect and protect from liabilities and reputational damages.[53]

2.9 *Information Exchange with Law Enforcement and Intelligence Bodies*

These – for obvious reasons – not published activities should serve to mutually provide information on technologies, players, delivery scenarios, and lessons learned. They can be ad hoc or on a regular basis.[54]

2.10 *Several Associations Issued Handbooks on Regulations*

In the beginning still as hard copies, they are now available as downloads, usually with references to websites of National Authorities.[55,56] OPCW has also issued useful brochures, such as the Declaration Handbook,[57] the Handbook on Chemicals[58] and the list of "Most Traded Scheduled Chemicals".[59] All of these can be useful resources to enable especially SMEs to comply with their national implementing legislation of the CWC and be prepared to receive inspections.

53 SAP, 'Global Trade Services' <https://learning.sap.com/products/supply-chain-management/global-trade-services>; Thomson Reuters, 'Global Trade Compliance Software' <https://tax.thomsonreuters.com/en/corporation-solutions/c/global-trade-compliance-software>; Christian Hauser, 'Trade-Control Compliance in SMEs: Do Decision-Makers and Supply Chain Position Make a Difference?' (2022) 179 Journal of Business Ethics 473 <https://link.springer.com/article/10.1007/s10551-021-04825-0>.

54 Interpol, 'Global Partnerships against Chemical and Explosives Terrorism' <https://www.interpol.int/Crimes/Terrorism/Chemical-and-Explosives-terrorism/Global-Partnerships-against-Chemical-and-Explosives-terrorism>.

55 e.g. Bundesamt für Wirtschaft und Ausfuhrkontrolle (BAFA), 'Chemical Weapons Convention' <https://www.bafa.de/EN/Foreign_Trade/Chemical_Weapons_Convention/chemical_weapons_convention_node.html>.

56 University of Dundee, *CWC Inspection Guide* (University of Dundee, February 2001) <https://www.lifesci.dundee.ac.uk/services/healthandsafety/other-topics/controlled_subs/chemical_weapons/CWC_inspection_guide.pdf>.

57 Organisation for the Prohibition of Chemical Weapons, *Declarations Handbook* (OPCW) <https://www.opcw.org/resources/declarations/declarations-handbook>.

58 Organisation for the Prohibition of Chemical Weapons, *Handbook of Chemicals* (OPCW) <https://www.opcw.org/sites/default/files/documents/2024/03/Handbook%20of%20Chemicals_2024.pdf>.

59 Organisation for the Prohibition of Chemical Weapons 'Most traded scheduled chemicals 2022' (OPCW 01 January 2022) <https://www.opcw.org/sites/default/files/documents/2021/12/Most%20Traded%20Scheduled%20Chemicals%202022%20%28MTSC%29.pdf>.

2.11 *Joint Government-Industry Exercises On-Site for Inspector Training*

Confidentiality as well as safety and security remained a major concern and initially a barrier to the support of chemical industry for the future CWC. Joint exercises helped to alleviate these concerns; however, see 3.1 for still valid issues regarding data security. To the best of the author's knowledge, there have been no breaches of confidentiality regarding inspections in chemical industry. Inspectors as well as escort teams from the National Authorities generally have a high degree of professionalism. For companies that receive inspections maybe only every ten years, knowledge retention remains a challenge.

2.12 *Table-Top Exercise on Schedule 2 Facility Agreement*

Verification Annex Part VII (17) specifies that "During the initial inspection, a draft facility agreement for the plant site shall be prepared unless the inspected State Party and the Technical Secretariat agree that it is not needed".

A workshop at an industrial site[60] led to the conclusion that the provisions of "shall … unless … agree" have proven to be useful to decrease the administrative burden on both sides by waiving this agreement if agreed.

3 Since Entry into Force

3.1 *Informing Member Companies about Their Future Responsibilities with i.a. Publications on Websites and Training Sessions*

As outlined above, the crucial role of chemical industry associations is to inform their members of existing and upcoming regulations. That has happened extensively in the case of the impending implementation of the CWC in the respective national legislations. National Authorities in some countries could not do that because they had no access to comprehensive listings of companies subjected to CWC requirements. Gaps are closing, and the future focus will be on those companies which should be declaring, but do not for a variety of reasons, especially lack of knowledge or national implementation. This should remain a priority since it places a disproportionate share of inspections on countries with sound and complete declarations.

60 Recollection of author

3.2 *Regular Meetings with National Authorities (NAs) for a Smooth Implementation*

There were and continue to be site visits for NAs to familiarize them with the operations of chemical facilities and vice versa. This is to facilitate and ease future inspection activities, which are extremely useful (see also 5.5). It needs to be noted that National Authorities' responsibilities may lie within government authorities that traditionally do not have intimate knowledge of chemical industry, such as interdependent supply chains, environmental and safety issues, data recording and reporting, intellectual property rights, labor rights and other issues. These site visits therefore turned out and continued to be extremely useful.

3.3 *Setting Up Organizational Structures within Companies to Manage the Declaration and Inspection Provisions*

As part of best management practices,[61] companies need to set up structures to implement the obligations arising from CWC national legislation. In some countries, it was also mandated by law to have a "CWC Responsible".[62] It remains a constant task, because managers tend to change jobs, and it may not always be assured that successors are aware of their future obligations. Therefore, as cited above by best management practices, it is the duty of every supervisor to ensure that his or her successor of a position in his area of responsibility has the knowledge, resources, and training needed to fulfill that position. That includes the persons themselves.

4 Current Status and Way Ahead

With the beginning of declarations and inspections, the cooperation between individual companies and industry associations, notably the ICCA,[63] with the

61 Adam Hayes 'Best Practices: Definition in Business, How to Develop, Examples' (Investopedia, 26 December 2022) <https://www.investopedia.com/terms/b/best_practices.asp>; Micheal O'Malley '10 Principles of Effective Organizations' (Harvard Business Review, 08 August 2022) <https://hbr.org/2022/08/10-principles-of-effective-organizations>; McKinsey & Company, 'In the Spotlight: Performance Management That Puts People First' (15 May 2024) <https://www.mckinsey.com/capabilities/people-and-organizational-performance/our-insights/in-the-spotlight-performance-management-that-puts-people-first>.

62 e.g. § 11 CWÜAG: Gesetze im Internet, Chemiewaffenübereinkommen (CWÜ) as amended by Article 1 of the Gesetz zur Änderung des Chemiewaffenübereinkommens und des Kriegswaffenkontrollgesetzes vom 13. Dezember 1994, Bundesgesetzblatt Teil II (1994), Nr. 50, 994 <https://www.gesetze-im-internet.de/cw_ag/BJNR195400994.html>.

63 International Council of Chemical Associations (ICCA) <icca-chem.org>.

OPCW entered a new phase. A cooperation agreement was approved by the ICCA Board and the Conference of States Parties to the CWC[64] establishing a Joint Steering Committee (JSC) and a Chemical Industry Coordinating Group (CICG) in 2015. Along with that came an increased participation in OPCW activities such as:

4.1 *The Flagship "Associate Programme"*[65]

It includes a three-week assignment in the chemical industry. Since 2000, more than 545 participants from 121 countries have attended (more than 30 companies worldwide), including annual lectures on trends in chemical industry by Cefic.[66]

4.2 *Global and Regional Workshops*[67]

The workshops include topics such as Safety and Security,[68] Integrated Chemicals Management,[69] Women in Chemistry[70] and others. Chemical industry experts – depending on the agenda – are participating either from the specific needs of the region or from a global perspective. There is a continuous exchange of mutual invitations between the OPCW and the ICCA (see above).

4.3 *Conferences of States Parties and Review Conferences*

The Chemical industry is invited to participate with plenary statements and participation in side-events. Every year, this is done either in person or via video message.[71] It is a constant reminder that the chemical industry is fully

---

64 Organisation for the Prohibition of Chemical Weapons, 'Our Partners' <https://www.opcw.org/about/our-partners>.

65 Organisation for the Prohibition of Chemical Weapons, 'Associate Programme' <https://www.opcw.org/resources/capacity-building/international-cooperation-programmes/associate-programme>.

66 Cefic (European Chemical Industry Council) <https://cefic.org/>.

67 Organisation for the Prohibition of Chemical Weapons, 'Capacity Building' (OPCW) <https://www.opcw.org/resources/capacity-building>.

68 Organisation for the Prohibition of Chemical Weapons, 'Chemical Safety and Security' (OPCW) <https://www.opcw.org/resources/capacity-building/international-cooperation-programmes/chemical-safety-and-security>.

69 Organisation for the Prohibition of Chemical Weapons, 'Executive Programme on Integrated Chemicals Management' (OPCW) <https://www.opcw.org/resources/capacity-building/international-cooperation-programmes/executive-programme-integrated>.

70 Organisation for the Prohibition of Chemical Weapons, 'Symposium on Women in Chemistry' (OPCW, 1 July 2021) <https://www.opcw.org/calendar/2021/07/01/symposium-women-chemistry>.

71 E.g. Organisation for the Prohibition of Chemical Weapons, 'Statement by René van Sloten on Behalf of Marco Mensink at the Fourth Special Session of the Conference of

supportive of the CWC and stands ready to provide its expertise to the OPCW and States Parties.

4.4 *The Scientific Advisory Board (SAB)*[72] *and the Advisory Board on Education and Outreach (ABEO)*[73]

From the onset, chemical industry representatives have been serving on both subsidiary bodies of the OPCW, providing input into developments of industry in general and helping promote awareness about the CWC. This includes participation in workshops to draft the SAB recommendations for the Review Conferences in Scientific and Technological Developments including one sponsored by BASF in Antwerp in 2022.[74]

4.5 *Annual Meetings of National Authorities and Annual Meetings of Chemical Industry with National Authorities*

National Authorities, national industry associations, and ICCA are regularly meeting to enhance cooperation and foster ways to promote the goals and objectives of the CWC.[75,76,77] Traditionally there are joint presentations for sharing best practices.

the States Parties to Review the Operation of the Chemical Weapons Convention' (OPCW Document RC-4/NAT.20 23) November 2018 <https://www.opcw.org/sites/default/files/documents/2018/11/rc4nat20%28e%29.pdf>.

72 Organisation for the Prohibition of Chemical Weapons, 'Scientific Advisory Board' (OPCW) <https://www.opcw.org/about/subsidiary-bodies/scientific-advisory-board>.

73 Organisation for the Prohibition of Chemical Weapons, 'Advisory Board on Education and Outreach' (OPCW) <https://www.opcw.org/about/subsidiary-bodies/advisory-board-education-and-outreach>.

74 Organisation for the Prohibition of Chemical Weapons 'Report of the Scientific Advisory Board on Developments in Science and Technology to the Fifth Special Session of the Conference of the States Parties to Review the Operation of the Chemical Weapons Convention' (OPCW Document RC-5/DG.1 22 February 2023) <https://www.opcw.org/sites/default/files/documents/2023/02/rc5dg01%28e%29.pdf>.

75 Organisation for the Prohibition of Chemical Weapons, 'Chemical Industry and National Authority Representatives Discuss Experiences of National Implementation' (OPCW) <https://www.opcw.org/resources/capacity-building/national-implementation-programmes/chemical-industry-and-national>.

76 Organisation for the Prohibition of Chemical Weapons, 'Annual Meeting of National Authorities' (OPCW) <https://www.opcw.org/resources/capacity-building/national-implementation-programmes/annual-meeting-national-authorities>.

77 E.g. Organisation for the Prohibition of Chemical Weapons, 'An invitation to participate in the fourth annual meeting of national authorities' (OPCW Document S/313/2002 16 July 2002) <https://www.opcw.org/sites/default/files/documents/S_series/2002/en/s-313-2002.pdf>.

4.6 *Industry Cluster*[78]

The Industry Cluster is an informal body of the OPCW, where issues – as the name says – concerning industry are discussed and submitted to the Executive Council. Discussions regarding updated on-site selection criteria are currently one of the topics.[79] Industry is invited to participate and contribute.

4.7 *The Hague Award*

"Established in 2014, the Award extends the legacy of the OPCW's 2013 Nobel Peace Prize 'for its extensive efforts to eliminate chemical weapons'. The Award is part of the OPCW's ongoing effort to highlight significant contributions made by individuals and organizations, widely from academia, researchers, chemical industry, and civil society to achieve a world free of chemical weapons".[80]

ICCA, among others, is a member of the panel for selection of the best candidates.

4.8 *Indicative Guidelines for Chemical Safety and Security in Small and Medium-Sized Enterprises to Foster the Peaceful Uses of Chemistry*

The lengthy title for a brochure is the result of two workshops with the participation of 11 experts from chemical industry of 8 countries, available for free on the website.[81] This is in accordance with Art. XI of the CWC.

78 Organisation for the Prohibition of Chemical Weapons, 'Verification Division' <https://www.opcw.org/about/technical-secretariat/divisions/verification>.

79 E.g. Organisation for the Prohibition of Chemical Weapons, 'Note by the Director-General Update Assessment of a methodology for the selection of schedule 3 plant sites for inspection' (OPCW Document S/1088/2013, 11 April 2013) <https://www.opcw.org/sites/default/files/documents/S_series/2013/en/s-1088-2013_e_.pdf>.

80 Organisation for the Prohibition of Chemical Weapons, 'OPCW Hague Award 2023 Open for Nominations' (OPCW, 19 June 2023) <https://www.opcw.org/media-centre/news/2023/06/opcw-hague-award-2023-open-nominations>.

81 Organisation for the Prohibition of Chemical Weapons, 'Indicative Guidelines for Chemical Safety and Security Management' (OPCW, 29 June 2021) <https://www.opcw.org/sites/default/files/documents/2021/06/OPCW%20Indicative%20Guidelines%20CSSM%2029062021%20Final_1.pdf>.

4.9 *Guidelines for Road Transport of Hazardous Chemicals*[82]

Similarly to the previous guideline, the brochure was published in September 2024.[83] It was recognized that road transportation is the weakest link in safety and security aspects of handling chemicals and therefore needs special consideration.

4.10 *Guidelines for "Know Your Customer"*[84]

As a third in a row, the draft guidelines will serve to raise awareness and help implementing ways to avoid getting chemicals into the wrong hands (see above 3.7) and will be published shortly together with accompanying checklists.

5 Closing Remarks

The increased involvement of chemical industry in Art. XI activities focusing on implementation of Nr. 2 (b) are only voluntary measures, as opposed to Art. VI and IX. However, they are strongly supported by the Responsible Care® initiative mentioned above. It is now recognized that the private sector is not only an important stakeholder and partner in implementation, but can be a resource, i.a. to:

- Share best practices
- Provide expertise about products, services, know-how and complex supply chains
- Use associations and networks to disseminate relevant information
- Strengthen consultation mechanisms between governments and industry
- Providing information about trends in chemical industry which could have an impact on the operations of the CWC.

---

82 Organisation for the Prohibition of Chemical Weapons, 'OPCW Supports Development of Guidelines for Road Transport of Hazardous Chemicals' (OPCW, 8 April 2022) <https://www.opcw.org/media-centre/news/2022/04/opcw-supports-development-guidelines-road-transport-hazardous-chemicals>.

83 <https://www.opcw.org/sites/default/files/documents/2024/09/OPCW%20Indicative%20Guidelines_Transport_English.pdf>.

84 Ministry of Defence, Sri Lanka, 'Russia appreciates Lanka's support at the 2023 International Army Games' (Ministry of Defence, Sri Lanka, 14 June 2024) <https://www.defence.lk/Article/view_article/27818>.

CHAPTER 6

The Role of the Chemical Industry in the Evolution and Implementation of the Norm against Chemical Weapons

Ralf Trapp

1 Introduction

The interaction between industry and governments in treaty negotiations and implementation is not unique for chemical weapons disarmament. Industry leaders, lobbyists and trade associations in other branches, too, have an interest in shaping government policies that affect their interests. They use multiple channels to communicate their views and concerns to policy and law makers as well as public audiences. Amongst others, industry aims at mitigating any damage that might result from what it sometime perceives as overregulation, and at promoting favourable conditions for its operations.

Areas of particular concern for industry often include the protection of its intellectual property, the minimisation of regulatory burden, favourable conditions for trade, and access to essential raw materials and services. At the same time, the industry has an interest in protecting and fostering its efforts to innovate, to grow and bring new products and solutions to the market, and to attract new clients.

The history of chemical weapons arms control and disarmament, too, includes many examples of how private industry has attempted to influence government decision-making on whether to use toxic chemicals as means of warfare, as well as whether and how to control or completely ban their use as weapons of war.

1.1 *The Nature of the Chemical Industry*

The chemical industry is a basic industry which supplies products to a wide range of other industries, as well as to consumers. Having emerged at the turn from the 19th to the 20th centuries, today's chemical industry is a mature enterprise. It remains highly competitive and innovative. A recent survey concluded that the sales of the global top 50 chemical companies combined to

 | DOI:10.1163/9789004739192_007

1.2 trillion US dollars in 2022, and that leading companies invested significant amounts of their sales into research and development.[1]

There is no universal definition of what constitutes the chemical industry. *Britannica* defines it as a "complex of processes, operations, and organizations engaged in the manufacture of chemicals and their derivatives,"[2] but recognises that the scope of the term is in part shaped by custom rather than logic. Chemicals manufacturing can range from upstream, extractive processes to downstream processes that manufacture chemical intermediates or, often after multiple conversions in different manufacturing units, final products that are put on the market. The processes used in the chemical industry can range from simple physical operations such as distillation or extraction (in CWC terminology "processing")[3] to chemical reactions in which new chemical entities are formed (in CWC terminology "production"),[4] or intermediates are chemically converted into other chemical products (in CWC terminology "consumption").[5]

The organisation of the chemical industry and the degree of back-integration of its operations vary from company to company and country to country, and change over time. There are large industrial complexes that process and convert raw materials to a wide variety of primary, secondary and tertiary intermediates and ultimately final products sold on the market. Such large chemical enterprises often operate in multiple locations and countries. On the other end of the spectrum, there are small and medium-size enterprises that specialise in a particular product or product group; in some cases, they are simply mixing (formulating) or repackaging chemicals they purchase from other manufacturers. Then there are companies that specialise in certain types of chemical processes based on their equipment suit, offering services to produce chemicals to customer specification or renting their facilities to clients for them to manufacture products to their own specifications.

From an arms control perspective, it is important to recall that there are multiple routes from different raw materials to the same final product, and that a particular product can have a range of uses in different industries. Furthermore, the market for chemical products is global, and both materials and services can be purchased from a variety of sources worldwide.

1 Alex Tullo: *C&EN's global top 50*. Chem. Engin. News 101 (24) (24 July 2023), pp. 21–30.

2 Encyclopedia Britannica, 'Chemical Industry (Encyclopedia Britannica) <https://www.britannica.com/technology/chemical-industry>.

3 CWC Art. II.12.b.

4 CWC Art. II.12.a.

5 CWC Art. II.12.c.

1.2 *Chemical Industry and Regulatory Systems*

Being a mature industry that handles hazardous material on a daily basis, the chemical industry is highly regulated. This is to a large degree the result of public health and environmental safety concerns, and hence a desire to apply good manufacturing practices (GMP). Regulations govern, amongst others, the manufacturing, storage, transportation, marketing and use of chemicals, the treatment of chemical wastes, limits to pollutant emissions into air and water, tolerable concentrations of hazardous chemicals in air, drinking water, food, consumer products, products used by other manufacturers, and many more.

The public image of the chemical industry at the time of the CWC negotiations was marked by the aftermath of the large-scale use of herbicides in the Viet Nam war, which had caused large-scale environmental damage and long-term health effects. Other incidents that had tainted the public view of the industry included two major industrial accidents: the release of the highly toxic 2,3,7,8-Tetrachlorodibenzo-p-dioxin ("dioxin") in 1976 from a chemical plant in Seveso (Italy),[6] and in Bhopal (India) the release in 1984 of highly toxic methyl isocyanate (MIC) which resulted in 2,000 people dying within a short period of time and tens of thousands injured.[7,8] Regulators responded to these incidents with what some in the industry perceived as overly harsh and costly regulations. Whether or not this view is shared, the regulatory framework within which the chemical industry is operating has become highly complex.

International treaties and initiatives that govern its operations in the safety and security domain include the 1997 Chemical Weapons Convention, UN Security Council Resolution 1540 (2004), export controls related to precursor chemicals coordinated by the Australia Group, the 1987 Missile Technology Control Regime (MTCR) which includes provisions on certain propellants and other chemicals, the Global Congress on Chemical Security and Emerging Threats set up in 2018 by Interpol with the support of the US Department of Homeland Security to counter the threat posed by malicious actors acquiring toxic and precursor chemicals through weak points in the supply chain, the

6 UK Health and Safety Executive, 'Case study: Icmesa chemical company, Seveso, Italy 1976' <https://www.hse.gov.uk/comah/sragtech/caseseveso76.htm>.

7 Edward Broughton, 'The Bhopal Disaster and Its Aftermath: A Review' (2005) 4 Environmental Health, 6.

8 UK Health and Safety Executive, 'Case study: Union Carbide India, Bhopal 1984' <https://www.hse.gov.uk/comah/sragtech/caseuncarbide84.htm>.

Programme Global Shield of the World Customs Organisation and supported by Interpol and the UN Office of Drugs and Crime (UNODC), the 1961 Single Convention on Narcotic Drugs as amended in 1988, the 1971 Convention on Psychotropic Substances, and the United Nations Convention Against Illicit Traffic in Narcotic Drugs and Psychotropic Substances of 1988. In addition, international and regional agreements pertain to such areas as transfers and transboundary movements of chemical materials and wastes, the transportation of chemical materials in the different transport modes, notifications of chemical accidents and incidents with potential transboundary impact, and more.

At the practical level, manufacturers and traders will have to comply with the laws and regulations of the country(ies) they are operating in. For example, in the European Union, regulatory instruments pertaining to the chemical industry include, most prominently, the 2012 EU's Seveso III Directive[9] and the 2017 EU Regulation on the registration, evaluation, authorisation and restriction of chemicals (REACH).[10] In addition, specific EU regulations govern the classification, labelling and packaging of products, prior informed consent with regard to exports of certain chemicals, dual use export controls, the marketing and use of biocidal products, the marketing of plant protection products, pollutant emissions from industrial installations, the inland transport of dangerous goods, the control of dual purpose chemicals which can be used to manufacture home-made explosives, market surveillance and product compliance, risks related to chemical agents at work, and drug precursors.

In the United States of America – another country that plays an important role in chemicals manufacturing and trade – the primary legislation covering hazardous chemicals is the Toxic Substances Control Act (TSCA) of 1976[11] as

9 Directive 2012/18/EU of the European Parliament and of the Council of 4 July 2012 on the control of major-accident hazards involving dangerous substances, amending and subsequently repealing Council Directive 96/82/EC, Official Journal of the European Union, L 197, 24 July 2012 <https://eur-lex.europa.eu/legal-content/EN/TXT/?uri=CELEX:32012L0018>.

10 Regulation (EC) No 1907/2006 of the European Parliament and of the Council of 18 December 2006 concerning the Registration, Evaluation, Authorisation and Restriction of Chemicals (REACH) <https://eur-lex.europa.eu/legal-content/EN/TXT/?uri=CELEX%3A32006R1907>.

11 United States Environmental Protection Agency (undated), 'Summary of the Toxic Substances Control Act' <https://www.epa.gov/laws-regulations/summary-toxic-substances-control-act#:~:text=The%20Toxic%20Substances%20Control%20Act%20of%201976%20provides%20EPA%20with,%2C%20drugs%2C%20cosmetics%20and%20pesticides>.

updated and amended in 2016 by the Frank R. Lautenberg Chemical Safety for the 21st Century Act.[12] Key provisions include the testing of chemical substances; pre-manufacture notifications for new chemical substances; requirements regarding record keeping; reporting requirements regarding new substances and mixtures; and certification, reporting and other requirements for exporters and importers. The US Environmental Protection Agency (EPA) manages a Chemical Substances Inventory listing more than 86,000 chemical substances that are manufactured, imported into and used in the United States.[13] The US Federal Hazardous Substances Act (FHSA) regulates precautionary labelling and packaging of hazardous chemical products.[14] Furthermore, the 2007 Chemical Facility Anti-Terrorism Standards (CFATS) and the Protecting and Securing Chemical Facilities from Terrorist Attacks Act 2014 (CFATS Act 2014) regulate chemical facilities which possess or use certain hazardous chemicals and prescribe security measures to reduce the risk of hazardous chemicals being weaponised by terrorists.[15]

Other jurisdictions have their own pertinent laws and regulations. For manufacturers and traders who operate on global markets, regulatory complexities result from diverging approaches in different jurisdictions. This explains the industry's desire for a "level playing field", and its willingness to take self-regulatory measures to prevent the adoption of additional hard laws.

1.3 *Chemical Industry and Chemical Warfare*

Another factor that frames the chemical industry's position on chemical weapons arms control is its past involvement as a supplier of materials for State chemical weapons programmes. During the First World War, leading chemists and industrialists in many countries promoted the use of toxic chemicals as an alternative to high explosives, given their perceived utility for breaking the stalemate of the trench warfare and a perception of them being "more humane" than conventional bombs and artillery. Also, after the First

12 US Congress (2016), Frank R. Lautenberg Chemical Safety for the 21st Century Act, Public Law 114–182 – June 22, 2016 <https://www.congress.gov/114/plaws/publ182/PLAW-114publ182.pdf>.

13 US Environmental Protection Agency, About the TSCA Chemical Substance Inventory <https://www.epa.gov/tsca-inventory/about-tsca-chemical-substance-inventory>.

14 US Consumer Product Safety Commission (2011), Federal Hazardous Substances Act (FHSA), Public Law 86–613; 74 Stat. 372, July 12, 1960 <https://www.cpsc.gov/s3fs-public/pdfs/blk_pdf_fhsa.pdf>.

15 Cybersecurity & Infrastructure Security Agency (undated), 'Chemical Facility Anti-Terrorism Standards (CFATS)' <https://www.cisa.gov/resources-tools/programs/chemical-facility-anti-terrorism-standards-cfats>.

World War, chemical industry remained an active player in the development and production of chemical weapons. For example, industry research conducted to develop new types of pesticides was repurposed for the development and production of nerve agents.[16]

Things began to change, however, during the 1980s. At this time, the US industry was struggling to repair its damaged public image after the large-scale use of herbicides during the Vietnam War. US private companies declined procurement calls from the US Army for the components of binary chemical weapons. The US chemical industry was no longer supportive of an offensive CW programme and began instead considering the practicalities of a CW prohibition.

This reflected a wider change in perception in the chemical industries worldwide following growing environmental concerns. Despite worries about the possible impact of a chemical weapons ban on its operations, chemical industry became a supporter of a CW ban. The reasons can be found both within the industry and in its understanding of its role in society, and in external pressures that affected its motivations. The ban needed to be technically sound, however, and it needed to take the industry's interests into account.

2 Involvement of the Chemical Industry in the Negotiations of the Chemical Weapons Convention

2.1 *Engagements between Industry and Negotiators*

Technical discussions about chemical weapons started in the 1970s, initially in an East-West context and then in a broader multilateral framework of what became the Conference on Disarmament. Textual and structural work on a treaty began during the early 1980s.

These negotiations were intergovernmental in nature. Other actors including the chemical industry were not directly involved. However, the negotiators recognised the need to reach out to these stakeholders given the unique character of the prospected treaty.[17,18] As a CWC became a possible future reality,

16 Jonathan B. Tucker: *War of Nerves: Chemical Warfare from World War I to al-Qaeda*, Pantheon Books New York (2006) 24–41.

17 Caitríona McLeish and Maarten Lak: *The role of civil society and industrial non-State actors in relation to the Chemical Weapons Convention*, in: W. Krutzsch, E. Myjer and R. Trapp: *A Chemical Weapons Convention Commentary*, OUP (2014), pp. 37–48.

18 Ian R. Kenyon and Daniel Feakes: The Creation of the Organisation for the Prohibition of Chemical Weapons – A case study in the birth of an Intergovernmental Organisation, T. M. C. Asser Press (2007) Chapter 9, pp. 179–204.

the chemical industry began to more clearly articulate its interests vis-à-vis the treaty. Not being a participant in the negotiations, however, it needed to find indirect channels to convey its views and concerns to governments. At the same time, governments looked at the chemical industry as a source of technical expertise as discussions about a possible verification system moved from exchanges about policy to specific verification concepts and procedures.

Step by step, industry participation became more systematic – a process that continued also after the end of negotiations. Industry remained engaged during the work of the Preparatory Commission which developed a host of technical and administrative procedures for the conduct of verification activities. It developed close contacts with the OPCW's Technical Secretariat after the implementation of the CWC began, and conveyed its concerns about the practical application of certain treaty provisions at their plants to governments and the OPCW.

2.2 *The CWC Negotiations*

Building on previous exchanges between the US Manufacturing Chemists Association (later Chemical Manufacturers Association (CMA) and today the American Chemistry Council (ACC)) and the US Arms Control and Disarmament Agency (ACDA),[19] the CMA set up a Chemical Weapons Disarmament Workgroup in the mid-1980s that met regularly with US government officials. Similar consultation mechanisms between governments and chemical industry were also established in Europe, Japan, Australia, India and some other countries. In countries with a centralised economy and/or State-owned industry, too, governments looked at the chemical industry for advice on technical issues as verification became more broadly accepted.

Chemical industry coordinated its position through national and regional trade associations, communicated with national governments, and looked for ways to present industry views and concerns to the negotiators. Key issues of industry concern included the composition of CWC control lists (the Schedules), the protection of confidential business information, the types of data that industry would be required to make available for declarations, and the modalities of conducting inspections of chemical plants.

Beginning in the mid-1980s, informal meetings and studies were organised by the Pugwash Conferences of Science and World Affairs (Pugwash) and the Stockholm International Peace Research Institute (SIPRI). These projects

19 Ian R. Kenyon and Daniel Feakes: The Creation of the Organisation for the Prohibition of Chemical Weapons – A case study in the birth of an Intergovernmental Organisation, T. M. C. Asser Press (2007) Chapter 9, 181.

built on previous such studies which, amongst others, had looked at how to verify the non-production of nerve gas, and in 1977, 1978 and 1979 had conducted visits to industrial facilities in Germany, the USA and Sweden.

In 1985, SIPRI and Pugwash convened a conference to discuss how the CWC could verify the non-production of chemical weapons.[20] The *rationale* of this meeting was that activities in the chemical industry could result in ambiguity and misunderstandings unless the CWC's compliance mechanisms could dispel such uncertainties about the nature of these activities and protect the chemical industry against unfounded accusations.

Subsequent SIPRI and Pugwash contributions to the evolution of the CWC's industry verification system included an analysis of technical verification concepts,[21] a study on national implementation,[22] a case study on the verification of dual use chemicals using Thiodiglycol as an example,[23] and a study on experiences from national trial inspections at industrial plants.[24]

All these activities helped deepen the engagement between industry and the arms control community. They provided channels of communication and helped negotiators understand how industry verification would work in practice. To tests the procedures, negotiators decided to conduct trials at chemical plants. Between 1988 and 1992, over 60 national and multilateral trial inspections were conducted. The chemical industry supported these efforts and opened its plants for the trials. This helped the chemical industry appreciate how future OPCW inspections might affect its operations, and at the same time it helped negotiators appreciate the practicalities of inspecting industrial facilities.

---

20 Stockholm International Peace Research Institute: The chemical industry and the projected Chemical Weapons Convention – Proceedings of a SIRPI/PUGWASH conference, SIPRI CBW Studies Series no. 4 and no. 5, volumes I and II, Oxford University Press (1986).

21 Stockholm International Peace Research Institute. Johan S. Lundin (ed.): Non-production in industry of chemical warfare agents: technical verification under a Chemical Weapons Convention, SIPRI CBW Studies Series no. 9 (Oxford University Press (1986).

22 Stockholm International Peace Research Institute. Thomas Stock and Ronald Sutherland: National implementation of the future Chemical Weapons Convention, SIPRI CBW Studies Series no. 11, Oxford University Press (1990).

23 Stockholm International Peace Research Institute. Johan S. Lundin (ed.): Verification of dual-use chemicals under the Chemical Weapons Convention: the case of thiodiglycol, SIPRI CBW Studies Series no. 13, Oxford University Press (1991).

24 Stockholm International Peace Research Institute. Ralf Trapp: Verification under the Chemical Weapons Convention: on-site inspection in chemical industry facilities, SIPRI CBW Studies Series no. 14, Oxford University Press (1993).

Beginning in 1987, informal meetings between negotiators and industry representatives were held alongside the negotiations in Geneva. The industry representatives would first consolidate their positions and proposals, and then meet informally with CD negotiators to receive briefings and present their views on specific issues. These meetings became regular events during the final phase of the negotiations, and were convened annually until 1991. The conversations were at times difficult, and some negotiators felt that certain industry position were not helpful.[25] Issues that drew particular attention included:[26]

- The protection of confidential information (submission of industry data, on-site inspections at chemical plants, sampling and analysis);
- The issue of "CW capable facilities" (facilities considered by negotiators to pose a risk to the CWC although they did not manufacture any precursors known from previous CW programmes; industry, on the other hand, considered the notion that some of its facilities might be "CW capable" as intolerable);
- Inspection protocols, with industry keen to minimise the operational and administrative burden associated with international on-site inspections at its plants;
- The use of monitoring technique and devices at chemical plants;
- The technical requirements for the future Inspectorate, as well as how to ensure that inspectors would be conducting themselves with high integrity, respect for the protection of confidentiality, and in a technically competent manner;
- The need to avoid any negative publicity as a result of verification activities by international inspection teams ("rumour damage").

2.3 *The Canberra Conference*

A major contribution to completing the CWC negotiations was the Government-Industry Conference against Chemical Weapons (GICCW) convened by the Australian government in collaboration with the Australian Chemical

25 Ian R. Kenyon and Daniel Feakes: The Creation of the Organisation for the Prohibition of Chemical Weapons – A case study in the birth of an Intergovernmental Organisation, T. M. C. Asser Press (2007) 182–183.

26 Ian R. Kenyon and Daniel Feakes: The Creation of the Organisation for the Prohibition of Chemical Weapons – A case study in the birth of an Intergovernmental Organisation, T. M. C. Asser Press (2007) 185. A range of informal industry position papers were also consulted.

Industry Association in September 1989.[27] 375 delegates from 66 countries met in Canberra, about half of them coming from national chemical industry associations. The European Union, the European Chemical Industry Council (CEFIC), and the United Nations, too, were present, and so were representatives of trade unions and of trade and industry ministries. It was estimated that 95 percent of the world's chemical manufacturing capacity was represented at the meeting.[28]

The conference set out to identify practical solutions to outstanding problems in the negotiations, and to convey a clear understanding of how the CWC would impact on the industry. It was an attempt to speed up the treaty negotiations and to ensure its effective implementation. Australia's Foreign Minister highlighted four key outcomes of the conference:[29]

- The first collective statement by the world's chemical industry of its commitment to assist governments in bringing about a total ban on chemical weapons;
- An extensive and continuing dialogue between governments and industry on issues relating to the conclusion and implementation of the treaty;
- The identification of measures that industry and governments would take in support of the objectives of the CWC;
- A renewed expression of commitment by governments to conclude and implement a comprehensive CWC at the earliest date.

The conference sent an important political signal in support of the early adoption and effective implementation of the CWC. An important aspect was the conduct of an Industry Forum, which adopted an Industry Statement that:[30]

- Expressed industry's unequivocal abhorrence of chemical warfare;

---

27 Timothy L. H. McCormack: Some Australian efforts to promote chemical weapons non-proliferation and disarmament, Australian Year Book of International Law (1992) 157–178, 166.

28 Ian R. Kenyon and Daniel Feakes: The Creation of the Organisation for the Prohibition of Chemical Weapons – A case study in the birth of an Intergovernmental Organisation, T. M. C. Asser Press (2007) 183; Government-industry conference against chemical weapons, National Convention Centre, Canberra 18–22 September 1989, Final Record published by the Department of Foreign Affairs and Trade Canberra, Australia, Annex II, Directory of Delegations.

29 Government-industry conference against chemical weapons, National Convention Centre, Canberra 18–22 September 1989, Final Record published by the Department of Foreign Affairs and Trade Canberra, Australia, 420.

30 Government-industry conference against chemical weapons, National Convention Centre, Canberra 18–22 September 1989, Final Record published by the Department of Foreign Affairs and Trade Canberra, Australia, 213.

- Expressed industry's willingness to work actively with governments to achieve a global ban on chemical weapons, and its willingness to contribute to the negotiation process;
- Affirmed its desire to foster international cooperation for the legitimate civil uses of chemical products, and its opposition to the diversion of its products for the manufacture of chemical weapons;
- Declared its support for efforts to conclude and implement the CWC at the earliest date;
- Expressed the belief that the only solution to the problem of chemical weapons was a global, comprehensive and effectively verifiable CWC;
- Expressed the strong hope that the negotiators would resolve urgently the outstanding issues and conclude the CWC at the earliest date;
- Stated its willingness to continue the dialogue with governments to prepare for the entry into force of an effective CWC which protects the free and non-discriminatory exchange of chemicals and transfer of technology for economic development and the welfare of all people. It indicated its willingness to participate in national measures designed to facilitate the early implementation of the CWC following its conclusion.

The Canberra Conference undoubtedly had a mobilising effect on the negotiations and added momentum to conclude the negotiations as early as possible. It also showed that industry and governments were able to sit together to discuss and resolve difficult issues where both had diverging views and ideas.

2.4 *The Final Phase of the CWC Negotiations*

The industry verification system was among the last issues to be agreed in the negotiations. The chemical industry provided advice on a wide range of technical issues, and supported the conduct of trial inspections to test the proposed industry inspection procedures. These trials continued until the end of the negotiations.[31]

Whilst an initial review of these trials in 1989 had concluded that the verification of non-diversion of toxic and precursor chemicals was feasible,[32] sub-

31 Stockholm International Peace Research Institute. Ralf Trapp: Verification under the Chemical Weapons Convention: on-site inspection in chemical industry facilities, SIPRI CBW Studies Series no. 14, Oxford University Press (1993), 110–111.

32 Stockholm International Peace Research Institute. Johan S. Lundin (ed.): Verification of dual-use chemicals under the Chemical Weapons Convention: the case of thiodiglycol, SIPRI CBW Studies Series no. 13, Oxford University Press (1991), 24.

sequent analyses began to point towards the need for a more qualitative approach.[33] Chemical industry experts had arrived at similar conclusions, and began to float the idea that the industry verification system should verify the absence of the production of certain high-risk chemicals rather than the diversion of precursor materials.

The trials also demonstrated that there are facilities outside the scope of the Schedules that could be misused for CW purposes, given their access to relevant chemicals and production equipment. The negotiators eventually included a regime for other chemical production facilities as Part IX of the Verification Annex. Industry bought into this approach partly because it avoided labelling some of its plants as "CW capable", partly because it came close to its own approach of "open access", and partly because it linked the OCPF regime to that for Schedule 3 facilities and thus limited the burden on industry.

Towards the end of the negotiations, industry associations issued position papers which commented directly on the evolving draft treaty text. In 1990, the European chemical industry association (CEFIC) issued two such statements: one on confidential business information, the other one on the Schedules of Chemicals.[34] The first was an analysis of the draft Annex on the Protection of Confidential Information. It contained a detailed review of the proposed provisions, a proposal for how to classify confidential information, and a review of the information that the industry would need to supply under the CWC. The aim of the statement was to anchor guidelines and decision directly into the treaty text. In practice, many of these issues were further elaborated by the Preparatory Commission as part of the OPCW Confidentiality Policy that was adopted at the first Session of the Conference of the States Parties.

The second CEFIC paper proposed a simplified approach to the Schedules, stressing that the classification under the Schedules should not hamper the use of chemical products that might be misused for CW purposes, nor hinder basic research or industrial development. This reflected a perception that including a chemical in Schedule 1 would effectively "ban" its future legitimate uses. Whilst many of the specific suggestions for the placement of certain chemicals were not taken on board by the negotiators, the classification prin-

33 Stockholm International Peace Research Institute. Johan S. Lundin (ed.): Verification of dual-use chemicals under the Chemical Weapons Convention: the case of thiodiglycol, SIPRI CBW Studies Series no. 13, Oxford University Press (1991), 24–25.

34 CEFIC statement on Confidential Business Information (1990); CEFIC Statement on Schedules (1990).

ciples set out by CEFIC were reflected in the Guidelines for the Annex on Chemicals.

In June 1991, as negotiations moved into their final phase, CEFIC and CMA issued a further position paper,[35] which was formally supported by the Japanese Chemical Industry Association, the Canadian Chemical Producers' Association and the Chemical Confederation of Australia. It restated the industry's support for a global ban on chemical weapons, and contained three different Statements, on:

- Challenge Inspection in the Civilian Chemical Industry (May 1991)
- Verification System within the Chemical Production (June 1991)
- Low Concentrations and Non-Isolated ("Captive Use") Chemicals (June 1991)

With regard to Challenge Inspection, industry's main concerns were a possible loss of confidential business information, undue interference with legitimate activities, and damage to a company's reputation even when a suspicion would have proven erroneous. In addition, the industry feared that challenge inspections at its plants would have significant resource implications. The statement set forth a number of proposals to minimise these risks, and concluded that, if properly managed, challenge inspections could be efficiently performed at industrial plants without excessively penalizing legitimate industry activities. Industry was willing to cooperate with the negotiators to define the conditions of a challenge inspection within the civilian chemical industry.

With regard to routine verification in the chemical industry, the industry took a major step towards facilitating the conclusion of the negotiations by offering free access to all its production sites. Inspections would be qualitative in approach. Rather than attempting to verify worldwide material flows, inspections would be based on an "anywhere and anytime" approach to detect illicit production of Schedule 1 chemicals. This "open invitation" would allow negotiators to design the verification regime for other chemical production facilities, and to adapt the regimes for Schedule 2 and 3 chemicals by giving them a more qualitative focus.

The third industry Statement related to mixtures of chemicals ("formulations" or "preparations") that contain certain amounts of Schedule 2 chemicals, to processes where scheduled chemicals appear as unavoidable by-products in the synthesis of other chemical products, and to situations where a Schedule 1 or Schedule 2 chemical is produced as an intermediate in

35 CEFIC and CMA positions on Chemical Weapons Convention issues affecting the chemical industry. Hearing June 1991.

a sequence of chemical reactions but never isolated and ultimately converted into another (unscheduled) chemical product ("captive use" or "non-isolated chemicals"). Industry concerns related to the risk that treaty-regulated chemicals would be found in chemical products that the manufacturers themselves were not aware of, or that restrictions might be applied to products it considered not relevant to the CWC. Industry was prepared to accept a degree of intrusion and regulation when these were justifiable given the risk that such materials posed. But there was a concern that if the concentration limits for mixtures containing scheduled chemicals would be set too low, many more industries would become subject to CWC reporting requirements, entailing more administrative control, a dilution of resources, and burdening in particular small and medium-sized manufacturers.

These issues turned out to be too difficult to be resolved in the negotiations. The Preparatory Commission, too, could not resolve them. These and other issues related to chemical industry verification were then transferred to the OPCW's facilitation process to resolve unresolved issues after the entry into force of the CWC. Pragmatic solutions were eventually found in negotiations that involved experts from governments, the Technical Secretariat as well as the chemical industry.

As the final phase of negotiations approached, Australia made a considered attempt to clean up the Rolling Text of the CWC to demonstrate that a compromise package *could* be achieved. This Australia Text was widely consulted with governments across the globe before it was introduced at the CD in 1992.[36] The chairman of the CD's Ad-Hoc Committee on Chemical Weapons, German Ambassador von Wagner, drew significantly on its structural and textual proposals, but there still remained issues where generally accepted compromises needed to be found. This became clear when he tabled his proposal of the "non-controversial text elements" of the draft CWC (document CD/CW/WP.400). A group of developing countries responded with additional comments and requests for change. In response, the Chairman drastically reorganised to *modus operandi* of the negotiations, in an effort to resolve as many outstanding issues as possible and at the same time provide him with the authority to make final compromise decisions where no consensus solutions could be found. This, then, enabled him to table a revised draft CWC

36 Conference on Disarmament document CD/1143 (1992). For a more detailed discussion see: Timothy L. H. McCormack: Some Australian efforts to promote chemical weapons non-proliferation and disarmament, Australian Year Book of International Law (1992), 157–178.

(document CD/CW/WP.400/Rev.1), and after final adjustments, the draft CWC was published in August 1992.[37] Contacts between experts from chemical industry and negotiators intensified during these final weeks. In some cases, countries actually included industry experts in their CD delegation.

3 Industry's Support for the Preparation for Entry into Force of the CWC

The involvement of the chemical industry continued during the work of the Preparatory Commission between February 1993 and the entry into force of the CWC on 29 April 1997. The commission prepared a wide range of procedures, guidelines, administrative directives for the implementation of the CWC, which were adopted by the Conference of the States Parties at its First Session in April/May 1997.

As in the past, industry was not a direct participant in the work of the Preparatory Commission. Some countries included industry representatives in their delegations, but by the end of 1993, industry voices about limited access to the Commission led to a decision to convene a combined meeting of chemical industry representatives and the Preparatory Commission's Expert Group on Chemical Industry Facilities. The first such meeting took place in October 1993, and trade associations from Austria, Brazil, Cuba, Finland, France, Germany, India, Israel, Japan, the Netherlands, Russia, South Africa, South Korea, Ukraine, the UK and the USA attended.[38] Subsequent meetings were conducted in April 1994 and June 1995, reinvigorating the engagement between negotiators and industry representatives. They were conducted less frequently than in the past, however, and discussions tended to rehash issues already discussed in Geneva. There were also attempts to reopen issues that had already been settled in the past, and some experts felt that industry had "done its bit".[39]

Many of the procedures developed by the Preparatory Commission further elaborated provisions of the CWC. This included the OPCW Health and Safety

37 Conference on Disarmament document CD/CW/WP.400/Rev.2.

38 Ian R. Kenyon and Daniel Feakes: The Creation of the Organisation for the Prohibition of Chemical Weapons – A case study in the birth of an Intergovernmental Organisation, T. M. C. Asser Press (2007), 191–192.

39 Ian R. Kenyon and Daniel Feakes: The Creation of the Organisation for the Prohibition of Chemical Weapons – A case study in the birth of an Intergovernmental Organisation, T. M. C. Asser Press (2007), 192.

Policy and the OPCW Confidentiality Policy, detailed inspection procedures for different types of inspections including guidelines on sampling and analysis and the designation of laboratories for off-site analysis, and technical specifications and operational requirements for inspection equipment. The Commission also adopted a general training scheme (GTS) for OPCW inspectors, and eventually hired inspector candidates to ensure that field operations could start right after the entry into force.

Many of these endeavours were supported by chemical industry. This was a recognition that "failure or serious problems in the early days of implementation can lead to an erosion of confidence in the Treaty, misunderstandings amongst states, and a loss of commitment."[40] Of particular importance was the industry's support for inspector training. Chemical companies offered access to their facilities to conduct mock inspections as part of the final training module.[41] This enabled the OPCW to recruit at entry into force 111 inspectors trained to the high standards required, among them 42 chemical production technologists/industrial chemists, 14 chemical production logisticians and 17 analytical chemists. By the end of 1998, the OPCW had on its staff a total of 205 fully trained inspectors.[42]

To facilitate the engagement with the chemical industry, the Preparatory Commission agreed in December 1993 that:[43]

- The Secretariat might conduct regular briefings for industry and Member States on issues important to industry
- The Secretariat would nominate officers as points of contact for industry on specific issues of interest to industry
- Member States should consult their national industries to assist with the development of national implementing legislation and to broaden awareness for the CWC
- Industry was invited to provide to the Secretariat its expertise in areas of interest for the industry through direct bilateral informal consultations and through providing the Secretariat with relevant data and papers

---

40 Government-industry conference against chemical weapons, National Convention Centre, Canberra 18–22 September 1989, Final Record published by the Department of Foreign Affairs and Trade Canberra, Australia, 150.

41 Ron Manley: Recruitment and training of inspectors (2007); Ian R. Kenyon and Daniel Feakes: The Creation of the Organisation for the Prohibition of Chemical Weapons – A case study in the birth of an Intergovernmental Organisation, T. M. C. Asser Press (2007), chapter 6, pp. 105–112.

42 Ibid., p. 111.

43 Preparatory Commission document PC-V/B/10 (15 December 1993), paras 2.3 and 4.9.

- The Secretariat could directly contact international chemical associations and, through Governments, national chemical associations to determine the likelihood of industrial facilities being offered for Module 3 (mock inspection) training.

This created direct channels of communication and collaboration between the chemical industry and the future OPCW Technical Secretariat.

In 1994, Switzerland submitted to the Preparatory Commission the details of a Swiss Training Programme for OPCW Inspectors (Industrial Verification) SWISSPRO.[44] It would train 60 candidate inspectors in the field of industry inspections, and had been elaborated in close cooperation with experts from the Swiss chemical industry. It included specialised training at chemical plants in Switzerland. In addition, companies in Germany, the Czech Republic, China and Japan made chemical plants available for the conduct of mock inspections.[45]

The involvement of the chemical industry in the work of the Preparatory Commission can be characterised as a shift from general engagements towards a more direct involvement of industry in the preparations for the early phase of CWC implementation. This was qualitatively different from the engagement between industry and negotiators during the CWC negotiations. Direct contacts between the provisional Technical Secretariat and industry supported national preparations for implementation, the conduct of regional seminars, and activities such as trial inspections in chemical industry facilities. Certain national chemical industry associations also provided logistical support to the panels that the provisional Technical Secretariat dispatched to locations in Europe, Africa, Latin America and Asia to interview potential inspector candidates.

These efforts signalled the general support by industry for the CWC. But they also aimed at ensuring that future inspections would be conducted in ways that would respect the concerns industry had about the protection of confidential business information, about the impact of inspection conduct on its operations and on plant safety, and about the possible impact of CWC inspections on the public image of their companies. Industry understood well that inspector training was crucial – as Will Carpenter of Monsanto had pointed out in Canberra, in addition to treaty language, the application

44 Preparatory Commission document PC-VII/B/WP.12 (27 June 1994).

45 Preparatory Commission document PC-XV/B/10 (6 November 1996), para. 2.4.

of the treaty would critically depend on guidelines, procedures and a well-trained Inspectorate.[46]

4 Contributions of the Chemical Industry after the Entry into Force of the CWC

The engagement by the chemical industry with the arms control community and regulators and its support for the CWC had been important for the development of a treaty that was technically sound and could be implemented at affordable costs to governments as well as industry. It was also important during the national ratification processes in countries with large private chemical industries such as the United States of America, European countries and Japan. But industry support and engagement did not stop at the entry into force of the CWC. Several factors were important in this regard:

- The interest of industry to be an actor rather than subject of how industry verification provisions would be implemented in practice;
- Its desire to press for consistent and equal CWC implementation across the globe;
- The need for companies to put in place internal mechanisms to ensure that they could comply with the national implementation requirements enforced by the National Authorities of States Parties and international inspections.

Furthermore, the Preparatory Commission had not been able to complete work on a number of issues, including:[47]

- Guidelines for provisions regarding scheduled chemicals in low concentrations, including in mixtures, in accordance with Part VII, paragraph 5, and Part VIII, paragraph 5, of the Verification Annex. (Paris Resolution, subparagraph 12(t))
- The model facility agreement for Schedule 2 plant sites covered under Article VI of the Convention
- The issue of whether or not the term "production by synthesis" used in Part IX includes biochemical and biologically mediated processes
- The method of reporting aggregate national data for Schedule 2 and 3 chemicals

46 Government-industry conference against chemical weapons, National Convention Centre, Canberra 18–22 September 1989, Final Record published by the Department of Foreign Affairs and Trade Canberra, Australia, 154.

47 Preparatory Commission Final Report, document PC-XVI/37 (1997), pp. 47–49.

- The tentative understandings in regard to discrete organic chemicals including PSF chemicals; "production" as defined in subparagraph 12(a) of Article II; and biochemical and biologically mediated processes in relation to scheduled chemicals
- Castor bean processing plants
- Past production of Schedule 1 chemicals at facilities having a capacity above 1 tonne for purposes not prohibited under the Convention on the basis of the understanding as reflected in subparagraphs 2.4 and 4.5 of PC-VIII/B/WP.10
- The meaning of the term "a State Party" in subparagraph 8(a)(i)(2) of Article II
- The model facility agreement for Schedule 3 facilities covered under Article VI of the Convention.

These and other unresolved issues were initially transferred to a facilitation mechanism managed by the Chairman of the Committee of the Whole of the First Session of the Conference of the States Parties.[48] In 1999, this mechanism was replaced by a facilitation process under the guidance of the Executive Council, which organised the work within a dedicated Working Group and eventually split the work into different "clusters", one of which dealing with issues related to chemical industry issues.

Several of the unresolved issues were resolved during the first intersessional period (notably the models for facility agreements in the chemical industry). Others were given to the Scientific Advisory Board (SAB); examples included Ricin reporting and a newly discovered issue related to Saxitoxin transfers for medical and diagnostic purposes. Yet others were split up into separate sub-items to be resolved one by one. Some issues remained unresolved for many years and some remain unresolved even today (such as the coverage of facilities producing discrete organic chemicals by biological or biologically mediated processes).

An added complication for the functioning of the industry verification system was the delayed submission of the industry declaration of the United States.[49] At the entry into force, the US had yet to enact its implementing legislation and thus lacked the regulatory basis to collect and submit to the

48 Organisation for the Prohibition of Chemical Weapons. Conference of the States Parties. Decision – Procedure for addressing unresolved issues during the first intersessional period. OPCW document C-I/DEC.70 (22 May 1997).

49 Ian R. Kenyon and Daniel Feakes: The Creation of the Organisation for the Prohibition of Chemical Weapons – A case study in the birth of an Intergovernmental Organisation, T. M. C. Asser Press (2007) Chapter 14, 272.

OPCW declaration data from private industry. This situation changed in 2000 when the US finally submitted its industry declaration.

But the delay of the US industry declaration meant that the implementation practice had evolved based on treaty interpretations that were not necessarily shared by the US and its chemical industry. Some 200 industry inspections in 40 States Parties had created a certain practice which, when read across to the US, resulted in a sudden increase in uncertainties reported by inspection teams. These uncertainties were not merely a reflection of different treaty interpretations, but also signalled structural changes in the industry. Certain CWC concepts (for example the definitions of the different structural units of a chemical production complex – plant site, plant and unit) no longer fitted the reality of industry operations. These issues were taken up between the Technical Secretariat and industry representatives in informal discussions, and pragmatic solutions were found which were subsequently endorsed by the First CWC Review Conference in 2003.[50]

Also, the US was not the only State Party that had not submitted a full Article VI declaration. Other countries, too, had either not declared any industry facilities or missed certain declarable plant sites in their submissions. The Technical Secretariat reported in 2003 that Colombia, Côte d'Ivoire, Kiribati, Nepal, Seychelles, Suriname, Turkmenistan, the United Republic of Tanzania and Yemen had yet to submit their initial declarations under Article VI. Even for several countries that had submitted industry declarations, there remained concerns about their completeness.[51] To help rectifying these deficiencies, the Technical Secretariat of the OPCW developed guidance documents to assist States Parties in identifying declarable industry facilities. In 2001, it set up a support project to assist States Parties by analysing public information sources to identify possible declarable industry facilities, using authoritative databases, industry directories and other public sources.[52] These activities were aimed at ensuring that the industries of different States Parties would be treated equally, mirroring a demand of chemical industry to ensure a "level playing field".

---

50 Ian R. Kenyon and Daniel Feakes: The Creation of the Organisation for the Prohibition of Chemical Weapons – A case study in the birth of an Intergovernmental Organisation, T. M. C. Asser Press (2007), 272.

51 Technical Secretariat Background Paper (First Review Conference 2003). Consolidated unclassified verification implementation report (April 1997–31 December 2002). OPCW document RC-1/S/6 (25 April 2003) 17–18.

52 Ian R. Kenyon and Daniel Feakes: The Creation of the Organisation for the Prohibition of Chemical Weapons – A case study in the birth of an Intergovernmental Organisation, T. M. C. Asser Press (2007) 275–276.

The relationship between the industry and the OPCW was changing, too. The Technical Secretariat now had the mandate under the CWC to *implement* international verification activities. This meant that specific technical issues would be taken up directly between industry associations and the Technical Secretariat. In some cases, joint projects were started such as the development of a spreadsheet identifying scheduled chemicals as a tool to support the preparation of industry declarations.

By the time of the first CWC Review Conference in 2003, the Technical Secretariat issued a consolidated unclassified verification report which listed the following still-unresolved issues which in its assessment impacted on the implementation of the industry verification regime:[53]

- Different interpretations by States Parties regarding the declaration of mixtures containing low concentrations of Schedule 2 chemicals.[54]
- Declaration of intermediates produced in captive use and how the low concentration limits would apply to mixtures from which the scheduled chemicals were not isolated and purified.[55]
- Chemical production facilities producing discrete organic chemicals that used biological or biologically mediated processes.[56]
- The discrepancy between declarations of exports and imports of scheduled chemicals declared annually by the exporting and importing State Party, respectively. These significant discrepancies signalled amongst others gaps, weaknesses and differences in national implementation systems.

There also was a need for additional guidance for companies to identify declarable scheduled chemicals, eventually resulting in the preparation of an OPCW Handbook on Chemicals.

Many of these issues were of concern to the chemical industry, or needed technical advice from it to be resolved. Direct exchanges between industry experts, officers of the Technical Secretariat and facilitators of the Executive

53 Technical Secretariat Background Paper (First Review Conference 2003). Consolidated unclassified verification implementation report (April 1997–31 December 2002). OPCW document RC-1/S/6 (25 April 2003) para. 7.5.

54 Technical Secretariat Background Paper (First Review Conference 2003). Consolidated unclassified verification implementation report (April 1997–31 December 2002). OPCW document RC-1/S/6 (25 April 2003) paras. 7.18–7.20.

55 Technical Secretariat Background Paper (First Review Conference 2003). Consolidated unclassified verification implementation report (April 1997–31 December 2002). OPCW document RC-1/S/6 (25 April 2003) paras. 7.21–7.22.

56 Technical Secretariat Background Paper (First Review Conference 2003). Consolidated unclassified verification implementation report (April 1997–31 December 2002). OPCW document RC-1/S/6 (25 April 2003) para. 9.6.

Council were used to share information, solicit advice and communicate concerns about proposed solutions.

A new channel that became available to industry for communicating its concerns and providing advice to the OPCW was the Scientific Advisory Board. The SAB was set up by the Director-General in September 1998. Amongst its 20 initial members (today 25) were several experts from chemical industry. This industry presence on the board continues until today, albeit at a lower level of representation. Perhaps as important is that much of the work of the SAB is done by Temporary Working Groups (TWGs), which are composed of several members of the SAB as well as external subject matter experts based on their specific expertise. TWGs have specific terms of reference on which to report, and their time and number of meetings are limited. Industry experts are included in these working bodies on a regular basis when the subject matter relates to issues concerning the chemical industry.

An early example concerned the application of the CWC rules on transfer notifications of Schedule 1 chemicals to exports of small amounts of Saxitoxin. The CWC requires a 30-days-in-advanve notification of any such transfer. However, this was not appropriate for transfers of small amounts of Saxitoxin for diagnostic and food contamination testing purposes, which sometimes needed to be shipped within days. The SAB organised a scientific conference with academic and industry experts familiar with the matter which confirmed the legitimacy of such short-notice transfers.[57] This advice was instrumental for the OPCW to adopt the first change to a CWC provision, the inclusion of a new paragraph 5bis in Part VI of the Verification Annex. This illustrates that pragmatic interaction between the Technical Secretariat, Member States, the SAB, and chemical industry can help find solutions to implementation problems when they occurred.

A further milestone in the interaction between the OPCW and chemical industry was the 2006 Industry and Protection Forum, organised by the OPCW in conjunction with the International Council of Chemical Associations (ICCA) and CEFIC. It discussed issues relating to the verification and implementation of the CWC from the perspective of the chemical industry, including the conduct of sampling and analysis during industry inspections.[58] At the time, the OPCW began piloting this inspection technique in chemical industry inspections. The Forum was an opportunity for industry representatives to present their views on a number of verification issues, including the need for the OPCW and National Authorities to assist chemical companies in under-

57 OPCW document C-III/DG.6 (6 October 1998).

58 OPCW document S/674/2008 (1 February 2008).

standing the CWC's declaration requirements, the desirability of educating chemical companies about the requirements emanating from sampling and analysis at industrial facilities, the use of analytical instruments in "blinded mode" to protect confidential information, the possibility – however unlikely – that hitherto unknown trace quantities of scheduled chemicals might be detected as impurities in products or intermediates, and the possibility that inspectors might want to use analytical facilities outside the inspected plant site that were located in the inspected country.[59]

The Forum also initiated a discussion of the OPCW's role in enhancing safety and security at chemical plants. This issue has become more prominent as the completion of the destruction of all declared CW stockpiles was approaching and the OPCW began to adjust its priorities towards the prevention of the re-emergence of chemical weapons. The CWC is increasingly seen as an instrument that can help to make it more difficult for malicious actors to use toxic chemicals.[60] The Industry and Protection Forum highlighted a number of challenges in this regard, including the need for a clearer assessment of the responsibilities, roles and activities of industry, governments, and international bodies. It drew attention to the role of the OPCW as a forum for consultation and cooperation among States Parties, including exchanges on best practices in chemical safety and security.

Speaking on behalf of the International Council of Chemical Associations (ICCA), Jack Gerard, President and CEO of the American Chemistry Council (ACC), stressed that the OPCW's work represented a notable example of cooperation between nations, between national chemical associations under the ICCA umbrella, and between governments and the ICCA. This cooperation was crucial for compliance with the obligations of the Convention, and the ICCA was ready to provide the requisite technical assistance and industry insight.[61]

In 2015, the ICCA-OPCW partnership was formalised by forming an ICCA-OPCW Steering Committee to coordinate joint activities in support of the CWC. This step underlines that the chemical industry regards its support of the CWC as a natural extension of its Responsible Care® Program: "In the negotiations that led to the CWC, the chemical industry has considered – and still considers itself - not only as subject to verification activities, but also as a

59 Ibid., paras. 41–49.

60 Ibid., para. 59.

61 Organisation for the Prohibition of Chemical Weapons, 'OPCW Industry and Protection Forum' (2007) <https://www.opcw.org/media-centre/news/2007/11/opcw-industry-and-protection-forum>.

partner and resource to governments and the OPCW. Over the years, our cooperation has intensified and matured. ICCA representatives participate in numerous events of the OPCW and offer their expertise in various subsidiary bodies. ICCA representatives also participated in the formulation of The Hague Ethical Guidelines."[62]

5 Motivations of the Chemical Industry to Support the Development and Adoption of the CWC

Beginning in 1985, the chemical industry has been developing its Responsible Care® initiative. This is a global voluntary initiative, which – beyond legislative and regulatory compliance – commits chemical companies, national chemical industry associations and their partners to:[63]

- Continuously improve the environmental, health, safety and security knowledge and performance of its technologies, processes and products over their life cycles so as to avoid harm to people and the environment;
- Use resources efficiently and minimise waste;
- Report openly on performance, achievements and shortcomings;
- Listen, engage and work with people to understand and address their concerns and expectations;
- Cooperate with governments and organisations in the development and implementation of effective regulations and standards, and to meet or go beyond them;
- Provide help and advice to foster the responsible management of chemicals by all those who manage and use them along the product chain.

The chemical industry has recognised that it finds itself increasingly under public scrutiny as its perceived responsibilities to society broaden. At the same time, it wants to maintain a secure environment for free and non-discriminatory trade in chemical products, and for further growth.[64]

Will Carpenter, at the time Vice President of Technology of the Monsanto Agriculture Company in St. Louis, USA, underlined in his plenary address to the Canberra Conference that the chemical industry would have to do far

62 International Council of Chemical Associations, 'OPCW Partnership' (International Council of Chemical Associations, 2024) <https://icca-chem.org/partnerships/opcw/>.

63 Cefic, 'Responsible Care' <https://cefic.org/responsible-care/>.

64 Government-industry conference against chemical weapons, National Convention Centre, Canberra 18–22 September 1989, Final Record published by the Department of Foreign Affairs and Trade Canberra, Australia, 216.

more than merely comply with the cwc. It would need to "help to refine and implement it." He pointed out that "in addition to being the right thing to do, it is in industry's self interest to serve this process as it can."[65] This summarises succinctly the two complementary reasons for the chemical industry to engage with the cwc:

- It supports the cwc as it prevents its products and technologies from being diverted for malicious purposes;
- At the same time, it has a keen interest to ensure that the mechanisms set up by the cwc will not unduly hamper its operations and its future development.

A survey of the industry statements delivered at the 1989 Canberra Conference allows to delineate further this motivation of the chemical industry for supporting the cwc. In no particular order, the primary motives for supporting the cwc that were presented in these statements included:

- Equality of process – restrictions must apply equally from company to company and country to country to avoid inequities and commercial disadvantages
- Any restrictions must be harmonised globally and meshed with existing regulations and controls
- Protection of intellectual property and of other confidential business information
- Ensure that negotiators and implementers appreciate the complex technical issues and avoid the creation of a mechanism that is not properly tuned to the conditions and requirements of the chemical industry
- Ensure that the system would not create unnecessary disruptions of, constraints on, or burdens or costs for the chemical industry

  The cwc must be effective, verifiable, economically feasible and technically workable
- Use of analytical methods and tools that are adapted to the context of the chemical production environment
- Focus the scope of the regulations on chemicals that have a proven relevance to the cwc, and avoid attempts to regulate the whole of the civil chemical industry or interfere with its legitimate business
- Prevent the hampering of the future development of chemical industry, of the transfer of its products and technologies, and of international cooperation in the peaceful uses of chemistry; investment in the development of chemical industry in developing countries must continue unhindered.

65 Ibid., pp. 148, 150.

At the same time, industry underlined that it can offer its business relations and management systems to reach these objectives in a globally coherent manner.[66]

6 Impact of the Industry Contributions on the CWC Regime

The engagement of the chemical industry with the negotiators of the CWC had a demonstrable impact on the design of the treaty and some of its provisions, as well as on subsequent OPCW guidelines and implementation practices.

Several key elements of the treaty text dealing with industry verification as well as national implementation can be traced back to industry positions. Whilst the text of the CWC remained the property of governments, industry association used indirect channels as well as direct interventions to provide ever more detailed comments and suggestions on key provisions and their practical application in chemical industry.

Industry's concerns about the protection of intellectual property and confidential business information was an important driver for the inclusion of the Confidentiality Annex in the CWC. The inclusion of such an Annex in an arms control treaty was an innovation in arms control – agreements by their very nature address the relations between States and concern the exchanges and handling of information belonging to governments. Such agreements do not usually concern themselves with the protection of information belonging to or originating from private enterprises. The inclusion of the Confidentiality Annex thus was a recognition that the CWC required the active involvement of the chemical industry, and that getting industry cooperation and compliance would require treaty provisions that would protect the industry's legitimate interests and prevent the disclosure or loss of confidential business information.

Equally, the chemical industry's input was instrumental for the design of the industry verification system of the CWC. Many of the concepts and ideas promoted by the chemical industry were incorporated into the provisions of the CWC – some in their entirety, others in part. Examples include the final CWC provisions on:

- The guidelines and criteria governing the composition of the Schedules
- The way in which inspectors are granted access to facilities not involved in the production of scheduled chemicals

66 Ibid., p. 153.

- The choice between a quantitative verification approach to detect the diversion of precursors from production and trade versus the qualitative approach aiming at verifying the non-production of Schedule 1 and other high-risk chemicals for CW purposes
- The purpose of sampling and analysis in chemical industry facilities, and the constraints that sampling and analysis in chemical plant environments must respect.

After the entry into force of the CWC, industry concerns about the impact of inspection activities on its operations were also reflected in relevant manuals, technical instructions and the quality assurance systems put in place by the OPCW Technical Secretariat. An example is the Inspection Manual, which was developed by the Technical Secretariat based on the CWC provisions, the guidance received from the OPCW's policy making organs, and feedback from industry during the work of the Preparatory Commission and the implementation of verification measures in industry.

The deployment of trainers and training centres from chemical companies as part of the General Training Scheme for OPCW inspectors provided another opportunity for chemical industry to directly influence the formation of the OPCW's initial corps of inspectors, and at the same time gave confidence to industry that future OPCW inspections would be conducted in ways that would not hamper its activities or compromise confidential business information.

At the same time, the Conference on Disarmament, the Preparatory Commission, and today the OPCW have benefited not a little from information, expertise and advice provided by chemical industry experts. McLeish and Lak highlighted the following ways in which non-governmental actors, including industry, can support the negotiations and implementation of the CWC:[67]

- Problem definitions
- Agenda setting and goal setting
- Enforcement of principles and norms
- Provision of information and expertise
- Public advocacy and mobilization
- Lobbying
- Direct participation in the formulation of international agreements

67 Caitríona McLeish and Maarten Lak: The role of civil society and industrial non-State actors in relation to the Chemical Weapons Convention, in: W. Krutzsch, E. Myjer and R. Trapp: A Chemical Weapons Convention Commentary, OUP (2014) 37–48, 43–4; based and expanding on C. Albin, 'Can NGOs Enhance the Effectiveness of International Negotiation?' (1998) 4(3) International Negotiation 371–387.

- Monitoring and other assistance with compliance
- Constituency building for committed officials
- Assisting national parliaments in their preparation for accession and national legislation, and informing them on national implementation and compliance.

Whilst industry input was essential during the development of the CWC provisions, the implementation of these provisions today benefits from internal governance measures adopted by chemical companies and promoted by industry trade associations. These internal compliance assurance measures are essential to ensure compliance with the provisions and obligations States have undertaken under the CWC, and contribute to the evolution of the regime as the conditions under which the treaty needs to function change as the result of scientific, technological and economic developments.

Acknowledgement

Thanks go to Dr Detlef Männig (Managing Director, Männig Consulting, Potsdam, Germany) and Dr Renate Becker-Arnold (retired, previously BASF Ludwigshafen, Germany) who supported the work on this study by providing insight in their experience with industry-OPCW relations in background discussions.

CHAPTER 7

Chemical Terrorism: Challenges to International Regime Norms by Non-state Actors, and Multilateral Responses

Alexander Kelle

1 Introduction

The prohibition of chemical weapons (CW) use has been agreed upon by states, who have codified such prohibition in the 1925 Geneva Protocol and the 1993 Chemical Weapons Convention (CWC). Thus, the normative guide-posts that are prohibiting CW use are applicable first and foremost to states in the international system and their conduct vis-à-vis each other. The agreed-upon nature of the norms, understood as "standards of behaviour defined in terms of rights and obligations,"[1] combined with the large number of CWC states parties – 193 at the time of writing – gives them an almost global reach. This ubiquity is supported by the presence of and the activities of the Organisation for the Prohibition of Chemical Weapons (OPCW), which has been set up under Article VIII of the CWC to support CWC states parties in their implementation of the treaty. In contrast to this institutional setup on the international level, the challenges posed to the norms against CW by non-state actors, such as terrorist groups, emanate from the sub-state level and efforts to counter CW terrorism will likewise have to focus on norm implementation on the level below the state.

In addition to the challenges posed by CW terrorism spanning different levels of authority and legitimacy from the sub-state to the international/global, the legal sources for addressing such challenges are varied. As demonstrated by the Geneva Protocol and the CWC, the laws of war on the one hand and international disarmament law on the other are providing clear guidance for state-level conduct, as is customary humanitarian international law, which also stipulates in Rule 74, as noted in the study by the International Committee of the Red Cross, that the use of chemical weapons is prohibited. Extending the 1925 Geneva Protocol prohibition and in line with the CWC the

1 Stephen D Krasner, 'Structural Causes and Regime Consequences: Regimes as Intervening Variables' (1982) *International Organization* 36(2) 185, 186.

 | DOI:10.1163/9789004739192_008

customary humanitarian international law prohibition of CW use applies to both international and non-international armed conflicts.[2] However, the normative framework provided by the CWC extends considerably beyond the prohibition of use, including preparatory activities such as development and acquisition of CW. In addition, the CWC provides additional normative guideposts for state behaviour that are relevant to countering the threat of chemical terrorism, such as the national implementation of regime norms agreed upon at the international level. While national implementation, or the internalization of regime norms, is important in this context, it is only one of several normative guideposts besides international cooperation and assistance as well as, potentially, inspections or investigations under the CWC.

United Nations Security Council Resolution 1540 (2004) represents an additional legal source in the fight against terrorism with weapons of mass destruction (WMD).[3] It has been described by one observer as "a rare international law in that it is mandatory for all United Nations Member States, brings together obligations under numerous single-technology focused treaties and agreements, focusses attention on the activities of non-state actors, and requires Member States to go beyond mere declarations of support for nonproliferation."[4] Despite early criticisms expressed over UNSC Resolution 1540, the operative paragraphs of Resolution 1540 strengthen several of the core norms of the CW prohibition regime, such as the ones on non-acquisition, non-transfer and non-use of CW, albeit with a focus on non-state actors, such as terrorist groups. To implement the resolution, the Security Council set up a Committee and established a group of nine experts.[5] Since 2004 the mandate of the Committee and the group of experts has been extended several times, most recently in November 2022, following the third comprehensive review of resolution 1540, for a period of ten years up to 2032.[6]

---

2 Jean-Marie Henckaerts and Louise Doswald-Beck, *Customary International Humanitarian Law, Volume I: Rules*, Cambridge: Cambridge Univ. Press, 5th Ed., 2010, pp. 259–263.

3 United Nations Security Council, *Resolution 1540 (2004) Adopted by the Security Council at its 4956th meeting*, document S/RES/1540 (2004), New York, 28 April 2004.

4 Seema Gahlaut, "United Nations Security Council Resolution 1540 Implementation: More of the Same or Brave New World", in *Strategic Trade Review*, 2019, 5(7), pp. 53–66, quote on pp. 53f.

5 For a discussion of Resolution 1540, criticism voiced and its early implementation see Alexander Kelle, *Prohibiting Chemical and Biological Weapons. Multilateral Regimes and Their Evolution*, Boulder, CO: Lynne Rienner, 2014, pp. 208–213.

6 United Nations Security Council, *Resolution 2663 (2022) Adopted by the Security Council at its 9205th meeting*, document S/RES/2663 (2022), New York, 30 November 2022.

Notwithstanding the terrorism focus of Security Council resolutions on WMD terrorism beginning with Resolution 1540, the CWC does provide the most comprehensive normative framework for dealing with the misuse of chemistry and the Organisation for the Prohibition of Chemical Weapons (OPCW) can provide much more substantial support for norm implementation than the 1540 Committee and its group of experts with the limited resources available to them. According to Michael Barnett and Martha Finnemore international organizations, such as the OPCW, serve a variety of functions that generally fall into three broad categories: classification and organization of information and knowledge, the fixing of meanings (i.e. naming or labelling the social context of action), and the diffusion of norms.[7] With respect to the latter, Barnett and Finnemore argue that international organizations "often act as conveyor belts for the transmission of norms and models of "good" political behaviour", and thus seek "to shape state practices by establishing, articulating, and transmitting norms that define what constitutes acceptable and legitimate state behavior."[8] With respect to the prohibition of chemical weapons such acceptable state behaviour is detailed in the provisions of the CWC.

This chapter will therefore focus on the CWC as the primary source of normativity and first provide a short overview of the regime norms that states parties have agreed to be bound by under the convention. It will then briefly describe the character of the terrorist threat by reference to a few instances of CW terrorism. This will be followed by a discussion of the tools available in the CW prohibition regime to address the terrorist threat to the norms of the regime. Here, a distinction will be made between measures based on normative guidance at the national and international levels, with a focus on the latter. The concluding section will summarize the argument, highlighting the multi-level nature of the global fight against chemical terrorism and the OPCW's role in it.

2 The Norms of the Chemical Weapons Prohibition Regime and Their Institutional Context

The text of the Chemical Weapons Convention (CWC) codifies several regime norms. These have been guiding state behaviour and the work of the OPCW

7 Michael N Barnett and Martha Finnemore, 'The Politics, Power, and Pathologies of International Organizations' (1999) *International Organization*, 53(3), in 699.

8 Ibid., p.713.

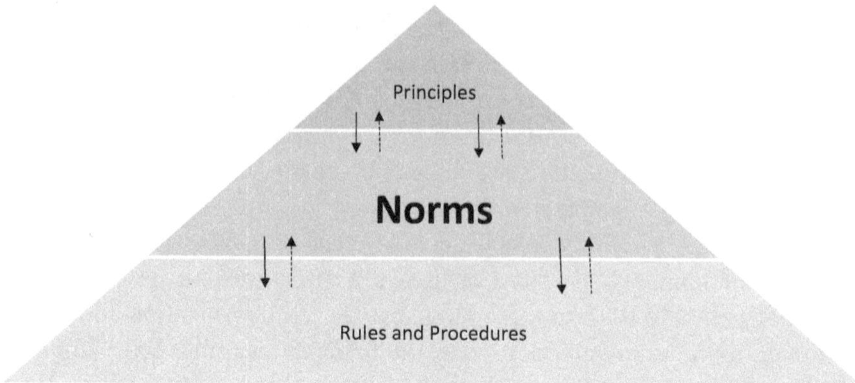

FIGURE 7.1 Regime pyramid consisting of principles, norms, rules, and procedures. Created by author.

since the CWC entered into force in April 1997. The fact that the norms of the CW prohibition regime do not exist in isolation, but in what has been termed a "norm cluster" makes them more resilient to challenges, such as contestation of their meaning or outright violations.[9] This paper follows the definitions by Krasner (1982: 186), according to which principles are "beliefs of fact, causation and rectitude", rules are "specific prescriptions or proscriptions for action", and "procedures are prevailing practices for making and implementing collective choice."[10]

This clustering of norms and embedding them in the broader institutional context with the principles as well as rules and procedures of the CW prohibition regime (Figure 7.1) establishes high hurdles for changing or amending the normative structure codified in the treaty text.

Thus, implementation of the CW prohibition regime was set on a particular path with the inclusion of a set of normative guideposts negotiated by the drafters of the CWC mostly during the second half of the 1980s. Most importantly among these, the "General Obligations" formulated in CWC Article I comprise the non-acquisition norm (which in turn includes the prohibition to develop, produce, or otherwise acquire CW), the non-retention norm, the non-transfer norm, the non-use norm (which is meant to guide regime participants' behaviour both in relation to CW and to riot control agents when used as a method of warfare), and the non-assistance norm.

9 Jeffrey S Lantis and Carmen Wunderlich, 'Resiliency Dynamics of Norm Clusters: Norm Contestation and International Cooperation' (2018) in *Review of International Studies*, 44(3), 570.

10 Krasner, note 1, p.186

Additional normative guideposts are the declaration norm in CWC Article III, the inspection norm expressed in Articles IV, V, and VI for different objects of verification, and the internalization norm in Article VII, which requires CWC states parties to enact implementing legislation and take a number of administrative steps, such as setting up a National Authority for domestic CWC implementation.[11] In addition, CWC Article IX contains the consultation, cooperation and investigation norms[12] and Article X spells out the assistance and protection norms. What is more, Article XI requires the non-interference in economic and technological development of CWC states.

The CWC, like all other non-proliferation, arms control and disarmament agreements, is a child of its time, i.e. the late 1980s/early 1990s. The then prevailing threat perception was still that of the Cold War and the chemical weapons arsenals of concern were those of the two superpowers and a few other states. As a result, the treaty text does not even mention non-state actors, such as terrorist groups. This notwithstanding, a combination of the wording of the general obligations in Article I of the CWC, and the internalization norm expressed in Art. VII allows extending the reach of the normative guideposts of the CW prohibition regime to terrorist groups or individuals too.[13]

According to CWC Articles I and II chemical weapons are "toxic chemicals and their precursors, except where intended for purposes not prohibited under the Convention, as long as the types and quantities are consistent with such purposes." This purpose based definition – sometimes referred to as the General Purpose Criterion – of a CW is complemented by the applicability of the above mentioned prohibitions at any time and to anybody. Thus, they are not limited to times of war – which was already covered by the 1925 Geneva Protocol – or states as the only actors concerned.

However, it is the primary responsibility of CWC states parties to implement the provisions of the treaty, in order to comply with the obligations they have undertaken. The OPCW Technical Secretariat established under

11 For a general discussion see Dana Zartner, 'Internalization of International Law' (2020), in Oxford Research Encyclopedias, International Studies.

12 The set of norms contained in CWC Art. IX, in contrast to the inspection norm expressed in Art. IV, V and VI, relates to non-compliance concerns and related fact-finding activities under the CWC.

13 For the wording of the different Articles of the CWC see <https://www.opcw.org/chemical-weapons-convention/articles>. This link was strengthened by UN Security Council Resolution 1540, which in its fifth preambular paragraph expresses support for existing multilateral treaties banning WMD and in operative paragraph 8 calls upon UN member states to promote full implementation of these treaties, and to adopt national rules and regulations to ensure their compliance with the obligations undertaken.

Article VIII of the CWC supports CWC states parties in fulfilling their obligations in certain areas. This division of labour also applies to the CW terrorism threat.

3 The CW Terrorist Threat: Cases, Actors, and a Spectrum of CW Agents

Although negotiations of the CWC were informed by the prevailing threat perceptions of the 1980s, in which the huge CW arsenals of the superpowers and those of other states were of primary importance, this threat perception began to change during the 1990s. The collapse of the former Soviet Union – with potentially easy access by rogue states and non-state actors to former weapons programme scientists and WMD materials – on the one hand, combined with domestic mass casualty events in the US – like the 1995 Oklahoma City bombing – led some influential decision-makers, like then US Senator Sam Nunn to conclude that terrorism with nuclear, biological and chemical weapons was now a major threat.[14] This perception was further reinforced by the sarin gas attack perpetrated by the Aum Shinrikyo sect in Tokyo in March 1995 and the unsuccessful attempts by the sect to produce biological weapons.[15] Finally, the combination of the mass-casualty terrorist attack on the twin towers of the World Trade Center in New York on September 11, 2001 and the anthrax letters sent to media outlets and US politicians shortly afterwards catapulted the spectre of CBW terrorism to the forefront of threat perceptions of security policy experts and decision-makers globally. Since then several more attempted or successful acquisition and/or CW use cases by terrorists have been documented. These include:

- CBRN training courses in Afghanistan conducted by Al-Qaeda operatives from 1999 to 2001;
- Training on and experiments with crude chemical agents at the Khurmal camp in northeastern Iraq by a terrorist group led by Abu Musab al-Zarqavi, resulting in several planned attacks (which were disrupted in time) with ricin or cyanide in some Western European states in early 2003;

14 Sam Nunn, 'Terrorism Meets Proliferation: A Post-Cold War Convergence of Threats' (1997) in *The Monitor: Nonproliferation, Demilitarization, and Arms Control* 1, 3(2), 3–4.

15 Milton Leitenberg, 'Aum Shinrikyo's efforts to produce biological weapons: A case study in the serial propagation of misinformation' (1999) 11(4), in Terrorism and Political Violence 149; William Rosenau, 'Aum Shinrikyo's Biological Weapons Program: Why Did it Fail?' (2001) in *Studies in Conflict & Terrorism*, 24(4), 289.

- In 2006–07 Sunni insurgents affiliated with Al Qaeda in Iraq built more than a dozen "Chlorine-augmented, vehicle-borne IEDs"; and
- Several chemical attacks took place on girl schools in Afghanistan in 2010; analysis of biomedical samples showed non-fatal levels of organophosphate poisoning.[16]

More recently, the OPCW UN Joint Investigative Mechanism (JIM) confirmed the use of CW by ISIL/Daesh in Syria in 2015 and 2016 and the United Nations Investigative Team to Promote Accountability for Crimes Committed by Da'esh/Islamic State in Iraq and the Levant (UNITAD) is investigating CW use in Iraq.

The JIM was established pursuant to UNSC Resolution 2235 (2015) and was tasked to identify, to the greatest extent feasible, individuals, entities, groups or Governments perpetrating, organizing, sponsoring or otherwise involved in the use of chemicals as weapons in Syria. In addition to CW use by the Syrian armed forces, the JIM confirmed Daesh use of sulfur mustard in Marea on 21 August 2015.[17] The JIM also concluded that ISIL was responsible for the use of sulfur mustard at Umm Hawsh on 15 and 16 September 2016.[18]

UNITAD was established through UN Security Council Resolution 2379 (2017) and has undertaken significant work to investigate the development and use of CW by Da'esh/ISIL in Iraq. According to its most recent (10th) report, UNITAD has expanded its investigation to additional CW attacks across Iraq and is currently "focusing on collecting and preserving evidence linked to 12 attacks."[19]

Overall, these cases show a variety of acquisition, training and use (attempts) related to a spectrum of CW agents ranging from classical chemical warfare agents, such as sulphur mustard, to toxic industrial chemicals, such as chlorine, in the context of improvised chemical devices. This is noteworthy as it seems to contradict the notion that there is a prototypical or most common

16 The first four examples are mentioned in Jonathan B Tucker, 'The Role of the Chemical Weapons Convention in Countering Chemical Terrorism' (2012) in *Terrorism and Political Violence*, 24(1), 107.

17 United Nations, *Letter Dated 24 August 2016 from the Secretary-General Addressed to the President of the Security Council* (24 August 2016) UN Doc S/2016/738; United Nations, *Letter Dated 21 October 2016 from the Secretary-General Addressed to the President of the Security Council* (21 October 2016) UN Doc S/2016/888.

18 United Nations, *Letter dated 26 October 2017 from the Secretary-General addressed to the President of the Security Council* (26 October 2017) UN Doc S/2017/904.

19 United Nations, *Letter dated 22 May 2023 from the Special Adviser and Head of the United Nations Investigative Team to Promote Accountability for Crimes Committed by Da'esh/Islamic State in Iraq and the Levant addressed to the President of the Security Council* (22 May 2023) UN Doc S/2023/367, 5.

type of CW acquisition or use by terrorists. Yet, the two regime norms most directly challenged by this are the non-acquisition and the non-use norms of the regime.

4 Addressing the Threat of Chemical Terrorism across Different Levels of Normativity and Agency

Norms of varying scope and legal "bindingness" that prohibit CW are situated at different levels across the international to national to sub-state spectrum. Tools to support such norms and their implementation can equally be identified across this spectrum. First, at the international level, measures undertaken by the OPCW – and to a more limited extent by the 1540 group of experts – support states in living up to the obligations they have undertaken under the convention.[20] Second, national legal norms and regulations, e.g. CWC implementing laws, specify measures that states must follow to comply domestically with CWC Articles VI and VII. Third, codes of ethics or conduct at the domestic level provide additional normative guidance, e.g. in the area of chemical security, for chemical industry. Given the global dimension of chemical industry and trade, such codes can also take on a transnational character.[21] In the following subsection, the domestic implementation of regime norms will be discussed briefly, before the remainder of this section will analyse how the threat of chemical terrorism is addressed at the regime level through the OPCW.

5 The Internalization Norm and Its Implementation in Guiding CWC State Party Action

International regime norms depend for their effectiveness on the internalization into national laws and regulations of regime members. More broadly, "the

20 In some regions, in particular in Europe, this international dimension is further bolstered by the activities of regional organisations, such as the EU. Analysing these regional efforts, however, is beyond the scope of this chapter. For more details on the EU, see Alexander Ghionis and Alexander Kelle, *The Chemical Weapons Convention After Its Fifth Review Conference: Key Issues For The European Union* <https://www.nonproliferation.eu/wp-content/uploads/2024/03/EUNPDC-87-CWC-after-RevCon5-2.pdf#new_tab> (accessed 17 May 2024).

21 See for example The Hague Ethical Guidelines, which have been drafted by a group of chemists in order to provide guidance on how to apply the norms of the practice of chemistry in support of the CWC; available at <https://www.opcw.org/hague-ethical-guidelines>.

internalization of international law into the fabric of domestic law significantly increases the likelihood that states feel obligated to comply."[22] The corresponding requirement for CWC states parties to internalize all the CWC's prescriptions and proscriptions for action is cutting across practically all aspects of CWC implementation. In this broad understanding, the internalization norm affects most of the normative guideposts for state action, subsumed under the heading of "core obligations" under the CWC.[23]

Thus, in the fight against terrorist acquisition and use of CW, most, if not all of these activities require the translation of the CWC's stipulations into the domestic sphere of states parties through domestic legal and administrative processes, and systematic follow-up, i.e. implementation activity. As summarized by Jonathan Tucker "Article VI sets out the ***functional basis*** of national implementation by stating that each member state 'shall adopt the necessary measures to ensure that toxic chemicals and their precursors are only developed, produced, otherwise acquired, retained, transferred, or used … for purposes not prohibited under this Convention.'"[24] He continues that Article VII provides the ***legal basis*** for national implementation by requiring that each member state "adopt the necessary measures to implement its obligations under this Convention."[25] [emphasis added]

While the CWC Art. VI does not specify what the "necessary measures" are, given the broad definitions under Articles I and II, there is an expectation for CWC states parties to adopt such measures in a way that terrorist activities would be covered.[26]

Comparing expectations of national implementation formulated in the treaty text to the actual track record of implementation by CWC states parties over the past 26 years shows a continuing discrepancy between normative guidance and state level conduct. While in the first few years after the CWC entered into force the CWC states parties and OPCW showed "a benign lack of interest in CWC national implementation", by 2003 they "were fully engaged with the issue."[27] The most visible sign of this heightened interest was the

22 Zartner, 2020, note 10.

23 As all CWC states parties are also members of the United Nations, operative paragraph 8 (b) of UN Security Council Resolution 1540 reinforces this obligation.

24 Tucker, note 15, p.111.

25 Idem.

26 The widespread uncertainty surrounding the issue of "necessary measures" has prompted the OPCW Technical Secretariat in 2016 to circulate discussion papers addressing the issue. See section on conceptual considerations below.

27 Lisa Tabassi and Scott Spence, 'Improving CWC implementation: The OPCW Action Plan' (2004), in *Verification Yearbook 2004*, 45.

national implementation action plan agreed upon by the Conference of the States Parties in October of that year. At that time about 60% of states parties had submitted a declaration to the OPCW under CWC Article VII (5) and about a third indicated that they had legislation in place covering all key areas of CWC implementation.

By 2012, i.e. 15 years after the CWC had entered into force, the action plan had led to an improvement of national implementation with Article VII declarations being submitted by three quarters of states parties and legislation covering all key areas reported by less than half of them.[28] Numbers have since grown, but as Table 7.1 shows, are still far from satisfactory, with around 70 of 193 states parties still lacking implementing legislation that would cover all areas that are key to the enforcement of the convention.

TABLE 7.1 Implementation of CWC Article VII

Cutoff date	Number of states parties	National authorities	Article VII declaration submitted	Legislation covering all initial measures
2003	154	126	94	51
2005	181	172	112	72
2008	184	177	126	82
19.08.2009	188	181	128	86
30.07.2010	188	185	135	87
29.07.2011	188	185	139	88
27.07.2012	188	186	141	88
31.07.2013	188	187	148	107
31.07.2014	190	188	152	112
31.07.2015	192	188	152	116
31.07.2016	192	189	156	118
31.07.2017	192	190	160	122
31.07.2018	193	190	162	122
31.07.2019	193	191	165	119
31.07.2020	193	192	172	119
31.07.2021	193	192	172	118

28 See the discussion in Kelle, note 5, pp. 135–138.

TABLE 7.1 Implementation of CWC Article VII (*cont.*)

Cutoff date	Number of states parties	National authorities	Article VII declaration submitted	Legislation covering all initial measures
31.07.2022	193	192	172	122
31.07.2023	193	192	179	128

SOURCES: VARIOUS ARTICLE VII IMPLEMENTATION REPORTS BY THE OPCW DIRECTOR-GENERAL, AS CONTAINED IN *REPORT BY THE DIRECTOR-GENERAL: OVERVIEW OF THE STATUS OF IMPLEMENTATION OF ARTICLE VII OF THE CHEMICAL WEAPONS CONVENTION AS AT 31 JULY 2023*, DOCUMENT C-28/DG.7, THE HAGUE, 6 SEPTEMBER 2023; *REPORT BY THE DIRECTOR-GENERAL: OVERVIEW OF THE STATUS OF IMPLEMENTATION OF ARTICLE VII OF THE CHEMICAL WEAPONS CONVENTION AS AT 31 JULY 2022*, DOCUMENT EC-101/DG.13, THE HAGUE, 9 SEPTEMBER 2022; *REPORT BY THE DIRECTOR-GENERAL: OVERVIEW OF THE STATUS OF THE IMPLEMENTATION OF ARTICLE VII OF THE CHEMICAL WEAPONS CONVENTION AS AT 31 JULY 2021*, DOCUMENT EC-98/DG.13, THE HAGUE, 14 SEPTEMBER 2021; *REPORT BY THE DIRECTOR-GENERAL: OVERVIEW OF THE STATUS OF THE IMPLEMENTATION OF ARTICLE VII OF THE CHEMICAL WEAPONS CONVENTION AS AT 31 JULY 2020*, DOCUMENT EC-95/DG.8, THE HAGUE, 4 SEPTEMBER 2020; *OVERVIEW OF THE STATUS OF THE IMPLEMENTATION OF ARTICLE VII OF THE CHEMICAL WEAPONS CONVENTION AS AT 31 JULY 2019*, DOCUMENT EC-92/DG.9, THE HAGUE, 26 AUGUST 2019; *OVERVIEW OF THE STATUS OF THE IMPLEMENTATION OF ARTICLE VII OF THE CHEMICAL WEAPONS CONVENTION AS AT 31 JULY 2018*, DOCUMENT EC-89/DG.9, THE HAGUE, 24 AUGUST 2018; *REPORT BY THE DIRECTOR-GENERAL: OVERVIEW OF THE STATUS OF THE IMPLEMENTATION OF ARTICLE VII OF THE CHEMICAL WEAPONS CONVENTION AS AT 31 JULY 2017*, DOCUMENT EC-86/DG.10, THE HAGUE, 24 AUGUST 2017; *OVERVIEW OF THE STATUS OF IMPLEMENTATION OF ARTICLE VII OF THE CHEMICAL WEAPONS CONVENTION AS AT 31 JULY 2015*, DOCUMENT EC-80/DG.14, THE HAGUE, 10 SEPTEMBER 2015; FIGURES FROM 2012 AND EARLIER ARE REPRODUCED FROM KELLE, NOTE 5, P.137

Furthermore, enacting national implementing legislation is only the first step in being able to enforce CWC prohibitions domestically. Not having these available seriously hampers further steps by states parties such as "the training and equipping of law-enforcement personnel and customs officials to detect, investigate, prosecute, and punish individuals or groups seeking chemical weapons."[29] Given these gaps in national implementation, implementation support from the international level through the OPCW gains in importance.

29 Tucker, note 15, p. 112.

6 Addressing the Threat of Chemical Terrorism at the International Regime Level: The Role of and Contributions by the OPCW

Creation of the OPCW is stipulated by Article VIII of the CWC. It establishes the three components of the organization in the form of the Conference of the States Parties (CSP), the Executive Council (EC) and an international bureaucracy – the Technical Secretariat of the organization. With the role assigned to the OPCW in implementing the convention,[30] several manifestations of the functions identified by Barnett and Finnemore – classification, the fixing of meanings, and norm diffusion – can be observed in the OPCW context. These will be discussed briefly in the following subsections.

6.1 *Conceptual Considerations and Organizational Responses to the Threat of Chemical Terrorism*

The terrorist attacks on 11 September 2001 against the United States and the anthrax letters sent through the US mail system shortly after the terrorist attack triggered a quick response by the OPCW. In early November the Director General submitted a note for the December 2001 Executive Council session, which contains an analysis of the provisions of the CWC "which apply to the danger of the terrorist use of chemical weapons, with a view to assisting in the development of an action plan for the OPCW's contribution to the global struggle against terrorism."[31] The paper identified CWC universality, the full implementation of the CW destruction norm (CWC Articles IV and V), Article VI (on activities not prohibited), the internalization norm expressed in Article VII, the assistance and protection provisions under Article X, and the international cooperation norm in Article XI as contributing to global anti-terrorist efforts. The Executive Council decision taken in the matter during its December 2001 session followed this classification of CWC elements as most relevant in the fight against CW terrorism. While the Council did not decide an action plan as proposed in the Director-General's note, it "established an open-ended working group ... and decided that the full and effective implementation of all the provisions of the Convention was in itself a contribution to global anti-terrorist efforts."[32]

30 The functions of the OPCW are detailed in CWC Article VIII.

31 OPCW, *Note by the Director-General. The OPCW and the Global Struggle against Terrorism* (9 November 2001) EC-XXVII/DG.3, p.1.

32 OPCW, *Report of the Implementation of the Convention in the Year 2001* (10 October 2002) C-7/3, p.4.

The key areas of CWC implementation that apply to the dangers of chemical terrorism identified in late 2001 have been guiding OPCW and state party action ever since, with the newly established open-ended working group on terrorism (OEWG-T) focussing on CWC universality, and the organisation in 2003 agreeing on an action plan on national implementation to strengthen the internalization norm.[33] Implementation of other provisions of the Convention continued as a matter of course and as such can be assumed to have had a positive side-effect of contributing to global anti-terrorism efforts. In addition, the OPCW established contacts with newly created counter-terrorism units in the United Nations system, such as the Committee established by the Security Council pursuant to Resolution 1540. It also joined the UN Counter-Terrorism Implementation Task Force (CTITF) in 2005. Overall, however, priorities of the OPCW during the first decade following the seminal EC decision of December 2001 continued to be associated with the verified destruction of declared CW stockpiles, for which major deadlines were set in 2007 and 2012.

During this period the OEWG-T served as the "main body giving shape to the counter-terrorism policies of the Organisation and advising on the position and activities of the Secretariat in this field."[34] As summarized in a French national working paper in 2009, the second CWC Review Conference in the previous year had given additional momentum to the work of the OEWG-T and the OPCW's work in the areas of assistance and protection under CWC Article X, and in relation to strengthening chemical safety and security in member states, including through the cooperation with chemical industry.[35] After the OPCW Director-General had submitted a summary document on the status of the OPCW's contribution to global anti-terrorism efforts to the Council in February 2010, the Council subsequently requested to receive such a note annually, so that it would remain informed about the organization's activities in this area.[36] Inter-organizational cooperation on countering chemical terrorism also increased during the first half of this dec-

33 OPCW, *Decision: Plan of Action Regarding the Implementation of Article VII* (24 October 2003) C-8/DEC.16.

34 OPCW, *Report of the Implementation of the Convention in 2010* (30 November 2011) C-16/4, p.31.

35 France, *The Open-Ended Working Group on Terrorism – A Platform for Promoting OPCW Active Engagement in the Global Anti-Terrorist Efforts*, document EC-57/NAT.6, The Hague: OPCW, 8 July 2009.

36 OPCW, *Report of the Sixtieth Session of the Executive Council*, document EC-60/3, The Hague: OPCW, 22 April 2010.

ade. In March 2014, for example, the then Chairperson of the 1540 Committee participated in the first OPCW OEWG-T meeting of that year.[37]

Subsequently, the OEWG-T in 2015 was complemented by a sub-working group on non-state actors in order "to discuss in more detail, and on the basis of three discussion papers issued by the Secretariat, the topics of: the legal accountability of non-State actors under the Convention ...; measures to prevent the hostile use of toxic chemicals ...; and ensuring an effective response to the hostile use of a toxic chemical ...."[38] While the sub-working group was open to the same state party representatives, its focus was less on general debates and more geared towards "supporting the OEWG in making practical recommendations on how the OPCW could further contribute to global anti-terrorism efforts."[39] The three discussion papers were complemented by a fourth one on the utility of CWC Article VI in the context of states parties' efforts to address chemical terrorism.[40] In addition to raising the profile of, and contributing to conceptual clarity on the substantive issues addressed in the four discussions papers, they had the additional effect of further establishing the role of the OPCW, and here in particular the Technical Secretariat, in the classification and organization of meaning concerning how CWC states parties could best use the provisions of the convention in their fight against chemical terrorism. The paper on Article VI is quite explicit in this regard by stating that its purpose is to "set out ways in which [CWC] Article VI ... and associated processes, mechanisms and information contribute to counter-terrorism efforts."[41] To this end the paper first highlights that Article VI "contains a very broad obligation, one that goes beyond the requirements of the current verification regime, in that it requires 'necessary measures' to be put in place for all 'toxic chemicals and their precursors', not just those listed in the Verification Annex."[42] The paper also proposes additional measures that states parties and the technical secretariat could take to improve implementation of Article VI and contains an annex that details

37 See the Annual Report of the 1540 Committee for 2014 as contained in UN Security Council document S/2014/958, p.9.

38 OPCW, *Report of the Implementation of the Convention in 2015* (30 November 2016) C-21/4, p.30.

39 OPCW, *Report of the Implementation of the Convention in 2015* (30 November 2016) C-21/4.

40 OPCW, *Note by the Technical Secretariat. The Contribution of Article VI to States Parties' Efforts to Counter Terrorism* (19 May 2016) S/1387/2016.

41 OPCW, *Note by the Technical Secretariat. The Contribution of Article VI to States Parties' Efforts to Counter Terrorism,* p.1.

42 Idem.

how – in the view of the secretariat – verification measures under Article VI contribute to counter-terrorism efforts.[43]

During the same period the OPCW-UN Joint Investigative Mechanism (JIM) was investigating CW use in Syria and found that both in 2015 and 2016 chemical weapons had been used by the so-called Daesh/ISIL in Marea and Umm Hawsh, respectively. In addition, the OPCW Technical Secretariat confirmed non-state actor use of sulphur mustard in northern Iraq after it had conducted Technical Assistance Visits to Iraq. CWC states parties strongly condemned the incidents, which "also underscored the imperative need for determined efforts in the area of countering chemical terrorism."[44]

The Executive Council provided further impetus to such efforts when it adopted a seminal decision in October 2017 on addressing the threat posed by chemical weapons use by non-state actors. The decision emphasized that any violation of any of the general obligations contained in CWC Article I by anyone, including non-state actors, would pose "a fundamental threat to the object and purpose of the Convention and to the achievement of a world free of chemical weapons".[45] More specifically, the decision includes a number of findings and calls to action for CWC states parties and the Technical Secretariat alike. For example, the decision underscores the role of the OPCW in preventing and responding to chemical terrorism and reaffirms that those responsible for CW use must be held accountable. It reminds states parties of their obligations under Article VI paragraph 2 to "adopt the necessary measures" and urges them to enact "comprehensive penal legislation" as required under Article VII.[46] The decision further encourages states parties to make use of mutual legal assistance arrangements and notes in this context the importance of assistance and capacity building more broadly in support of national implementation. The decision also reaffirms that the right of states parties to request assistance also extends to the threat of use or use of CW by non-state actors. With a view to the Technical Secretariat, the decision requests an

43 Ibid., pp. 5–6. The Secretariat returned to the topic of Article VI implementation in a further discussion paper discussion paper issued by the Secretariat entitled *The Implementation of Article VI as a Contribution to Countering Chemical Terrorism* in May 2018 (document S/1622/2018), which discussed in particular the obligation for States Parties to adopt the "necessary measures" under Article VI to control the use of toxic chemicals and their precursors.

44 OPCW, *Report of the Implementation of the Convention in 2016* (29 November 2017) C-22/4, p.4.

45 OPCW, *Decision. Addressing the Threat Posed by the Use of Chemical Weapons by Non-State Actors* (13 October 2017)EC-86/DEC.9.

46 OPCW, *Decision. Addressing the Threat*, p.3.

enhancement of "its capacity-building programmes that facilitate the sharing of chemical safety and security best practices among States Parties, on a voluntary basis".[47] In addition, it tasks the Secretariat to examine how it could assist states parties in investigating and prosecuting non-state actors and countering chemical terrorism more broadly.[48] Thus, the October 2017 Council decision reinforced the framing of counter-terrorist measures under the CWC prevailing since its December 2001 decision, reflected positively on both conceptual and programmatic work undertaken since by the Secretariat and states parties, but also sought to identify areas for further improvement.

Several of these issues were further discussed in some detail during the first conference convened by the OPCW on countering chemical terrorism in June 2018. The key objectives of the conference were to "explore the threat of chemical terrorism, to discuss and share strategies for preventing and responding to acts of chemical terrorism, and to consider how to ensure the legal accountability of non-State actors."[49] Presentations and discussions during the conference highlighted the need for risk assessments, international cooperation efforts, assistance and protection activities ranging from the international to regional to the national level, and comprehensive national implementation measures. As noted by the chairperson of the sub-working group on non-state actors, Ambassador Maria Teresa Infante of Chile during the closing session of the meeting, the structure of the conference would be a good template for CWC states parties to "follow in ensuring that they are equipped to counter the threat of chemical terrorism."[50] In addition, the fact that the OPCW hosted this conference with the participation of several external experts further established the OPCW as one of the central actors in the global network of multilateral institutions and international organizations seeking to counter terrorism with WMD.

While OPCW programmatic activities in support of the various normative guideposts outlined above continued as a matter of routine CWC implementation, the salience of the global fight against terrorism has increased more recently in the OPCW context when reviewing CWC implementation and planning ahead. Most notably, chemical terrorism has been treated as a topic in its own right during the review process leading up to the Fifth CWC Review Conference in May 2023. Reviewing the operation of the treaty in relation to global

---

47 Idem.

48 Idem.

49 OPCW, *Note by the Technical Secretariat. Summary of the Conference on Countering Chemical Terrorism, OPCW Headquarters, 7–8 June 2018* (16 July 2018) S/1652/2018, p.1.

50 Ibid., p.9.

anti-terrorism efforts, CWC states parties stressed that universality and the full and effective national implementation play a key role in countering chemical terrorism, as well as the relevance of chemical safety and security to prevent the misuse of toxic chemicals by non-state actors. In addition the importance of the cooperation and assistance norms and the right to protection against chemical terrorism under CWC Article X were recognised, as were the capacity building activities undertaken by the Technical Secretariat and the role of the United Nations, including the obligations stemming from UN Security Council resolution 1540 in this context.[51]

In addition, the new OPCW Medium-Term Plan (MTP) for 2024–2028 notes that knowledge about toxic chemicals, including chemical weapons, becomes ever more widely accessible. Therefore, "the Organisation will need to continue strengthening its capabilities to deal with non-State actors, especially terrorist groups, organised criminal groups, and individuals."[52] In the context of reducing risks associated with incidents involving toxic chemicals, the MTP reiterates the Technical Secretariat's role in the global fight against terrorism and "the development, more broadly, of a chemical security culture"[53] among states parties and the wider stakeholder community. In addition, the plan emphasizes the OPCW's collaboration with other international organisations in the fight against terrorism. In particular, it foresees that the organisation will maintain and strengthen its role in this area "by deepening its existing cooperative activities with partners, while at the same time examining potential partnerships with other organisations."[54]

In sum, the OPCW – both its policy making organs and the Technical Secretariat – since 2001 has engaged in a variety of activities to support the global fight against terrorism by classifying certain regime norms as relevant in this context, by providing a platform for exchange by states parties on their activities in this context and by supporting states parties in implementing relevant norms. As discussed above, there is still room for improvement in relation to realization of the internalization norm, i.e. implementation of CWC Article VII. The following subsection, will briefly review OPCW activities in relation to the assistance and protection norms as tools in the fight against chemical terrorism.

51 Personal communication from participant in the OEWG to prepare the Fifth CWC Review Conference.

52 OPCW, *Note by the Technical Secretariat. Medium-Term Plan for the Organisation for the Prohibition of Chemical Weapons 2024–2028* (14 August 2023) EC-104/S/1* C-28/S/1, p.2.

53 Ibid., p.8.

54 Ibid., p.12.

6.2 *Use of the Assistance and Protection Norms to Counter Chemical Terrorism*

Already the first Secretariat paper on chemical terrorism in 2001 included implementation of the assistance and protection norms expressed in Article X for consideration by the Executive Council. The Director-General at the time suggested to increase readiness of the OPCW to provide "effective and timely assistance to victims of chemical weapons use, in order to save human lives and to reduce human suffering, while striving to minimise the impact of terrorist chemical attacks."[55] OPCW activities in this regard would complement those of CWC states parties under Article X, which include the provision of emergency assistance and protection to any state party that is exposed to or threatened with chemical weapons. Importantly, Art. X (8) does not distinguish between a state and a non-state perpetrator. Assistance provided by states parties may take the form of a financial contribution to a voluntary fund managed by the OPCW. Member states could also donate certain items of chemical defence equipment either on a bilateral basis or through the organisation. In addition, Article X stipulates that within 24 hours after the receipt of a request for assistance, the OPCW Director-General must launch an investigation of the alleged chemical attack, irrespective of the type of perpetrator, to establish relevant facts "to provide foundation for further action."[56] After another 72 hours he shall submit a report to the Executive Council, which has then to deal with the issue. The organisation is thus involved in different ways in the implementation of the assistance norm, alongside states parties, who under Article X are both entitled to request such assistance and obliged to provide it.[57] Below are a few examples to illustrate this multilevel approach to implementation of the assistance norm.

- In 2010 "the Secretariat continued to conduct long-term national capacity-building projects on development and improvement of protection against chemical weapons for personnel who are involved in emergency response", with a specific focus of three events in Mexico "in preparation for the Pan-American Games in 2011."[58]

---

55 OPCW, *Note by the Director-General. The OPCW and the Global Struggle against Terrorism*, 2001, p.2.

56 See CWC Article X (9) for further details.

57 As noted previously, a state party request for assistance can also be addressed by the Technical Secretariat in the form of a Technical Assistance Visit, such as the ones to the UK in 2018 and Iraq in 2016. Timelines and other procedural elements are more flexible in the case of TAVs.

58 OPCW, *Report of the OPCW on the Implementation of the Chemical Weapons Convention in 2010* (20 November 2011) C-16/4, p.15.

- In 2014 the OPCW Technical Secretariat conducted several courses and trainings to assist with CWC state party preparedness in different areas. In July of that year it provided a platform the Fourteenth Annual Workshop to Coordinate Assistance and Protection under Article X,[59] in September it held – jointly with South Africa – an assistance and protection course for instructors from African states parties to the CWC,[60] and in October it convened a regional course on medical aspects of assistance and protection against CW for CWC states parties for Latin America and the Caribbean in Cuba.[61]
- The latter theme was further developed in 2018 when the Technical Secretariat as part of its capacity-building programme began "focusing on the institutional preparedness of Member States' hospitals to provide care and remain operational in the aftermath of a mass casualty chemical terrorism event [... in order] to expand the chemical emergency capacity of OPCW Member State hospitals to receive, treat, and manage a sudden influx of contaminated patients."[62]
- From 23 September to 5 October 2023 the OPCW and Algeria jointly conducted a "multi-component chemical emergency response capacity-building exercise for the Africa region ("CHEMEX Africa"), in Algiers in order to "enhance African States Parties' capacities to respond to chemical emergencies, including incidents and attacks perpetrated by non-State actors."[63]

As these examples covering a period of more than a decade show, the OPCW Technical Secretariat has continuously assisted CWC states parties in developing their capacities for protection against CW, including attacks perpetrated by terrorists. This has taken the form of providing a platform for states

59 OPCW, *Note by the Technical Secretariat. Fourteenth Annual Workshop to Coordinate Assistance and Protection under Article X of the Chemical Weapons Convention, Madrid, Spain, 1–3 July 2014* (1 May 2014) S/1178/2014.

60 OPCW, *Note by the Director-General, Call for Nominations for the Third Assistance-and-Protection Course from African States Parties, Tshwane, South Africa, 1–12 September 2014* (11 June 2014) S/1188/2014.

61 OPCW, *Note by the Director-General. Call for Nominations for a Regional Course on Medical Aspects of Assistance and Protection against Chemical Weapons for States Parties in the Latin America and Caribbean Region, Havana, Cuba, 20–23 October 2014* (3 July 2014) S/1195/2014.

62 OPCW, *Note by the Director General. Status of the OPCW's Contribution to Global Anti-Terrorism Efforts* (12 February 2019) EC-90/DG.8, p.8.

63 OPCW, *Note by the Technical Secretariat: CHEMEX Africa (Multi-Component Chemical Emergency Response Capacity-Building Exercise for the Africa Region), Algiers, Algeria, 23 September - 5 October 2023* (27 June 2023) S/2185/2023, p.1.

parties to exchange best practices, but has also reached into the domestic sphere of OPCW member states by dealing directly with emergency preparedness practitioners and first responders around the globe. This clearly illustrates the multi-level nature of the response to chemical terrorism pursued by the OPCW. It also demonstrates the importance of the OPCW Technical Secretariat in inculcating certain standards of behaviour in states parties when implementing the assistance norm in the protection against chemical terrorism.

7 Summary and Conclusions

Terrorism is a crime committed for political purposes at the sub-state level. Given the sometimes transnational character of terrorism, including chemical terrorism, a number of international institutions and prohibition regimes have been created to address the issue globally. The CWC and its implementing organization, the OPCW, play a pivotal role in supporting the global fight against terrorism, with a view to the misuse of toxic chemicals by non-state actors, including terrorists.

The prohibition of chemical weapons use is supported by different bodies of international law, including humanitarian international law, UN Security Council resolutions addressing WMD terrorism since resolution 1540 (2004), and international disarmament law. Among these, the latter body of law, in the form of the Chemical Weapons Convention, reinforced by law promulgated by the UN Security Council, is providing the clearest guidance for internationally agreed-upon state-level conduct in relation to this non-state actor threat.

The Chemical Weapons Convention does not explicitly deal with chemical terrorism. However, the prohibitions in CWC Article I in combination with the provisions of Article VII extend the non-use norm and other regime norms to terrorism with CW. Unfortunately, more than a quarter-century after the CWC entered into force in 1997, 70 of the 193 CWC states parties have not yet enacted domestic legislation covering all key aspects of the convention. This deficit in implementing the internalization norm has potentially negative effects in the fight against chemical terrorism, when for example perpetrators of such acts cannot be prosecuted due to lacking domestic laws.

In addition to supporting CWC states parties through a variety of capacity building activities related to improved Article VII implementation, the OPCW has engaged in a wide range of activities that are falling into the different categories identified by Barnett and Finnemore for international organisations more broadly. The OPCW Technical Secretariat shortly after the 9/11 terrorist attacks and the mailing of anthrax letters in the US engaged in the classification and organization of information and knowledge by outlining relevant provisions of the CWC that are applicable to the fight against terrorism. Subsequent OPCW activities that fall into this category can be found for example in the discussion papers provided by the secretariat for states parties' consideration during the meetings of the OEWG on terrorism and its subgroup on non-state actors.

In addition to the diffusion of the internalization norm mentioned above, the OPCW Technical Secretariat was instrumental in strengthening implementation of the assistance and protection norms. In this context, the OPCW developed its convening power through events like the first terrorism conference in The Hague in June 2018, but also through more regular events like the annual workshops to coordinate assistance and protection under the CWC. Working with different stakeholder groups in CWC states parties the OPCW has supported emergency responders on the domestic level of CWC states parties and thereby established itself as an important actor in the multi-level fight against chemical terrorism.

CHAPTER 8

The Prohibition of Chemical Weapons and the ECtHR: A Complementary Approach?

Elisabeth Hoffberger-Pippan

1 Introduction

The Chemical Weapons Convention[1] (CWC) constitutes one of the most successful arms control treaties. Experts in the field of chemical weapons attribute the CWC's eminence *inter alia* to 7 July 2023 when the United States of America announced the destruction of all stockpiles of its former chemical weapons program.[2] The largest part of the Convention's success, however, is owed to its main body, the Organisation for the Prohibition of Chemical Weapons (OPCW) ensuring the implementation of the Convention and offering a forum of consultation as well as cooperation among CWC States Parties.[3] The CWC also has a comprehensive verification regime forming part of an Annex to the CWC with the possibility of updating the list of scheduled chemicals regularly.[4]

However, the CWC lacks a *successful* enforcement mechanism, let alone one that would allow individuals to seek redress for violations of the Convention. Moreover, the exact scope of application of the CWC is still not entirely clear, and divergent views among CWC States Parties persist. To overcome these pitfalls and compensate for at least some of these shortcomings, the role of the European Convention of Human Rights (ECHR) should also be considered. Even though the ECHR is – logically – completely silent on issues related to arms control, let alone the use of chemical weapons, it might have relevance in case chemical agents were used in contravention of human rights law, es-

1 Convention on the Prohibition of the Development, Production, Stockpiling and Use of Chemical Weapons and on their Destruction (adopted 3 September 1992, entered into force 29 April 1977) 1975 UNTS, 33757.

2 US Department of Defense, Press Release, 'US Completes Chemical Weapons Stockpile Destruction Operations' (7 July 2023) <https://www.defense.gov/News/Releases/Release/Article/3451920/us-completes-chemical-weapons-stockpile-destruction-operations/> (accessed 15 April 2024).

3 Art VIII CWC (n 2).

4 See the Annex on Implementation and Verification to the CWC (n 2).

 | DOI:10.1163/9789004739192_009

pecially the right to life. In the past, the European Court of Human Rights (ECtHR) has already rendered three judgments relevant for arms control-related issues: *Finogenov vs. Russia*,[5] *Carter vs. Russia*,[6] and *Navalnyy vs. Russia*.[7] While both in *Finogenov vs. Russia* and *Navalnyy vs. Russia* the Court dealt with the (mis-)use of chemical agents by actors attributable to a state – one time as a perceived "counter-terrorism effort" and one time as an attempted targeted assassination – in *Carter vs. Russia* the Court addressed the use of a *radioactive* substance by state agents for a targeted assassination. Even though *Carter vs. Russia* does not deal with the use of a chemical agent, the Court's findings – especially concerning the question of the extraterritorial applicability of the ECHR – might have relevance for future scenarios in which chemical weapons, for example, are used for targeted assassinations.

The following text aims to ascertain to what extent the ECtHR could play a complementary role by overtaking functions that the CWC is unable to perform. This contribution will focus on three areas. First, the ECHR provides an almost "unlimited" material scope of application in case of attacks with chemical agents by State agents or other individuals attributable to a State. Unlike the CWC, where discussions on the Convention's material scope of application remain, the ECHR would apply to *all* chemical agents if certain human rights are implicated. Second, while discussions on the applicability of the CWC to targeted assassinations remain, the ECtHR has shown a clear commitment to hold States responsible for targeted assassinations including assassinations in an extraterritorial context. In *Carter vs. Russia*, for example, the ECtHR applied a conceivably broad notion of jurisdiction within the meaning of Article 1 ECHR. And third, the ECtHR seems to have changed its very own approach towards arms control and human rights in more general terms. While, initially, in *Finogenov vs. Russia*, the Court was reluctant to deal with issues related to arms control, the Court actively engaged with the CWC explicitly in *Navalnyy vs. Russia*.

The text then concludes with an analysis of these observations showing that the ECHR and the ECtHR, respectively, could indeed assume complementary roles when it comes to the use of chemical weapons. The numerous substantive hurdles, such as the still contested scope of application of the

5 ECtHR, *Finogenov and Others v Russia* (Application Nos. 18299/03 and 27311/03, Final Judgment of 4 June 2012).

6 ECtHR, *Carter v Russia* (Application No. 20914/07, Final Judgment of 28 February 2022).

7 ECtHR, *Navalnyy v Russia* (No. 3) (Application No. 36418/20, Final Judgment of 6 September 2023).

CWC, could be overcome and individuals, finally, would have the possibility to seek redress in case chemical agents were used against them.

2 Procedural and Substantive Hurdles When Seeking Redress in Case of Chemical Attacks

The CWC does not entail an enforcement mechanism for individuals in case of chemical weapons use. Furthermore, the scope of application of the CWC is still not entirely clear and has been contested by (some) States Parties throughout the years. These two aspects will be elucidated in more detail in the following section to better understand how and to what extent the ECHR and the ECtHR respectively could assume a complementary function concerning the CWC.

2.1 *The Lack of Enforcement Mechanisms for Individuals in the CWC*

The CWC faces significant challenges in terms of enforcement, especially when it comes to enforcement mechanisms for individuals. The CWC allows States Parties to bring questions related to the interpretation or implementation of the Convention in front of the International Court of Justice (ICJ) pursuant to Article XIV para 2 CWC, but no such proceedings have hitherto been instituted.[8] Furthermore, such proceedings would only apply between States but individuals themselves would not have the possibility to claim, for example, reparations.[9] In addition and in light of recent chemical weapons attacks, CWC States Parties have decided to establish an International Support Network for victims of chemical weapons as well as a voluntary trust fund for this purpose in 2011.[10] However, the ISN does not guarantee that individual cases will be heard under all circumstances and the procedure in front of the ISN can most certainly not be compared to official legal proceedings in terms

8 Article XIV para 2 CWC. For more details see Martina Buscemi, 'Ensuring Compliance with International Obligations Applicable to CBRN Weapons: Supervisory Mechanisms, Sanctions, and Inter-State Litigation' in Andrea de Guttri et al. (eds), *International Law and Chemical, Biological, Radio-Nuclear (CBRN) Events* (Brill – Nijhoff 2022) 456–480.

9 For more details see Jonathan Herbach, 'Settlement of Disputes' in Walter Krutzsch, Eric Myjer and Ralf Trapp (eds) *The Chemical Weapons Convention: A Commentary* (OUP 2014) 387–396 (387).

10 OPCW, Conference of the States Parties, Decision: Establishment of the International Support Network for Victims of Chemical Weapons and the Establishment of a Voluntary Trust Fund for this Purpose (2 December 2011) C-16/DEC.13 <https://www.opcw.org/sites/default/files/documents/CSP/C-16/en/c16dec13_e_.pdf> (accessed 15 April 2024).

of access to records or inspection of files.[11] In contrast, Proceedings before the ICJ would take place between CWC States Parties, and the interests of individuals could only be considered indirectly. It is thus imperative to investigate which avenue individuals could take instead.

2.2 *The Contested Scope of Application of the CWC*

In addition to the fact that the CWC does not entail enforcement mechanisms for individuals, the exact scope of application of the Convention is, alas, still disputed. Questions relating to the scope of application of the CWC mainly revolve around two questions: the specific context in which it applies as well as the question of whether the use of *all* chemical weapons is prohibited and if answered in the affirmative, if such prohibitions are absolute. State authorities may lawfully use force either during armed conflict[12] or during peacetime. When used in armed conflict, weapons may be deployed against enemy combatants provided that such use is in line with applicable international (and

11 Article XIV para. 2 CWC. For more details see Martina Buscemi, 'Ensuring Compliance with International Obligations Applicable to CBRN Weapons: Supervisory Mechanisms, Sanctions, and Inter-State Litigation' in Andrea de Guttri et al. (eds) *International Law and Chemical, Biological, Radio-Nuclear* (CBRN) Events (Brill – Nijhoff 2022) 456–480.

12 There are two types of armed conflict in international law. International armed conflict (IAC) refers to an armed conflict between two or more states, whereas non-international armed conflict refers to an armed conflict taking place between State armed forces and a (or more) non-state armed group(s) or to several non-state armed groups fighting against each other. For a definition of IAC see Common Article 2 to the Geneva Conventions of 1949 as well as Article 1 (4) Additional Protocol I to the Geneva Conventions. For NIAC see Article 1 Additional Protocol II to the Geneva Conventions. Geneva Convention (I) for the Amelioration of the Condition of the Wounded and Sick in Armed Forces in the Field (adopted [illegible] August 1949 [illegible] Geneva Convention for the amelioration of the condition of the wounded, sick and shipwrecked members of the armed forces at sea (adopted 12 August 1949 entered into force 21 October 1950) 75 UNTS No. 971; Geneva Convention (III) relative to the Treatment of Prisoners of War. Geneva, 12 August 1949, UNTS Vo. 75 I No. 972; Geneva Convention (IV) relative to the Protection of Civilian Persons in Time of War (adopted 12 August 1949 entered into force 21 October 1950) 75 UNTS No. 973; Protocol additional to the Geneva Conventions of 12 August 1949, and relating to the protection of victims of international armed conflicts (Protocol I) (adopted 8 June 1977 entered into force 7 December 1978) 1125 UNTS No. 17512. Protocol Additional to the Geneva Conventions of 12 August 1949 and relating to the protection of victims of non-international armed conflicts (Protocol II) (adopted 8 June 1977 entered into force 7 December 1978) 1125 UNTS No. 17513. For a full list of all IHL treaties see ICRC, International Humanitarian Law Database, <https://ihl-databases.icrc.org/en/ihl-treaties> (accessed 15 April 2024). For more on conflict classification see Emily Crawford and Alison Pert, International Humanitarian Law (2nd edition, CUP 2020) 54–95.

domestic) law. When used in peacetime, State authorities can employ weapons as a measure of law enforcement. In common parlance, law enforcement refers to measures that are aimed at "enforcing laws, maintaining public order, and managing public safety."[13] A typical measure of law enforcement is riot control. For example, police forces frequently use pepper spray, tear gas, or water cannon to disperse rioting crowds. Sometimes such weapons are also used to apprehend individuals. It is important to note that measures of law enforcement may also be taken on the territory of a country that is engaged in armed conflict. In the case of occupation, for example, the occupying power has the legal obligation to maintain security and public order and may thus even resort to force against individuals or groups of people. The question of whether the CWC applies both in armed conflict and in peacetime during law enforcement is challenging as the Convention employs difficult and sometimes contradictory terminology.

2.2.1 The Contested Material Scope of Application of the CWC: Are All Chemical Agents Prohibited at All Times?

Similar discussions have revolved around the CWC. The CWC prohibits *inter alia* the use of chemical weapons under *any* circumstances but simultaneously stipulates that chemical weapons are "[t]oxic chemicals and their precursors, except where intended for purposes not prohibited under this Convention, as long as the types and quantities are consistent with such purposes."[14] Article II para. 9 lit d then proceeds by stating that "law enforcement including domestic riot control" constitutes a purpose, which is not prohibited under the Convention. But substantial problems remain, especially because of the qualifier in Article I CWC according to which the use of CW for purposes not covered by the Convention is permitted – as long as the types and quantities of such weapons are compatible with such purposes. Most authors take the view that even RCAS, for example, can be used in law enforcement provided that the types and quantities of the RCAS dispersed are in line with such purposes. There have been ample of debates as to whether all chemical agents or only those explicitly mentioned in the Convention's Annex are prohibited under the CWC. The broad terminology of the CWC seems to be sufficiently clear according to which *all* chemical agents are prohibited except for those which do not fall under one of the exceptions specifically enumerated in the Convention itself. And yet, a number of CWC

13 US Bureau of Justice Statistics <https://bjs.ojp.gov/topics/law-enforcement> (accessed 15 April 2024).

14 Article II(1)(a) CWC.

States Parties, including Russia, have argued that chemicals, which are not listed in the Annex, can never be prohibited, especially if used in a law enforcement context (which Russia claimed to be the case in the Moscow theatre siege).[15] The position taken by Russia clearly contradicts the wording of the CWC, which stipulates that even for domestic riot control, only such chemicals can be used which are employed "in types and quantities" that are compatible with such purposes. Most authors in the literature contend that this terminology places particular limits on the question of what kind of chemical agents can actually be used. According to them, RCAS would be permitted (provided that certain criteria are fulfilled) but incapacitants, that is to say, chemical agents which have a significantly stronger impact on human health by *inter alia* affecting the central nervous system, would not be allowed. In 2018, the OPCW Scientific Advisory Board emphasized that the continued use of certain chemical agents (including incapacitants) in law enforcement contexts "resulted in permanent harm and death due to an irreversible action on life processes". In 2021, a statement of CWC States Parties when addressing the question of whether incapacitants, such as a derivative of fentanyl could be used in domestic riot control clarified that "such permitted use does not include the 'aerosolised use' of CNS chemicals, such as fentanyl"[16]. To conclude, the scope of application of the CWC is still not entirely clear as different views among CWC States Parties remain. Despite the Convention's use of a qualifier "in types and quantities" some States, such as Russia, still argue that the use of incapacitants in law enforcement contexts does not contradict the Convention. Such diverging views jeopardize the Convention's efficacy and ultimately leads to the erosion of the Convention's normative power.

2.2.2 The Contested Material Scope of Application of the CWC: The Special Case of Targeted Assassinations

Targeted assassinations, that is to say, the intentional use of force against individuals, especially dissidents and other political opponents, either on a country's own territory or abroad, cannot qualify as measure of law enforcement proper. Targeted assassinations can, in contrast to the use of force in law

15 The Guardian, 'Russia names gas used to end siege', <https://www.theguardian.com/world/2002/oct/30/russia> (accessed 29 February 2024).

16 Congressional Research Service, 'Illicit Fentanyl and Weapons of Mass Destruction: International Controls and Policy Options' (28 March 2022) <https://crsreports.congress.gov/product/pdf/IN/IN11902> (accessed 29 February 2024). See also CWC, Conference of the States Parties, Decision: Understanding Regarding the Aerosolised Use of Central Nervous-System Acting Chemicals for Law Enforcement Purposes, C-26/DEC.10 (1 December 2021).

enforcement, almost never be justified from a legal perspective. The intentional use of force against an individual outside the ambit of armed conflict would only be permissible if the individual in question constitutes a threat to life or limb of oneself or others.[17] Hitherto most cases of targeted assassinations had little to do with a concrete physical threat a person poses. Rather, targeted assassinations were almost always cold-blood attempts to eliminate regime critics. Especially Russia has a comparative long history of (attempted) targeted assassinations by using chemical agents,[18] including the attempted murder of *Alexey Navalnyy*, who died on 16 February 2024 while in Russian custody.[19] The most important question is whether targeted assassinations are covered by the CWC.[20] Chemical agents play a significantly larger role when it comes to targeted assassinations from an arms control perspective. It is important to note that the CWC is completely silent on targeted assassinations. However, the broad terminology of Article I CWC according to which the use of chemical weapons under *any* circumstances is prohibited, suggests the conclusion that the CWC applies to targeted assassinations. Hitherto, targeted assassinations have not been dealt with by investigative and fact-finding mechanisms respectively such as the Investigation and Identification Team (IIT),[21] the OPCW-UN Joint Investigative Mechanism (JIM)[22] and the OPCW Fact-Finding Mission (FFM).[23] The OPCW itself, however, has played quite a

17 For a comprehensive overview on the right to life see Stuart Casey-Maslen, *The Right to Life: An Interpretative Manual* (CUP 2021) 141–180.

18 Dasha Litvinova, 'Nerve agents, poison and window falls. Over the years, Kremlin foes have been attacked or killed' (Associated Press 25 August 2023) <https://apnews.com/article/prigozhin-navalny-putin-assassination-russia-wagner-plane-crash-5d4f8506b89bfa8848fd88529701db7c> (accessed 15 April 2024).

19 Lucy Papachristou, 'What we know about Alexey Navalny's death in Arctic prison' (Reuters, 19 February 2024) <https://www.reuters.com/world/europe/Alexey-navalnys-death-what-do-we-know-2024-02-18/> (accessed 15 April 2024).

20 See, for example, The New Killer Pathogens: Countering the Coming Bioweapons Threat (Foreign Affairs, 17 April 2018) <https://carnegieendowment.org/2018/04/17/new-killer-pathogens-countering-coming-bioweapons-threat-pub-76009> (accessed 15 April 2024).

21 OPCW, Investigation and Identification Team, <https://www.opcw.org/iit> (accessed 15 April 2024). See also OPCW, Technical Secretariat, Fourth Report by the OPCW Investigation and Identification Team Pursuant to Paragraph 10 of Decision C-SS-4/Dec. 3, "Addressing the Threat from Chemical Weapons Use" Marea (Syrian Arab Republic) – 1 September 2015 (22 February 2024) S/2255/2024.

22 OPCW-UN Joint Investigative Mechanism (JIM), <https://www.opcw.org/media-centre/news/2016/11/opcw-executive-council-adopts-decision-regarding-opcw-united-nations> (accessed 15 April 2024).

23 OPCW, Fact Finding Mission, <https://www.opcw.org/fact-finding-mission> (accessed 15 April 2024). See also OPCW, Note by the Technical Secretariat, Report of the OPCW-

substantial role when it comes to targeted assassinations, for example, in case of the attempted assassination of *Alexey Navalnyy*.[24] Germany requested the Technical Secretariat pursuant to Article VIII subparagraph 38 lit e) CWC to provide technical assistance regarding the poisoning of *Alexey Navalnyy*.[25] It is important to note that Article VIII subparagraph 38 lit e) CWC stipulates that States Parties can request the Technical Secretariat for Assistance with regard to questions relating "to the implementation of this Convention". The wording of this provision within the meaning of Article 31 para 1 Vienna Convention on the Law of Treaties[26] together with the Technical Secretariat's willingness to proceed with said request thus clearly supports the argument that the CWC applies in the broadest possible sense including scenarios of targeted assassinations. However, given the limited possibilities for States Parties to enforce the Convention (with the clear exception of Article XIV para 2 CWC allowing States to institute proceedings before the International Court of Justice, which had limited to no relevance in practice thus far), compliance with the relevant legal obligations largely depends on the willingness of States Parties. As long as some States Parties call into question the applicability of the CWC to targeted assassinations, a broad reading of the various provisions in the CWC is futile.[27] It is therefore paramount to investigate whether the ECHR and the ECtHR respectively could be considered in the alternative to overcome an impasse that has been created by States Parties not endorsing the approach

Fact Finding Mission Regarding an Alleged Use of Toxic Chemicals as a Weapon in Al-Yarmouk, Syrian Arab Republic on 22 October 2017 (22 February 2024) S/2254/2024.

24 See, for example, OPCW Technical Secretariat, Correspondence from Germany to the OPCW Requesting Technical Assistance in the Case of Mr. Alexey Navalny and Associated Documents (3 August 2021) S/1979/2021.

25 OPCW, Note by the Technical Secretariat, Correspondence from Germany to the OPCW Requesting Technical Assistance in the Case of Mr. Alexei Navalny, and Associate Documents (3 August 2021) S/1979/2021. See also OPCW, OPCW Provides Technical Assistance to Germany Regarding Allegations of Chemical Weapons Use Against Alexei Navalny (17 September 2020) <https://www.opcw.org/media-centre/news/2020/09/opcw-provides-technical-assistance-germany-regarding-allegations-chemical> (accessed 15 April 2024).

26 Vienna Convention on the Law of Treaties (adopted 23 May 1969, entered into force 27 January 1980) 1155 UNTS No. 18232.

27 See, for example, the critical remarks by Russia regarding Germany's request for technical assistance to the Technical Secretariat. Correspondence Between OPCW and Permanent Representation of the Russian Federation to the OPCW, from 1/10/2020 to 21/12/2020, in Relation to a Request for a Technical Assistance Visit to the Russian Federation Under Subpar. 38(e), Article VIII of the CWC (21 December 2020) <https://www.opcw.org/sites/default/files/documents/2020/12/Correspondence%20ODG_RF%20re%20TAV.pdf> (accessed 15 April 2024).

according to which the CWC applies to targeted assassinations. It is exactly these discrepancies that make it all the more important to look at other institutions and assess whether they could better and most importantly sufficiently address *inter alia* targeted assassinations, especially from a victim's perspective.

3 The Potential Role of the ECtHR for Seeking Redress in Case of Chemical Attacks

The ECtHR observes compliance with and implementation of the European Convention of Human Rights[28] (ECHR) as well as related Protocols.[29] Hitherto, the Court has mostly dealt with chemical weapons[30] in the form of so-called less-lethal weapons in law enforcement scenarios, such as the use of tear gas and pepper spray for the dispersal of violent demonstrations[31] but

28 Convention for the Protection of Human Rights and Fundamental Freedoms (adopted 4 November 1950, entered into force 3 September 1953) ETS No. 005.

29 Protocol to the Convention for the Protection of Human Rights and Fundamental Freedoms (20 March 1952, entered into force 18 May 1954) ETS No. 009; Protocol No. 4 to the Convention for the Protection of Human Rights and Fundamental Freedoms, securing certain rights and freedoms other than those already included in the Convention and in the first Protocol thereto (adopted 16 September 1963, entered into force 2 May 1968) ETS No. 046; Protocol No. 6 to the Convention for the Protection of Human Rights and Fundamental Freedoms concerning the abolition of the death penalty (adopted 18 April 1983, entered into force 1 March 1985) ETS No. 114; Protocol No. 7 to the Convention for the Protection of Human Rights and Fundamental Freedoms (adopted 22 November 1984, entered into force 1 November 1988) ETS No. 117; Protocol No. 12 to the Convention for the Protection of Human Rights and Fundamental Freedoms (adopted 4 November 2000, entered into force 1 April 2005) ETS No. 117; Protocol No. 13 to the Convention for the Protection of Human Rights and Fundamental Freedoms, concerning the abolition of the death penalty in all circumstances (adopted 3 May 2002, entered into force 1 July 2023) ETS No. 187; Protocol No. 16 to the Convention for the Protection of Human Rights and Fundamental Freedoms (adopted 2 October 2013, entered into force 1 August 2018) CETS No. 214.

30 The term biochemical weapon is mostly used to describe weapons which fulfill the criteria of biological as well as chemical weapons. Often of biological origin, such agents are synthesized and transformed into chemical agents to be used, inter alia, by police forces and other law enforcement authorities. For more details see Elisabeth Hoffberger-Pippan, *Less-Lethal Weapons under International Law* (n 23) 45–55. For the purpose of simplification these weapons will be termed "chemical weapons" throughout the text.

31 See, for example, ECtHR, *Navalnyy v Russia* (n 11).

also in custodial settings.[32] Only in a limited number of cases, the Court has addressed issues related to chemical attacks outside a *clear* law-enforcement context. In *Finogenov vs. Russia*,[33] Russian authorities explicitly referred to an anti-terror operation. Critics of the judgment argued, that the incident had taken place in the context of an ongoing non-international armed conflict (NIAC) between Russia on the one hand and Chechen rebel forces, on the other, and that the ECtHR failed to address this issue adequately when dealing with the merits of the case.[34] In *Navalnyy vs. Russia*,[35] the Court dealt with the use of a chemical agent in the context of an attempted targeted assassination in the territory of Russia. And even though the Court dealt with a radioactive and not a chemical agent in *Carter vs. Russia*[36], the case deserves closer attention because of the far-ranging approach the Court has taken as regards the extraterritorial applicability of the ECtHR, which certainly will have repercussions for any future assassination attempts, including those involving chemical agents. Before undertaking a closer examination of these three cases, a few preliminary remarks on the ECtHR and the question of jurisdiction seem imperative to assess the Court's potential role in the case of chemical weapons attacks – whether in the territory of States Parties to the ECHR or in an extraterritorial context.

3.1 *The Jurisdiction of the ECtHR: Preliminary Remarks*

Initiating a case before the ECtHR requires the fulfillment of certain criteria. At the outset, it is important to note that either States themselves according to Article 33 ECHR or individuals according to Article 34 ECHR can submit complaints arguing that a States Party to the ECHR has violated the Convention or either of the Protocols it is bound to. Individual cases by far outnumber interstate complaints. Since the establishment of the European Commission of Human Rights, which was succeeded by the ECtHR, 37 inter-state cases have been brought before the Court.[37] By contrast, more than 75,000 individual

32 See, for example, ECtHR, El-Asmar v Denmark (Application no. 27753/19, Final Judgment, 3 January 2024).

33 ECtHR, *Finogenov and Others v Russia* (n 5).

34 Cf. Daragh Murray, *Practitioners' Guide to Human Rights Law in Armed Conflict* (OUP 2016) 98. See also Stuart Wallace, *The Application of the European Convention on Human Rights to Military Operations* (CUP 2019) 83–86.

35 ECtHR, *Navalnyy v Russia* (n 7).

36 ECtHR, *Carter v Russia* (n 6).

37 See ECtHR, 'Inter-state applications', <https://www.echr.coe.int/inter-state-applications> (accessed 5 February 2024). It is important to note that each case is being counted

cases have been submitted to the Court.[38] Despite the significant disparity between inter-state and individual complaints, inter-state applications seem to have gained more prominence in the last years.[39] Hitherto, the ECtHR has only dealt with individual complaints in the context of chemical weapons use and individual complaints will likely remain the primary avenue to seek redress in case individuals have been attacked with chemical weapons, either within a targeted assassination or in armed conflict.[40]

The Court can only deal with individual complaints after the exhaustion of local remedies "according to the generally recognised rules of international law" and "within a period of four months from the date on which the final decision was taken".[41] The obligation to exhaust local remedies is reflective of customary international law, as, was inter alia confirmed by the ICJ in the *Interhandel Case*.[42] Moreover, numerous human rights treaties have established similar criteria, such as in Article 41 para 1 lit c) International Covenant of Civil and Political Rights (ICCPR)[43] as well as Article 2 and 5 para 2 lit b) of the Optional Protocol to the ICCPR,[44] Article 46 of the American Convention

---

separately (*Georgia vs. Russia I* counts as one case; *Georgia vs. Russia II* counts as a second case). The list includes both pending and completed inter-state applications.

38 For more details see Geir Ulfstein and Isabella Risini, 'Inter-State Applications under the European Convention on Human Rights: Strengths and Challenges', *EJIL Talk!* (24 January 2020), <https://www.ejiltalk.org/inter-state-applications-under-the-european-convention-on-human-rights-strengths-and-challenges/> (accessed 5 February 2024).

39 Ibid.

40 For the sake of completeness, it should be mentioned at this point that at least theoretically, States Parties to the ECHR could also issue inter-state complaints in the case of chemical weapons use by another States Party. This, in turn, raises the question of whether States aiming to lodge a complaint with the Court, would be obliged to invoke the various mechanisms established by the CWC first because (in case the impugned State allegedly violated the CWC at the same time), arguably, the CWC constitutes a self-contained regime. A thorough analysis would expand the scope of this contribution (apart from the fact that inter-state complaints are not the focus of this text). For further reading on the concept of self-contained regimes in international law, see, however, Eckart Klein, 'Self-contained regime' in *Max Planck Encyclopedia of Public International Law* <https://opil.ouplaw.com/display/10.1093/law:epil/9780199231690/law-9780199231690-e1467?prd=EPIL> (accessed 5 February 2024).

41 Article 35 ECHR.

42 ICJ, *Interhandel Case* (*Switzerland v United States of America*), Preliminary Objections, Judgment of 21 March 1959, ICJ Reports 1959, 29.

43 International Covenant on Civil and Political Rights (adopted 16 December 1966, entered into force 23 March 1976) 999 UNTS No. 14668.

44 Optional Protocol to the International Covenant on Civil and Political Rights (adopted 16 December 1966, entered into force 23 March 1976) 999 UNTS No. 14668.

of Human Rights[45] and Articles 50 and 55 para 6 of the African Charter on Human and Peoples' Rights.[46] Thus, individuals seeking redress for human rights violations because of a chemical weapons attack have to – first and foremost – refer to domestic remedies. However, the chances of success or of fair proceedings might be significantly hampered in case State agents (or other individuals attributable to the State) use chemical weapons against individuals. It is important to note that "[a]pplicants are only obliged to exhaust domestic remedies which are available in theory and in practice at the relevant time and which they can directly institute themselves – that is to say, remedies that are accessible, capable of providing redress in respect of their complaints and offering reasonable prospects of success".[47]

3.2 *Judgments by the ECtHR with Relevance from an Arms Control Perspective: Facts of the Cases*

At least three judgments rendered by the Court have a nexus to arms control-related issues. First, in *Finogenov vs. Russia*,[48] the Court for the first time dealt with the use of an incapacitating chemical agent, presumably a derivative of fentanyl. The agent was employed by Russian armed forces in a scenario they described as "anti-terror operation". Second, in *Carter vs. Russia*,[49] the Court dealt with the targeted assassination of Russian dissident *Alexander Litvinienko* when two former KGB agents used a radioactive substance to kill *Litvinienko* in a London hotel bar. Even though the substance was not a chemical but a radioactive agent,[50] the conclusions drawn from the Court's judgment – especially its approach towards the ECHR's extraterritorial applicability – might have a bearing on the potential use of chemical weapons in the future. Last but not least, in *Navalnyy vs. Russia*,[51] the ECtHR dealt with the at-

45 American Convention of Human Rights (adopted 22 November 1969) <https://www.cidh.oas.org/basicos/english/basic3.american%20convention.htm> (accessed 5 February 2024).

46 African Charter on Human and Peoples' Rights (1981) <https://au.int/sites/default/files/treaties/36390-treaty 0011_ african_charter_on_human_and_peoples_rights_e.pdf> (accessed 5 February 2024).

47 ECtHR, 'Practical Guide on Admissibility Criteria' (31 August 2023) <https://www.echr.coe.int/documents/d/echr/Admissibility_guide_ENG> (accessed 5 February 2024). See also ECtHR, *Sejdovic v Italy* (Application No. 56581/00, Grand Chamber Judgment of 1 March 2006) para. 46; ECtHR, *Paksas v Lithuania* (Application No. 34932/04, Grand Chamber Judgment of 6 January 2011) para. 75.

48 ECtHR, *Finogenov and Others v Russia* (n 5).

49 ECtHR, *Carter v Russia* (n 10).

50 Ibid., paras. 14–18.

51 ECtHR, *Navalnyy v Russia* (n 11).

tempted assassination of Russian dissident and opposition leader *Alexey Navalnyy*. While the Court has abstained from explicitly referring to an arms control treaty so far, it fully endorsed the CWC in *Navalnyy vs. Russia*. The following chapter will thus delve deeper into these judgments and explain how the ECtHR has assumed a complementary role in arms control related issues.

3.2.1 Finogenov vs. Russia

On 23 October 2002, a group of approximately 40 people belonging to the Chechen separatist movement stormed Moscow's "Dubrovka" theatre. Equipped with machine guns, they stormed the building and took more than 900 people hostage. The ordeal lasted for three days. The terrorists booby-trapped the building and positioned 18 suicide bombers close to the hostages.[52] Following this event, a rescue operation ensued which faced a number of challenges. On 26 October 2002, Russian security forces pumped a derivative of fentanyl into the theatre's ventilation system. Russian special security forces stormed the building, shooting most of the suicide bombers while unconscious, several other suicide bombers died during gunfire which ensued after they had tried to resist.[53] Because of that operation, more than 730 hostages could be rescued. However, it is also important to note that because of the gas, 129 hostages died. A total of 102 hostages died right on the spot, 3 of which were killed during gunfire, 21 hostages died during evacuation and transportation, whereas six people died in the hospital. Russian forces were heavily criticized for their behavior, especially for not having provided sufficient care for those affected by the gas.[54] Applicants described the scene as chaotic.[55] Some victims were transported in public busses to the hospital,[56] whereas others suffocated from choking without being provided sufficient medical care.[57] One of the victims was the brother of the main applicant and his fiancée. *Finogenov inter alia* complained that Russian authorities have not taken sufficient measures to investigate his brother's death and the death of his fiancée.[58] The Court concluded that Russia had violated Article 2 ECHR – not because it has decided to use the gas after all – but because it has not

52 ECtHR, *Finogenov and Others v Russia* (n 5) para. 8.
53 Ibid., para. 22.
54 Ibid., para. 24.
55 Ibid., para. 25.
56 Ibid., para. 176.
57 Ibid., para. 178.
58 Ibid., para. 123.

provided sufficient medical care to the victims of the attack including *Finogenov*'s brother and his brother's fiancée.[59]

3.2.2 Carter vs. Russia

In *Carter vs. Russia* the ECtHR dealt with the poisoning of Russian dissident *Alexander Litvnienko*. His wife instituted proceedings before the ECtHR alleging that Russian forces had assassinated her husband by using a nuclear agent.[60] *Litvinienko* has formerly worked as KGB agent but was, *inter alia*, accused of having abused official authority. In 2001, he and his wife were granted asylum in the UK. They changed their names to *Edwin Redwald Carter* and *Maria Anna Carter* respectively. Both were granted citizenship on 13 October 2006.[61] While in the UK, *Litvinienko* evidently undertook consulting activities for British intelligence services and also private security work which involved preparing "due diligence" reports for companies seeking to find out information about Russian business contacts.[62] On November 2006, *Litvinienko* met two former KGB agents, *Andrey Lugovoy* and *Dmitry Kovtun*. They met in the bar of the hotel where both *Lugovoy* and *Kovtun* were staying.[63] According to official records, *Litvinienko* drank a cup of green tea which was already at the table when he entered the hotel. After approximately 20 minutes, the meeting ended. Only a couple of days later *Litvinienko* was admitted to the hospital as he had started to develop severe symptoms of poisoning, such as vomiting and diarrhea. While first being suspected of suffering from a rather severe form of gastroenteritis, the hospital confirmed that *Litvinienko* had been poisoned with plutonium on 23 November 2006. Only a couple of weeks later *Litvinienko* died. The Court arrived at the conclusion that both *Andrey Lugovoy* and *Dmitry Kovtun* had poisoned and thus assassinated *Litvinienko*. Acting as agents of the Russian State, the Court held Russia liable for having violated, *inter alia*, Article 2 ECHR.[64]

---

59 For more on the *Finogenov* case see Stuart Wallace, *The Application of the European Convention of Human Rights to Military Operations* (CUP 2019) 35–40.

60 ECtHR, *Carter v Russia* (n 10).

61 Ibid., paras. 5–10.

62 Ibid., paras. 11–12.

63 Ibid.

64 Ibid., paras. 170–172.

3.2.3 Navalnyy vs. Russia

On 20 August 2020, Alexey Navalny, founder of the Anti-Corruption Foundation (an NGO), flew from Tomsk to Moscow.[65] In the plane he suddenly suffered severe symptoms of poisoning and even fell unconscious. Only two days later, Navalny was flown to Germany to a medical hospital where tests were made in order to find out the cause of his physical condition. He fell into a medically induced coma and after he could be woken up again, he had to go through months of rehabilitation.[66] In November 2020, the German labs published their results according to which "the applicant's samples had revealed unequivocal proof of the presence of a chemical nerve agent from the Novichok group of substances prohibited under the Chemical Weapons Convention". Proceedings were initiated against Russia for *inter alia* violating the right to life.[67] It is important to note that the right to life by implication obliges States Parties to conduct an effective investigation "in case an individual has sustained life-threatening injuries".[68] This obligation also applies in case the perpetrators were not state agents. The Court applies a number of parameters in order to assess whether a State has undertaken an effective investigation, such as "the adequacy of the investigative measures, the promptness and reasonable expedition of the investigation, the involvement of the victim or next of kin and the independence of the investigation. They are criteria which, taken jointly, enable the degree of effectiveness of the investigation to be assessed"[69]. As a response to the attack against *Navalnyy*, Russia had conducted a so-called pre-investigation, which, according to the Russian legal system, does not lead to the punishment of those responsible for the attack. Russia claimed to have undertaken a thorough review by questioning witnesses and by conducting several forensic tests. However, no documentation of these steps was provided to the Court. And even after the OPCW – based on a request by Germany for technical assistance – has warned that a chemical nerve agent had been used, Russia abstained from conducting a thorough investigation in this regard claiming that Germany did not cooperate adequately.[70] Again, no documentation could be provided to the Court substantiating Russia's claims. In light of these circumstances the Court arrived at the conclusion

65 ECtHR, *Nalvanyy vs. Russia* (No. 3) (Application No. 36418/20), Final Judgment of 6 September 2023, para. 5.

66 Ibid., para. 9.

67 Ibid., para. 129.

68 Ibid., para. 130.

69 Ibid., para. 132.

70 Ibid., paras 150–152.

that "[t]he inquiry conducted by the domestic authorities fell short of being public and made no allowance for the victim's right to participate in the proceedings. Furthermore, the inquiry failed to explore the allegations of a possible political motive for the attempted murder, as well as possible involvement or collusion by State agents, and did not follow up on the reported use of a substance identified as a chemical weapon prohibited by international and domestic law. As such, it was not capable of leading to the establishment of the relevant facts and the identification and, if appropriate, punishment of those responsible and therefore could not be considered adequate".[71] Furthermore, as already indicated, it was difficult to determine whether the perpetrators of the attack were state agents or private actors. In both cases, Russia was under an obligation to undertake a thorough investigation. The Court observed that the development as well as the use of the chemical nerve agent used required substantial knowledge, preparation and organization. Thus, according to the Court, the attack "could hardly be achieved by individuals unconnected to State agencies".[72] Reports by *Bellingcat* and *The Insider* corroborated this assumption while Russia failed to explore sufficiently the probable involvement of State agents.[73]

3.3 *The Prohibition of Chemical Weapons and the ECtHR*

The following section sets out to clarify in which way and to what extent the ECtHR complements existing arms control treaties in the field of chemical weapons, most notably the CWC. In addition to the fact that the CWC does not offer individuals the possibility to seek redress directly for chemical attacks, at least three additional aspects deserve greater attention. First, while no consensus as regards the material scope of application of the CWC has been achieved thus far, the situation is far less complex in the case of proceedings before the ECtHR. Given the broad and human rights-centric terminology of the ECHR, *all* chemical weapons could eventually be scrutinized by the ECtHR as long as the use of such weapons potentially violates human rights that are enshrined in the ECHR, such as the right to life. Second, while it is not entirely clear whether the CWC applies in case of targeted assassinations, the ECtHR seems to be an alternative avenue to seek redress in case chemical weapons are used for (attempted) targeted assassinations.[74] The ECtHR has made it

71 Ibid., para. 160.

72 Ibid., para. 156.

73 Ibid., paras. 158–158.

74 ECtHR, *Nalvanyy v Russia* (No. 3) (Application No. 36418/20, Final Judgment of 6 September 2023) paras. 159–161.

unmistakably clear that the ECHR applies in such scenarios including in an extraterritorial context.[75] The third refers to the question of whether the ECtHR is actively willing to engage with arms control treaties and to refer to these treaties in contentious proceedings. While the ECtHR was reluctant to do so in *Finogenov vs. Russia*,[76] it took a more assertive approach in *Navalnyy vs. Russia* highlighting its willingness to engage with arms control treaties explicitly thereby heralding a new era in the Court's jurisprudence.[77]

3.3.1 The "Unlimited" Material Scope of Application of the ECHR: Focusing on the Procedural Limb of Article 2 ECHR and Shifting the Burden of Proof

Discussions on the exact material scope of application of the CWC abound. One of the most pertinent issues refers to the question of whether aerosolized incapacitating agents affecting the human's central nervous system are covered by the CWC in cases of law enforcement.[78] While the vast majority of CWC States Parties have a broad understanding of the CWC's material scope of application,[79] it is particularly Russia, Iran, Syria, and China that take a more conservative (and often legally unconvincing approach).[80] By contrast,

75 ECtHR, *Carter v Russia* (n 10) para. 146.

76 Cf. Noelle Quénivet, 'The Moscow Hostage Crisis in the Light of the Armed Conflict in Chechnya' (2013) 4 *Yearbook of International Humanitarian Law* 348–372.

77 ECtHR, *Nalvanyy v Russia* (No. 3) (Application No. 36418/20, Final Judgment of 6 September 2023) paras. 20 – 21 and paras. 29 –30.

78 CWC, CSP-24 Report, Conclusion of the general debate and the Schedule amendment decision(s), Number 4 – Thursday 28th November 2019, <https://www.cbw-events.org.uk/CSP-24-04.pdf> (accessed 15 April 2024).

79 Cf. United States of America, Statement by Mr. Thomas Dinanno, Senior Bureau Official and Deputy Assistant Secretary for Defence Policy, Emerging Threats, and Outreach at the Twenty-Fourth Session of the Conference of the States Parties (25 November 2019) C-24/NAT.4. See also the Report of the Scientific Advisory Board on the dangers of nerve agents more generally. Report of the Scientific Advisory Board on Developments in Science and Technology for the Fourth Special Session of the Conference of the States Parties to Review the Operation of the Chemical Weapons Convention (30 April 2018) RC-4/DG.1 paras. 300 – 302. In 2021, finally, the CSP took the decision that the aerosolized use of nerve agents in law enforcement is incompatible with the CWC. See CSP, Decision Regarding the Aerosolized Use of Central Nervous System-Acting Chemicals for Law Enforcement Purposes (1 December 2021) C-26/DEC.10. On the voting procedure regarding the CSP more generally see Article VIII para. 18 CWC.

80 Islamic Republic of Iran, Joint Statement on behalf of 4 Delegations (People's Republic of China, the Islamic Republic of Iran, Russian Federation and the Syrian Arab Republic) delivered by the Delegation of the Islamic Republic of Iran at the 26th Session of the Conference of States Parties of the OPCW under the Subitem 26.1 "Any Other Business" on the Draft Decision entitled "Understanding Regarding the Aerosolized Use of Central

the ECtHR would most certainly be willing to adjudicate matters involving the use of *any* kind of chemical agent as long as specific human rights, such as the right to life, are implicated. This involves a broad range of potential agents including RCAs, incapacitants, and – obviously – chemical agents that are considered lethal (those which render death inevitable).[81] The ECtHR has already rendered judgments that involved the use of RCAs and incapacitants.[82] All these cases, however, mainly involved scenarios of law enforcement. The Court has not (yet) dealt with chemical attacks in the context of armed conflict.[83] This is deplorable, especially in light of recent chemical attacks. It is important to bear in mind that in the case of chemical attacks, identifying the perpetrator(s) might be challenging, if possible at all. *Navalnyy vs. Russia* is a case in point. The perpetrators of the attack could not be identified, nor could it be established whether they were acting as non-state actors, private individuals or state agents. However, given the fact that *Navalnyy* was under intensive surveillance, the poisoning by a private person would – according to the Court – not go unnoticed. Rather, the probability that state agents had poisoned *Navalnyy* was high from the very beginning obliging Russia to investigate their possible involvement.[84] The Court reiterated that "[t]he development and use of such chemicals required time, skill and a level of organisation that could hardly be achieved by individuals unconnected to State agencies. Concealing any such activities over a substantial period of time would also appear unlikely".[85] Thus, even though the exact perpetrators could not be identified, the Court held Russia accountable, inter alia, for not having undertaken a thorough investigation into their identity. Thus, in the case of chemical attacks where the identity of the perpetrators is unknown, the ECHR might nevertheless come into play in case the relevant State in question does not undertake sufficient measures to investigate incidents of chemical weapons use. In such cases, the Court seems to focus on the "procedural limb" of Article 2 ECHR.[86] *Carter vs. Russia* was slightly different. While

---

Nervous System-Acting Chemicals for Law Enforcement Purposes (29 November 2021) C-26/NAT.68.

81 Elisabeth Hoffberger-Pippan, *Less-Lethal Weapons under International Law* (n 23) 89–160.

82 See, for example, *Tali v Estonia* (Application No. 66393/10, 13 February 2014); *Abdullah Yaşa and Others v Turkey* (Application No. 44827/08, 16 October 2013); *Borbála Kiss v Hungary* (Application No. 59214/11, 26 June 2012).

83 He would have had the chance in *Finogenov v Russia* (n 9), though.

84 ECtHR, *Nalvanyy v Russia* (n 11) para. 156.

85 Ibid.

86 Ibid., para. 160.

the identity of the perpetrators was clear,[87] the Court still had to ascertain whether they had been acting in their private capacity or as state agents. Similar to its approach in *Navalnyy vs. Russia*, the Court held that "[w]hile there existed a theoretical possibility that the assassination of Mr Litvinenko might have been a 'rogue operation' not involving State responsibility, the information needed to corroborate this theory lies wholly, or in large part, within the exclusive knowledge of the Russian authorities, which moreover asserted exclusive jurisdiction over Mr Lugovoy and Mr Kovtun by invoking the constitutional protection against extradition. In these circumstances, the burden of proof was shifted onto the authorities of the respondent State, which were expected to carry out a meticulous investigation into that possibility, identify those involved in the operation and determine whether or not Mr Lugovoy's and Mr Kovtun's conduct was directed or controlled by any State entity or official, which is a factor indicative of State responsibility".[88] The Court went on to hold that "[t]he Government, however, have not made any serious attempt either to elucidate the facts or to counter the findings arrived at by the United Kingdom authorities. In fact, they have failed to engage with any fact-finding efforts, whether those conducted in the United Kingdom or those undertaken by the Court".[89] Thus, in cases where the identify of the perpetrators has been established but where it is necessary to ascertain whether they are to be considered "state agents" Article 2 ECHR obliges States Parties to undertake adequate measures to investigate the incident and to help identify the nature of the perpetrators. It was especially Russia's refusal to cooperate, which ultimately incentivized the Court to shift the burden of proof to the Russian authorities. The Court then arrived at the conclusion that the two KGB agents were attributable to Russia and that by poisoning *Litvinienko*, had violated the right to life according to Article 2 of the ECHR.[90] To conclude, the Court – in contrast to the CWC – could address and scrutinize *all* chemical agents as long as human rights are implicated. The trickier question relates to the identification of the perpetrators and their attributability to a State Party. In both *Navalnyy vs. Russia* and *Carter vs. Russia,* the Court has demonstrated – either by focusing on the procedural limb of Article 2 ECHR or by mandating a shift of the burden of proof to the accused State – that it is more than willing to hold those accountable, who have violated the law.

87 ECtHR, *Carter v Russia* (n 10) para. 157.
88 Ibid., para. 166.
89 Ibid., para. 167.
90 Ibid., paras. 170–172.

3.3.2 The ECtHR's Clear Commitment in the Case of Targeted Assassinations

Victims of chemical attacks may institute proceedings before the ECtHR provided that certain conditions are met and certain criteria are fulfilled, such as the exhaustion of local remedies.[91] In addition, the Court would also need to affirm jurisdiction in case of alleged chemical weapons use in an extraterritorial context. This was clearly the case in *Carter vs. Russia* where two former KGB agents flew to London to meet with *Litvinienko* in a hotel bar.[92] The Court assumed that the poison, a radioactive agent called polonium-10, was put into the tee *Litvinienko* was offered upon entering the hotel bar.[93] In an extraterritorial context, the Court only affirms to have jurisdiction in case a State Party to the ECHR exercises effective control over territory[94] as would be the case with occupation (territorial model of jurisdiction) or a State agent exerts authority and control over an individual as would be the case with custodial settings[95] in armed conflict or security operations[96] (spatial model of jurisdiction).[97] In case of a chemical weapons attack by a States Party to the ECHR on

91 Article 35 ECHR.

92 *Navalnyy v Russia*, on the other hand, was a purely domestic case and thus did not raise any questions regarding extraterritoriality. See *Navalnyy v Russia* (n 11) para. 5.

93 Other sources of so-called primary contamination, understood as "evidence of direct contact between the radioactive substance and the surface on which it was deposited" was found in the hotel rooms where the two former KGB agents had been staying as well as in the boardroom where both of them met *Livtinienko* for the first time. See ECtHR, *Carter v Russia* (n 10) para. 155.

94 ECtHR, *Loizidou v Turkey* (Preliminary Objections) (Application No. 15318/89, 23 March 1995) para. 62; ECtHR, *Bankovic v Belgium and 16 other contracting States* (Application No. 52207/99, 12 January 2001) paras. 44–47, 50, and 70–80; ECtHR, *Ilaşcu and Others v* [illegible] ECtHR, *Al-Skeini and Others v the United Kingdom* (Application no. 55721/07, 7 July 2011) paras. 138–140.

95 ECtHR, *Al-Jedda v the United Kingdom* (Application No. 27021/08, 7 July 2011); ECtHR, *Hassan v the United Kingdom* (Application No. 29750/09, 16 September 2014); ECtHR, *Manitaras and Others v Turkey* (Application No. 54591/00, 3 June 2008); ECtHR, *Öcalan v Turkey* (Application No. 46221/99, 12 May 2005).

96 ECtHR, *Pad and Others v Turkey* (Application No. 60167/00, 28 June 2007).

97 ECtHR, *Al-Skeini and Others v the United Kingdom* (Application no. 55721/07, 7 July 2011) paras. 138–139 and 133–137. See also Marko Milanovic, Jurisdiction and Responsibility: Trends in the Jurisprudence of the Strasbourg Court in Anne van Aaken and Iulia Motoc (eds.) *The European Convention of Human Rights and General International Law, European Society of International Law Studies* (OUP 2018) 97–111 (98). For further reading see also Rick Lawson, Life after Bankovic: On the Extraterritorial Application of the European Convention of Human Rights in Fons Coomans and Menno T. Kamminga (eds.) *Extraterritorial Application of Human Rights Treaties* (Intersentia 2004) 83–124; Michael

the territory of a third country, the ECtHR might deny having jurisdiction unless the relevant State in question exercises control over the territory where the chemical attack occurred or state agents exercise authority and control over individuals.[98] Russia was obviously not exercising territorial control over parts of the territory of the UK and the case was also not dealing with, e.g. a custodial setting where State agents exercised authority and control over a person. In *Carter vs. Russia*, the Court affirmed to have jurisdiction because of the radioactive agent's *effects*. The use of the radioactive agent by the two former KGB agents constituted "physical power and control over the life of Mr. Litvinenko in a situation of proximate targeting"[99] which was tantamount to scenarios where state agents unquestionably exercised authority and control over an individual, such as in custodial settings. The Court's broad understanding of "authority and control" in situations of targeted assassinations will certainly have repercussions for future proceedings before the Court including cases of chemical weapons use, at least in cases of targeted assassinations where the potential victim can be identified and where the attack can be conducted precisely against that individual (as was the case in *Navalnyy vs. Russia*). The Court's approach in *Carter vs. Russia* shows that the Court is willing to adjudicate matters related to targeted assassinations in an extraterritorial context and the use of (potentially) lethal substances.[100]

3.3.3 The ECtHR and Its Gradual Shift towards Complementarity

The third and final observation addresses the question of how the Court deals with the CWC and thus with arms-control-related issues in a broader context. As will be demonstrated in the following sections, the Court has, previously, abstained from explicitly engaging with the CWC but in *Navalnyy vs. Russia*, a rather recent judgment, it changed its approach and fully engaged with the CWC demonstrating a shift towards stronger complementarity. The following

O'Boyle, The European Convention of Human Rights and Extraterritorial Jurisdiction: A Comment on 'Life after Bankovic' in Fons Coomans and Menno T. Kamminga (eds.) *Extraterritorial Application of Human Rights Treaties* (Intersentia 2004) 125–140;

98 See William A. Schabas, The European Convention of Human Rights: A Commentary (OUP 2015) 100–101; see also Extra-territorial jurisdiction of States Parties to the European Convention on Human Rights, fact sheet, available at <https://www.echr.coe.int/documents/d/echr/fs_extra-territorial_jurisdiction_eng> (accessed 15 April 2024).

99 ECtHR, *Carter v Russia* (n 10) paras. 157–158.

100 In order for Article 2 ECHR to apply it is not necessary that the substance indeed had lethal effects. The potential of having lethal affects suffices for the Court to scrutinize an incident along the lines of Article 2 ECHR. For more on "lethality" and "potentially lethal effects" see Elisabeth Hoffberger-Pippan, *Less-Lethal Weapons under International Law* (n 23) 100–104.

section commences with an analysis of *Finogenov vs. Russia* and the approach that was taken by the Court there. The text will then proceed with an analysis of *Navalnyy vs. Russia* and elaborate in more detail how and to what extent the Court engaged with the CWC and whether or not the CWC had a factual impact on the Court's line of legal reasoning.

3.3.3.1 *The Court's Restrictive Approach in* Finogenov vs. Russia

In *Finogenov vs. Russia*, the ECtHR had to deal with a purely internal issue where the scope of application of the ECHR was quite clear from the very beginning. Nevertheless, account should be taken of the fact that the Court did not address the situation between Russia and the Chechen rebel forces from the perspective of international humanitarian law (IHL) but solely from a law enforcement point of view. The Court more or less automatically assumed that the situation lay within the realm of law enforcement without even slightly touching upon the fact that the impending conflict between Russia and the rebels had been qualified as non-international armed conflict (NIAC) by several authoritative sources.[101] This is deplorable as the Court would have had the chance to delve deeper into the relationship between human rights and humanitarian law – albeit not in an extraterritorial context. The reluctance of the Court to determine the exact nature of the conflict (law enforcement in peacetime or armed conflict) leaves many questions unanswered. Furthermore, in *Finogenov vs.* Russia, the Court held Russia liable for, *inter alia*, having violated the right to life within the meaning of Article 2 ECHR but the Court did not base its findings solely on the fact that an incapacitating chemical agent had been *used*. Only the combination of the use of the aerosolized chemical agent paired with insufficient medical care led the Court to determine that Russia had violated the right to life.[102] Furthermore, the ECtHR abstained from mentioning the CWC even though its relevance in the case was obvious. The reason for the Court's approach may lay in the fact that the OPCW itself had not addressed the Moscow siege in greater detail nor did it condemn Russia for the use of the nerve agent in this "anti-terror" oper-

101 See, for example, Stuart Casey-Maslen, *The Right to Life under International Law: An Interpretative Guideline* (CUP 2021) 190–191; Noelle Quénivet, The Moscow Hostage Crisis in the Light of the Armed Conflict in Chechnya (2013) 4 *Yearbook of International Humanitarian Law* 348–372.

102 Cf. Johan Vorland Wibye, 'Beyond Acts and Omissions – Distinguishing Positive and Negative Duties at the European Court of Human Rights' *Human Rights Review* (2022) 23, 479–502 (483).

ation.[103] At an open OPCW Meeting in 2009, *Michael Crowley* at least addressed the Moscow siege and its potential relevance for the CWC and the OPCW respectively.[104] Given the fact that the OPCW itself did not address the Moscow siege, the decision by the ECtHR not to engage with CWC to avoid any interference with the CWC and the impression of taking decisions anticipatorily is comprehensible.

3.3.3.2 *Embracing Complementarity in* Navalnyy vs. Russia

The general approach by the Court changed in *Navalnyy vs. Russia*. It was primarily Germany that brought the CWC into play. On 2 September 2020, it announced "that the results of the tests carried out on the applicant's samples had revealed unequivocal proof of the presence of a chemical nerve agent from the Novichok group of substances prohibited under the Chemical Weapons Convention"[105]. Furthermore, Germany requested the OPCW "to help analyse evidence related to the Navalny case"[106] pursuant to Article VIII para 38 lit (e) of the CWC. In its findings, the ECtHR took the opportunity to address the CWC and the assessment made by the OPCW. It, *inter alia*, cited the findings of the OPCW investigative team. On 6 October 2020, for example, the OPCW Technical Secretariat issued a summary of the report on the findings of the investigative team by stating "that the results of the analysis demonstrated that the applicant had been exposed to a toxic chemical acting as a cholinesterase inhibitor. The biomarkers of the cholinesterase inhibitor found in his blood and urine samples had similar structural characteristics to the toxic chemicals belonging to Schedules 1.A.14 and 1.A.15 in the Annex on Chemicals to the CWC. This cholinesterase inhibitor was not listed in the Annex on Chemicals to the CWC".[107] But also the Parliamentary Assembly of the Council of Europe became active. On 26 January 2022, it adopted Resolution 2423[108] stating that there was ample evidence "that the applicant had been poisoned with an organophosphorus cholinesterase inhibitor whilst in Russia. It

103 Please check with Ralph Trapp.

104 Michael Crowley, 'Dangerous Ambiguities: Regulation of incapacitants and riot control agents under the Chemical Weapons Convention', OPCW Open Forum Meeting (2 December 2009) <https://www.opcw.org/sites/default/files/documents/CSP/C-14/open-forum/Dangerous-Ambiguities-Regulation-of-Riot-Control-Agents-and-Incapacitants-under-the-Chemical-Weapons-Convention_Rev.1.pdf> (accessed 31 March 2024).

105 ECtHR, *Navalnyy v Russia* (n 11) para. 15.

106 Ibid., para. 20.

107 Ibid., para. 29.

108 Council of Europe Parliamentary Assembly, 'Poisoning of Alexey Navalny' Resolution 2423 (2022).

pointed out that five different tests had established that the poison was structurally related to a group of chemicals generally referred to as "Novichok", an extremely toxic nerve agent known to have only been produced in State laboratories of the USSR and, reportedly, Russia".[109] The Parliamentary Assembly did not only call upon Russia to comply with its obligations under the ECHR but also under the CWC. And on 30 December 2020, the Special Rapporteur on extrajudicial, summary or arbitrary executions and the Special Rapporteur on the promotion and protection of the right to freedom of opinion and expression, appointed by the UN Human Rights Council sent a letter to Russian authorities claiming inter alia that "the time of the chemical weapon attack the applicant had been under the intensive surveillance of the intelligence agencies, making it very unlikely that third parties could act without their knowledge, and that there was clear evidence that Novichok was a chemical weapon developed by the Russian government".[110] The ECtHR not only cited all these different sources but it used these arguments to support its own legal analysis. Russia's non-compliance with the obligation to carry out an independent investigation into Mr. Navalny's poisoning was, *inter alia*, derived form the findings made by the OPCW investigative team: "the obligation to investigate the possible poisoning took on a new dimension after the German government's announcement concerning the evidence obtained with the assistance of the Organisation for the Prohibition of Chemical Weapons (OPCW) indicating that the applicant's poisoning had been caused by a chemical nerve agent from the Novichok group (see paragraphs 15 and 20 above). Russia, as a party to the Chemical Weapons Convention (CWC), was under an obligation to investigate in criminal proceedings any activities breaching the prohibition of chemical weapons, which was, moreover, incorporated as a specific provision in the Criminal Code (see paragraphs 73–75 above). It follows that under international and domestic law, Russia was required to open a criminal investigation with a view to establishing the origin of the prohibited substance, as well as to identify those responsible for the applicant's ingestion of the substance".[111] The ECtHR's clear-cut commitment to the CWC and its openness to take into consideration the findings of the OPWC are telling. It is the first time the Court clearly shows a willingness to take into consideration arms control-related measures – even in cases, which are difficult to categorize, such as the poisoning and attempted murder of *Alexey Navalnyy*.

109 ECtHR, *Navalnyy v Russia* (n 11) para. 82.
110 Ibid., para. 86.
111 Ibid., para. 150. See also para. 151 on the CoE Parliamentary Assembly.

3.3.3.3 *Interim Conclusion*

In light of the above considerations, it seems that the ECtHR does play a complementary role with regard to arms control, especially in the context of the CWC. While the Court has entirely abstained from delving deeper into arms control-related issues in both *Finogenov vs. Russia* and *Carter vs. Russia*, it has taken a far more progressive – and in the eyes of the author long overdue – approach towards complementarity instead of "regime isolation". Account should be taken of the fact, however, that in *Navalnyy vs. Russia*, the chemical agent used was listed in the Annex of the CWC and thus undoubtedly prohibited. In *Finogenov vs. Russia*, on the other hand, a "derivative of fentanyl" was used, which was not listed in the Annex and thus raised the question of whether the use of the chemical agent could have violated the CWC for other reasons. As adumbrated above, the use of the derivative of fentanyl and the alleged violation of the CWC led to lengthy discussions culminating in a decision in 2021 when CWC States Parties finally clarified that the use of chemical agents was generally permitted for the purposes of domestic riot control (with the respective qualifier "in types and quantities) but that "that such permitted use does not include the "aerosolised use" of CNS chemicals, such as fentanyl".[112] It might well be the case that Court – because of the rather complicated legal situation – intentionally abstained from delving deeper into issues related to the CWC in *Finogenov vs. Russia*, whereas it referred to both the CWC and OPCW in *Navalny vs. Russia*. This, in turn, might have severe implications for future proceedings as only those chemicals, which are listed in the Annex to the CWC, would certainly trigger the ECtHR's engagement with the CWC and the OPCW as reference material. In addition, account must be taken of the fact that because of Russia's war of aggression against Ukraine and its persistent violation of international law, CoE States Parties decided[113] to suspend Russia's membership. In any case, it was high time for the Court to take a more progressive approach and fully embrace complementarity. Hopefully, the Court will also do that in the case of chemical agents that

112 Congressional Research Service, 'Illicit Fentanyl and Weapons of Mass Destruction: International Controls and Policy Options' (28 March 2022) <https://crsreports.congress.gov/product/pdf/IN/IN11902> (accessed 15 April 2024).

113 Council of Europe, Committee of Ministers, 2.3 Situation in Ukraine – Measures to be taken, including under Article 8 of the Statute of the Council of Europe (1426ter meeting, 25 February 2022) CM/Del/Dec(2022)1426ter/2.3. See also Council of Europe, Committee of Ministers, Resolution CM/Res (2022) 1 on legal and financial consequences of the suspension of the Russian Federation from its rights of representation in the Council of Europe, CM/Res (2022), 1.

are not listed in the Annex to the CWC. The biggest hope, certainly, is that no such weapons will ever be used in the future but that is, most probably, mere utopia.

4 Conclusion

This contribution was concerned with the question of whether the ECtHR can assume a complementary role in relation to the CWC. The CWC does not offer individuals the possibility to seek redress for chemical weapons attacks. Recent case law of the ECtHR has demonstrated that the Court might be an alternative avenue. Apart from the fact that the ECtHR offers individuals the possibility to seek redress directly, the previous analysis has identified at least three additional advantages. First, while the material scope of application of the CWC is not entirely clear, the ECtHR could, potentially, scrutinize the use of *all* chemical agents as long as human rights under ECHR are implicated, most notably the right to life. Questions relating to the CWC's material scope of application became obvious in the context of the Moscow theatre siege in 2002. Russia, among others, argued that only those aerosolized nerve agents are covered by the CWC, which are listed in the Annex attached to it. This is certainly not the prevailing view among CWC States Parties and the literature also clearly suggests otherwise, but Russia maintains this position. The ECtHR, on the other hand, would not be faced with such discussions. It has rendered judgments on the use of a derivative of fentanyl, Novichok, and even radioactive substances, such as polonium-10. It sufficed for the Court that these substances had the potential of being lethal and thus fell under the purview of the right to life. Second, lengthy discussions have revolved around the question of whether the CWC, in particular, applies in [illegible] of (attempted) targeted assassinations. Even though there seems to be a tendency to argue in the affirmative, CWC States Parties have hitherto not reached a consensus. The ECtHR, on the other hand, has made unmistakably clear that it is willing to affirm jurisdiction in case of targeted assassinations including in an extraterritorial context. It has taken an extensive approach as regards the ECHR's extraterritorial scope of application in *Carter vs. Russia* where it held that both former KGB agents had authority and control over the victim because the substance they used (polonium-10) had effects that were tantamount to actual physical control as would be the case in custodial settings, for example. And third, the ECtHR has shown that it is now willing to actively engage with arms control treaties. It has successfully done so in *Navalnyy vs. Russia* – a case of an attempted targeted assassination – whereas in *Finogenov vs. Russia,* it was still reluctant to engage in arms control-related matters. Admittedly, the Court probably did not delve deeper into the CWC in *Finogenov vs. Russia* because the OPCW itself had hardly touched upon this issue. It seems plausible that the Court did not aim to touch upon issues related to arms control to avoid any unwanted, anticipatory interference with the CWC regime. The situation was completely different in *Navalnyy vs. Russia* where the OPCW was requested to offer technical assistance by Germany. The organization concluded that *Navalnyy* had been exposed to the chemical nerve agent Novichok. Building upon and relying on the OPCW's findings, the ECtHR held that "[t]he need to investigate the possible involvement of State agents was therefore clearly present from the outset. Moreover, after the OPCW's confirmation of the use of the substances classified as chemical weapons, this line of investigation should have become a priority".[114]

In light of the above, it is safe to assume that the ECtHR will play an even greater role in case of future chemical weapons attacks. One can only hope that they do not occur in the future, but such thoughts are mainly wishful thinking. A deteriorating geopolitical climate rather suggests otherwise. The Court relied on the OPCW where it made sense, mainly to substantiate its own arguments but it never interfered with the OPCW. Unfortunately, Russia has left the ECHR. But there is a glimpse of hope that Russia can return one day as a law-abiding nation fully embracing the ECHR.

114 ECtHR, *Carter v Russia* (n 10) para. 156.

CHAPTER 9

A (Too) Loose Link? Revisiting the OPCW's Conventional and Implied Powers to Investigate Chemical Weapons Use

Kristoffer Burck

1 Introduction

The Chemical Weapons Convention (CWC) represents one of the most comprehensive regimes prohibiting an entire class of weapons. In contrast to some other disarmament treaties, the drafters of the CWC enshrined in the treaty text an elaborate system on verifications, trust-building measures, and inspections, knitting a quilt of different procedures to assure compliance with its provisions. Yet, when faced with continuous chemical weapons use in the context of the Syrian civil war, a majority of states parties decided to not invoke the procedures to investigate such use under the Convention. Instead, states, through the different organs of the Organization for the Prohibition of Chemical Weapons (OPCW) established several ad hoc mechanisms with differing mandates, ranging from assuring destruction of declared chemical weapons, i.e. the Declaration Assessment Team over establishing whether chemical weapons have been used, i.e. the Fact Finding Mechanism (FFM) to identifying those responsible for such chemical weapons use, i.e. first the Joint Investigative Mechanism (JIM), mandated by the United Nations Security Council (UNSC) and later the Investigation and Identification Team (IIT), solely mandated by the OPCW.

These mechanisms have played a preeminent role in ascertaining facts, investigating specific cases, and providing methodologically sound evidence to ascertain violations of the prohibition of chemical weapons use. Since their establishment, the FFM in 2014 and the IIT in 2018, they have published numerous reports, covering several instances of alleged chemical weapons use. At time of writing in early 2024, the FFM has published 20 reports, covering 71 instances of alleged use of chemical weapons, finding 20 cases where chemical weapons were used. The IIT has published four reports, finding reasonable grounds to believe the Syrian armed forces were responsible in five instances

 | DOI:10.1163/9789004739192_010

and the non-state actor Islamic State in Iraq and Levante in one instance of chemical weapons use.[1]

Roughly ten years after the FFM was established and five years after the IIT became operational, disagreements on their method of work and unaddressed questions on the legal mandate of the IIT persist. Some states maintain a consistent and continuous rejection of the IIT's entire mandate while other states already enter discussions on potential future mechanisms that might be modeled after the Syrian experiences. Indeed, at the last Conference of States Parties (CSP) in November 2023, a majority passed a decision that contained, besides a call to enforce collective measures against Syria, a request to the Technical Secretariat of the OPCW to build investigative capabilities.[2] The need to reflect on the legal basis of ad hoc investigative mechanisms and specifically the IIT is exacerbated two factors: Firstly, when the mandate to establish the IIT was passed,[3] state representatives as well as OPCW officials made ambiguous and conflicting statements on the exact legal basis of the mechanism. As discussed in detail later, voices in favor of the decision referred to moral obligations of the OPCW, others linked to expressed conventional provisions for investigating alleged use, while others, including the then OPCW Director-General Ambassador Üzümcü, referred to implied or inherent powers of the organization. Secondly, the decision to establish the IIT at the time only saw scarce academic discussion on its assumed legal basis. While considerable discourse emerged on the political implications of the decision,[4]

1 Compare: OPCW (2023), *Note by the Technical Secretariat, Accession of the Syrian Arab Republic to the Chemical Weapons Convention: Ten Years on* (S/2213/2023), paras 30, 40 and OPCW (2024), *Note by the Technical Secretariat - Fourth Report by the OPCW Investigation and Identification Team - Marea (Syrian Arab Republic)* (S/2255/2024), para 3.

2 OPCW (2023), *Decision, Addressing the Threat from Chemical Weapons Use and the Threat from Future Use* (C-28/DEC.12), para 2.

3 The basis of this was provided in a Special CSP Session that authorized the OPCW Technical Secretariat to create a mechanism with attribution functions. See: OPCW (2018), *Addressing the Threat from Chemical Weapons Use* (C-SS-4/DEC.3), para 10.

4 See exemplary: Oliver Meier and Trapp, 'Playing Politics with Chemical Weapons? The UK's Initiative on Chemical Weapons Accountability' (*Bulletin of the Atomic Scientists*, 20 June 2018) <https://thebulletin.org/2018/06/playing-politics-with-chemical-weapons-the-uks-initiative-on-chemical-weapons-accountability/> (accessed 20 February 2024); Una Becker-Jakob, 'Countering the Use of Chemical Weapons in Syria: Options for Supporting International Norms and Institutions' 16; Oliver Meier, 'Chemical Weapons Attacks: The End of Anonymity. Organisation for the Prohibition of Chemical Weapons to Identify Perpetrators' 8; Gregory D Koblentz, 'Chemical-Weapon Use in Syria: Atrocities, Attribution, and Accountability' (2019) 26 The Nonproliferation Review 575; For a retrospective evaluation see: Alexander Kelle, 'The CWC at 25: From Verification of Chemical-Weapons Destruction to Attribution of Their Use' [2023] The Nonproliferation Review, 1.

only few addressed the legal justification of the mandate. Few contributions engaged the question of whether the OPCW had sufficient powers to create the IIT.[5] Yet, these all in their own respect overlook vital aspects, most prominently a differentiation between implied and inherent powers of international organizations.

In consideration of continuous contestation on a state level, a paucity of discussions on the legal foundation by scholarly sources and the need of a stocktaking for potential future mechanisms, this chapter will reengage the OPCW's powers to set up investigative mechanisms. To do this, the chapter will first set forth applicable conceptions of powers of international organizations, then present the CWC's conventional provisions for investigations into alleged chemical weapons use as well as the organizational framework of the IIT and proceed to discuss whether the IIT's mandate may or may not constitute a lawful act by the OPCW. The chapter closes by presenting some concluding remarks with a specific focus on potential future mechanism.

2 Doctrines on Powers of International Organizations

The theory of implied powers marks an essential concept in the law of international organizations. It developed over time, mainly through jurisprudence of the Permanent Court for International Justice (PCIJ), later the International Court of Justice (ICJ). Additionally, the Court of Justice of the European Union (CJEU) and its predecessor organs,[6] have had a significant impact on the theory of implied powers, which is recognized by scholars as impacting this concept beyond the regional reach of the CJEU.[7] This jurisprudence and scholarly

5 See for example: Mirko Sossai, 'Identifying the Perpetrators of Chemical Attacks in Syria' (2019) 17 Journal of International Criminal Justice 211; Alexander Orakhelashvili, 'The Attribution Decision Adopted by the Opcw's Conference of States Parties and Its Legality' (2020) 17 International Organizations Law Review 664; Tuuli Haataja, 'The Authority and Scope of Activities of the OPCW – Decision to Establish a Mechanism to Attribute Responsibility for Chemical Weapons Use in Syria' (National Defence College Finland 2020) <https://www.doria.fi/handle/10024/177686>.

6 For ease of reference these will also be referred to as CJEU throughout this text, while acknowledging that the respective Courts did indeed have different mandates and names throughout the different stages of European integration.

7 Jan Klabbers, *An Introduction to International Organizations Law* (Third edition, Cambridge University Press 2015) 57; On the general role of the EU and the CJEU in developing concepts of international law applicable to International Organizations see: Jed Odermatt, 'The Development of Customary International Law by International Organizations' (2017) 66 International and Comparative Law Quarterly, 491.

commentary underwent significant changes over time and do not present a uniform understanding of this theory. Instead, several approaches can be subsumed under the concept of implied powers of international organizations and their acts as legal persons under international law, which are presented and discussed below.

2.1 *The Emergence of Implied Powers Doctrine*

Implied powers emerged from the need to ascertain the distribution of powers between central and local governments in a federalized system.[8] With the formation of international organizations, holding legal personality, this theory found first application in international law in the PCIJ's Advisory Opinion on the *Greco-Turkish Agreement* in 1928.[9] The Court found that certain, non-explicit powers of an international body could be deducted from other explicit powers.[10] This concept effectively provided for an expansion of powers, allowing an international organization to act in areas in which it did not have explicitly attributed competence as long these were sensibly linked to an explicit power. This concept was reinforced by ICJ Advisory Opinions in 1949[11] and 1954,[12] further widening the scope of implicit powers to also find implied powers in acts that are necessary for the functioning of the organization. This approach was shared by the CJEU (then European Community for Coal and Steel), finding that powers can be necessarily implied if they are required for an organization to usefully fulfill its mandate.[13] The courts thereby established the concept of *effet utile*,[14] which allows for impli-

8 Viljam Engström, *Understanding Powers of International Organizations: A Study of the Doctrines of Attributed Powers, Implied Powers and Constitutionalism - with a Special Focus on the Human Rights Committee* (Åbo akademis förlag = Åbo Akademi University Press 2009), 25.

9 PCIJ (1928), *Interpretation of the Greco-Turkish Agreement of December 1st, 1926, Advisory Opinion,* PCIJ Publication Series B (16).

10 Ibid., p. 20. Compare also: Klabbers (n 7), 57.

11 ICJ (1949), *Reparation for Injuries Suffered in the Service of the United Nations, Advisory Opinion,* ICJ Reports 1949, p. 174.

12 ICJ (1954), *Effect of Awards of Compensation made by the UN Administrative Tribunal, Advisory Opinion,* ICJ Reports 1954, p. 47.

13 ECJ (1956), *Fédération Charbonnière de Belgique v High Authority of the European Coal and Steel Community* [1956] ECJ Case 8–55. In the following referred to as *Fedechar* decision.

14 Klabbers (n 8) 57; See generally on the role of the *effet utile:* Michael Potacs, 'Effet utile als Auslegungsgrundsatz' (2009) 44 Europarecht, 465.

cation of powers where they are necessary to attain a specific objective of the Convention.[15]

These early judgments identified the existence of implied powers in cases where these could be sensibly deducted from and were necessary in the fulfillment of explicit powers transferred to the organization.

2.2 *Implied and Inherent Powers*

In the following years, two decisions, the ICJ Advisory Opinion on *Certain Expenses*[16] and the CJEU *ERTA*[17] case significantly widened the scope of powers of international organizations, leading some authors to conclude that an entirely new theory is necessary to describe this source of powers, i.e. the doctrine of inherent powers.[18] Both courts partially moved away from linking an implied power to an explicitly mentioned power. Instead, they held that powers could be assumed if they are necessary to achieve the general object and purpose of the treaty. Following from this, Seyersted positioned the doctrine of inherent powers as diametrically opposed to inherent powers.[19] Instead of searching a link to an expressed power in the constituent document, inherent powers are an outflow of the legal personality of the international organization. This personality necessitates certain powers to achieve the object and purpose of the organization, which are to be assumed, even if they are not mentioned in the organization's treaty. The limit would ultimately only be in those areas where the constituent document expressly prohibits such powers, meaning that acts are *ultra vires* only if they have nothing to do with the wider object and purpose of the organization.[20]

This very extensive concept of inherent powers received wide criticism for its internal incoherence, its lack of a judicious framework to determine the objective purpose of an organization, and most strikingly for casting aside the

15 ECJ (1977), *Draft Agreement Establishing a European Laying-up Fund for Inland Waterway Vessels* [1977] ECJ Opinion 1/76. In the following referred to as *Laying-up Fund.* See on this: Engström (n 8), 63.

16 ICJ (1962), *Certain Expenses of the United Nations, Advisory Opinion*, ICJ Reports 1962, p. 151.

17 ECJ (1971), *Commission of the European Communities v Council of the European Communities* [1971] ECJ Case 22–70. In the following referred to as *ERTA* decision.

18 Finn Seyersted, *Common Law of International Organizations* (Brill | Nijhoff 2008) 65 <https://brill.com/view/title/15122> (accessed 9 February 2024); Klabbers (n 7), 60.

19 Seyersted (n 18), 65.

20 Enzo Cannizzaro and Paolo Palchetti, 'Ultra Vires Acts of International Organizations' in Jan Klabbers (ed), *Research handbook on the law of international organizations* (Paperback ed, reprint, Edward Elgar 2014), 377.

core concept of state sovereignty by majorly disregarding the importance of the constituent document in representing the intent of the drafting states.[21] The theory of implied powers, besides its severe criticism by scholars, also received no significant support by states. While no state expressly endorsed this concept in an official setting, the United Kingdom and the United States in the Human Rights Council vehemently opposed any insinuation of inherent powers.[22] The same is now true for a considerable number of states in the OPCW with even those advocating for the IIT's creation trying to tie the competence to create this mechanism to expressed powers in the CWC, as discussed in detail below.

3 Implied and Attributed Powers

In line with academic and state criticism, the ICJ and CJEU also somewhat reversed their extensive interpretation of powers from the *Certain Expenses* Advisory Opinion and the *ERTA* decision by returning back to a necessary link to expressed powers. The ICJ in its Advisory Opinion on *Legality of Use of Nuclear Weapons* (*WHO*) held that international organizations such as the World Health Organization can exercise implied powers, which are however limited to the principle of specialty and need to be linked to explicit purposes assigned in the constituent document by member states.[23] Likewise, the CJEU applied a more restricted approach to implied powers in its *ECHR* and *Tobacco Advertising* decisions, stating that implied competences would necessitate a link to explicitly attributed competences or otherwise would be rendered *ultra vires* acts.[24]

The return to such a restrictive interpretation by the two courts represents a revitalization of the perimeters limiting implied powers, already proposed by ICJ Judge Hackworth in his dissenting opinions in *Reparations for Injuries* and *Effect of Awards*. According to this, certain powers of an international organization may be implied for the fulfillment of its attributed tasks but are confined to those that are necessary to achieve such explicitly granted

21 Klabbers (n 7) 65–67.

22 Engström (n 8), 222.

23 ICJ (1996), *Legality of the Threat or Use of Nuclear Weapons, Advisory Opinion,* ICJ Reports 1996, p. 226, para 25.

24 ECJ (1996), *Accession by the Community to the European Convention for the Protection of Human Rights and Fundamental Freedoms* [1996] ECJ Case C-2/94, paras 23–25. and ECJ (2000), *Federal Republic of Germany v European Parliament and Council of the European Union* [2000] ECJ Case C-376/98, paras 78–80.

powers.[25] Necessity requires an assessment that no other less intrusive measures and acts would be suitable to achieve the same objective.[26] An additional important constraint articulated by Hackworth, and now arguably returned to by ICJ and CJEU jurisprudence, is found in the principle that implied powers cannot "*supplant or vary* [,] *express powers*".[27] A similar approach was taken by Judge Quintana in his dissenting opinion on *Certain Expenses*, stating that implied powers cannot "*be invoked when explicit powers provide expressly for the eventualities under consideration*".[28] Following from the reaffirmed principle that implied powers are a corollary of the intent of the drafters, they logically cannot be invoked to justify acts which deviate from the specifical acts foreseen in the constituent document.

Implied powers are a necessary doctrine to ensure the effective functioning of international organizations. Judicial and scholarly opinions on the exact extent underwent significant changes over time and continue to see disagreement. Nevertheless, it appears that in the current jurisprudence and academic discourse, the significantly wider concept of inherent powers is rejected. Instead, acts based on implied powers, are only assumed to be *intra vires* if they are necessary to attain an explicit objective in the constituent document, link to an attributed power, and do not vary or supplant such express powers.[29]

4 Conventional Provisions for Investigations

Returning to the legal basis for investigations into alleged use of chemical weapons under the CWC, the convention does indeed foresee several proced-

---

25 Judge Hackworth (1949), *Reparation for Injuries Suffered in the Service of the United Nations, Dissenting Opinion*, ICJ Reports 1949, p. 199.

26 German constitutional law scholarship and jurisprudence has adopted an extensive definition of the term necessity as part of its proportionality assessment. Similar approaches, though less detailed, are also observed in comparative constitutional law as well as in international law. See: Erich Vranes, 'Der Verhältnismäßigkeitsgrundsatz Herleitungsalternativen, Rechtsstatus und Funktionen' (2009) 47 Archiv des Völkerrechts 1, 11.

27 Judge Hackworth (1954), *Effect of Awards of Compensation made by the UN Administrative Tribunal, Dissenting Opinion*, ICJ Reports 1954, p. 80.

28 Judge Quintana (1962), *Certain Expenses of the United Nations, Dissenting Opinion*, ICJ Reports 1962, p. 245–246.

29 See more extensive on the return to the narrower conception of implied powers: Andrzej Gadkowski, 'The Doctrine of Implied Powers of International Organizations in the Case Law of International Tribunals' (2016) 6 Przegląd Prawniczy Uniwersytetu im. Adama Mickiewicza 45, 57.

ures, depending on the concrete situation. Reactions to an alleged violation of the Convention can generally follow three ways: Clarification Requests through article IX (3–7) CWC, Assistance Requests through article X (9) CWC, and Challenge Inspections through article IX (8–25). Additionally, the Verification Annex, a legally binding appendix to the Convention, provides specifics on how investigations should be conducted in Part XI.

The least invasive procedure are Clarification Requests, which do not constitute investigations in themselves but rather represents a less-adversive form of ad hoc dispute settlement that is very much in line with the CWC's focus on confidence and compliance.[30] This provision allows any state part, having doubts about the compliance of another party, to request clarification. Concretely, the requested party has to provide adequate information addressing these doubts, or otherwise the OPCW Director-General may establish a group of experts to issue a report on the situation of concern, based on all available information.[31] It is up to the requesting state to decide whether such a clarification is satisfactory and in case concerns persist, the state can request a special session of the OPCW Executive Council to recommend measures in order to resolve the situation.[32] If concerns remain, the requesting state can escalate further by requesting a Challenge Inspection.[33]

The Assistance Request procedure under article X CWC allows states parties to request an investigation if it considers that chemical weapons have been used against it.[34] The main focus of such requests is however to establish the extent of assistance needed by the affected state and thus primarily seeks to establish whether chemical weapons were used against that state, not to identify those responsible.[35] An affected state could however invoke both articles IX and X and thereby trigger different requests at the same time.[36]

---

30 Thilo Marauhn, 'Article IX: Consultations, Cooperation, and Fact Finding' in Walter Krutzsch and others (eds), *The Chemical Weapons Convention: a commentary* (Oxford University Press 2014), 302.

31 Art. IX (4) (b) and (e) CWC.

32 Art. IX (4) (f) CWC.

33 It is, however, important to note that a prior request for clarification is not a necessary condition to directly request a challenge inspection. Another option is to request a Special Session of the Conference of States Parties to recommend further measures. See Art. IX (7) CWC.

34 See Art. X (8) (a) CWC.

35 Per Runn, 'Verification Annex, Part XI' in Walter Krutzsch and others (eds), *The Chemical Weapons Convention: a commentary* (Oxford University Press 2014), 643.

36 Ibid., 646.

The third procedure to react to alleged use, the Challenge Inspection, is the closest to comparable ad hoc Fact Finding efforts in other regimes. The Convention provides a right to each state party to request an ad hoc on-site investigation on the territory of any other state party to resolve questions of non-compliance, which duly include the potential use of chemical weapons.[37] The inspected party is obligated to provide access to the inspected site and assist the inspection team.[38] The team then issues a report that contains details on the inspection activities, including the access granted to the team.[39] This report shall also contain any information that might serve to identify the origin of the chemical used, in case the team collects such information.[40] The wording here is however somewhat ambiguous: while the purpose of the investigation is arguably to establish whether the investigated state is in violation of the CWC by using a chemical weapon,[41] the paragraph utilizes a conditional phrase,[42] indicating that obtaining such information is not of the highest priority but rather to be seen as a side effect of the investigation.[43] This ambiguity should not be mistaken to reflect a lack of attention by the drafters. On the contrary, the exact procedures and extent of challenge inspections was one of the more intensely debated parts of the Convention, as is evident from the *traveaux preparatoire.*[44] Taking this into account, it appears likely that the conditional phrasing was used to not bar the inclusion of evidence, whilst not making attribution the focus of the investigation.

In any case, the report produced by the inspection team should only present facts and not enter into an evaluation of those, let alone make findings on non-compliance as this is the exclusive authority of the Executive Council.[45] The CWC's drafters quite deliberately entrusted the Council with the politico-

---

37 Art. IX (8) CWC. These requests can only be denied by a three-quarter majority in the Executive Council in cases where the request is considered abusive. Compare art. IX (17) CWC.

38 See Art. IX (12) (b) and (20) CWC.

39 Part X (59) Verification Annex CWC.

40 Part XI (26) Verification Annex CWC.

41 Runn (n 35), 654.

42 Compare: Part XI (26) Verification Annex CWC.

43 With a different view see Abe, who concludes that para. 26 suggests attribution to be inherent to the OPCW's powers. This analysis does, however, not consider the exact phrasing of this paragraph, omitting the conditional nature of the formulation. Tatsuya Abe, *Syrian Chemical Weapons and International Law* (Springer Nature Singapore 2023), 60.

44 Conference on Disarmament (1990), *Report of the ad-hoc Committee on Chemical Weapons to the Conference on Disarmament, CD/1033,* p. 216. See also: Marauhn (n 30), 304.

45 Compare Art. IX (22) (a) CWC and see for an in-depth discussion: Ibid., 324.

legal evaluation of the outcome of an investigation. This construction ultimately allows an evaluation to remain inconclusive on whether a violation has taken place, even if the factual basis might indicate a certain outcome. This political scope for assessment is essential to the Convention's preference on amicable solutions to ensure compliance over ascribing responsibility or as Marauhn put it: "[...] *the object and purpose of the challenge inspection is not to label a non-compliant State Party as a perpetrator, but to rebuild the confidence between all States Parties* [...]".[46]

While the CWC, with its Challenge Inspection provides for a remarkably detailed and far reaching instrument for fact finding, this article has not yet been invoked in the Convention's history. This restraint may be caused by states, in most cases, choosing to pursue less intrusive avenues of ensuring compliance,[47] which would very much be in the cooperative spirit enshrined in the Convention. Yet, for the situation in Syria, this explanation does not hold, as the most recent ad hoc mechanisms established to investigate allegation of chemical weapons use, the IIT, was at the very least as intrusive as the article IX procedure, an aspect further discussed in the following section.

5 Ad Hoc Investigative Mechanisms

Reacting to repeated allegations of chemical weapons being used in the Syrian civil war, several ad hoc fact-finding mechanisms were created. The following section briefly presents and contrasts mandate, legal basis and space within the organizational system of the most relevant mechanisms, the FFM, JIM, and IIT.

The FFM was established in 2014 by the OPCW Director-General as a response to continued reports of chemical weapons use in Syria. It is based on the Director's broad authority to uphold the object and purpose of the Convention, received a general endorsement by the Executive Council and was accepted by Syria.[48] Its mandate only includes to determine whether toxic chemical have been used as a weapon in Syria,[49] and is therefore significantly narrower than a potential challenge inspection. Article IX (2) CWC allows to

46 Ibid., 325.

47 As suggested by Marauhn: Ibid., 327.

48 See: OPCW (2014), *Note by the Technical Secretariat – Summary Report of the Work of the OPCW Fact-Finding Mission in Syria Covering the Period from 3 to 31 May 2014* (S/1191/2014), Annex 2, para 4.

49 Compare: <https://www.opcw.org/fact-finding-mission> (accessed 20. February 2024).

establish by mutual consent of the parties involved any inspection procedure that might be better suited to resolve concerns about non-compliance,[50] again signifying the conciliatory character of the Convention.[51] In light of Syria's consent, the FFM's deviation from the standard procedures for ad hoc investigations falls undoubtedly within the legal framework of the Convention and the legality of the mandate itself has not been challenged by any state party.[52]

The UNSC in 2015 passed resolution 2235, which created the JIM as a joint mission between the UN and the OPCW. The JIM's mandate entailed to identify those responsible for chemical weapons use in Syria, including their organizers and sponsors, in those cases that have been ascertained by the FFM.[53] This mandate entailing identification and attribution of responsibility represents the first instance of a newly emerging attribution norm,[54] not foreseen in a strict sense in the CWC. While this decision was transmitted into the OPCW's framework by the Director-General,[55] the authority of creating the JIM and the responsibility to implement it, primarily rested with the UNSC as the primary organ in relation to maintenance of international peace and security. The Security Council's authority to create subsidiary organs in the area of peace and security, such as the JIM, is undisputed and the mandate is further bolstered by the fact that the resolution was passed unanimously.[56] The JIM investigated nine of the 23 cases of chemical weapons use confirmed by the FFM, attributing responsibility to the Syrian government for four incidents from 2014 to 2017 and the terrorist group ISIS in two others.[57] In 2017, the

---

50 Abe argues that the FFM is nevertheless still reliant on an implied power but similarly concludes that the competence here is clearly supported due to Syria's consent. See: Abe (n 43), 56.

51 See also: Marauhn (n 30), 307.

52 Although there have been challenges to the FFM's conduct of investigations and alleged partiality of the investigation, these did not question the FFM's mandate as such. See exemplary: OPCW (2022), *Statement by Ambassador Shulgin - Permanent Representative of the Russian Federation to the OPCW at the Ninety-Ninth Session of the Executive Council under Agenda Item 7(e)* (EC-99/NAT.51).

53 UNSC (2015), *Resolution 2235* (S/2235/2015), para 4 and 5.

54 Kelle (n 4), 6.

55 OPCW (2015), *Note by the Director-General dated 11 August 2015* (S/1302/2015).

56 See: UNGA (1991), *Declaration on Fact-finding by the United Nations in the Field of the Maintenance of International Pace and Security* (A/46/59/1991) and the related commentary by: Sir Kenneth Keith, 'Declaration on Fact-Finding by the United Nations in the Field of the Maintenance of International Peace and Security' United Nations Audiovisual Library of International Law.

57 See: UNSC (2016), *Letter Dated 10 June 2016 from the Secretary-General Addressed to the President of the Security Council* (S/2016/530); UNSC (2016), *Letter Dated 24 August 2016 from the Secretary-General Addressed to the President of the Security Council* (S/2016/738);

UNSC did, however, not renew the JIM's mandate, mainly following from Russia not agreeing with the mechanisms independent findings and objecting to its continuation without significant methodological changes.

At the initiative of the United Kingdom, the OPCW convened a special session of the CSP in 2018 with the expressed goal to transfer the JIM's mandate entirely to the OPCW.[58] The UK's draft to task the Technical Secretariat with putting in place arrangements to attribute responsibility in cases where the FFM established chemical weapons use, was adopted through majority decision.[59] The decision's mandate indeed very much mirrored the JIM's tasks, with the small exception that the new mechanism was not instructed to also identify the organizers and sponsors of chemical weapons attacks but to focus on perpetrators only.[60] The Technical Secretariat established the IIT accordingly with reporting lines to the Director-General.[61] The IIT has so far investigated nine cases, resulting in three reports and attribution of responsibility for chemical weapons attacks to the Syrian armed forces in five cases.[62] The different IIT reports comprised of ample evidence, followed established guidelines for international fact-finding, and their findings were incremental in further establishing the horrific violations of international law committed by the Syrian armed forces.[63] Criticism by Russian diplomats mostly followed a pervading pattern of discrediting the work through a flood of allegations in order to sow distrust in the mechanism's work.[64]

Since the FFM was a less intrusive form of investigation consented to by Syria and the UNSC's mandate to establish the JIM was uncontested, only the IIT's legality remains questionable. The following sections will therefore pre-

UNSC (2016), *Letter Dated 21 October 2016 from the Secretary-General Addressed to the President of the Security Council* (S/2016/888); UNSC (2017), *Letter Dated 26 October 2017 from the Secretary-General Addressed to the President of the Security Council* (S/2017/919).

58 Kelle (n 4), 7.

59 Of 152 participating state parties, 82 states voted in favor, and 24 states, including, among others, Russia, China, Iran, India, South Africa, and Syria, voted against. See: OPCW (2018), *Report of the Fourth Special Session of the Conference of the States Parties* (C-SS-4/3), para 3.15.

60 OPCW (2018) (C-SS-4/Dec.3), para 10.

61 OPCW (2019). *Report by the Director-General. Progress in the Implementation of Decision C-SS-4/Dec.3 on Addressing the Threat from Chemical Weapons Use* (EC-91/DG.20).

62 Compare: <https://www.opcw.org/iit> (accessed 20. February 2024).

63 Wissam Aldien Aloklah, 'International Efforts Against Impunity for the Use of Chemical Weapons in Syria' (2022) 20 Journal of International Criminal Justice 541, 555–558.

64 Kristoffer Burck, 'Muddying the Waters: Official Russian Disinformation on Chemical and Biological Weapons' (2023) 2023 PRIF Spotlight.

sent the different conceptions of powers invoked to justify the IIT's mandate and assess their viability.

6 The Powers to Establish the IIT

Notwithstanding that the IIT's findings are both methodologically sound and politically highly relevant, the legality of its mandate remains questionable. Especially if OPCW seeks to reflect on how ad hoc investigations could be improved, a candid discussion of the legal basis is however vital to maintain sufficient support of the Convention.

6.1 *Implied or Inherent Powers?*

The Decision at the Special Session did not reference any of the existing conventional provisions for investigations in articles IX and X CWC as its legal basis. Instead, the Decision draws the legal mandate to establish the IIT from the general powers of the OPCW to act in order to promote the Convention's object and purpose.[65] The Decision does however mention paragraph 26 of Part XI Verification Annex without providing any further language on why this paragraph is referenced.[66] As described above, this specific paragraph purports that if any evidence relating to the origin of a chemical weapon is uncovered, this should be included in the report. It appears that the drafters of the Decision attempted to indicate their conviction that paragraph 26 provides for a conventional provision for attribution without feeling confident enough to make this claim explicit. The IIT is therefore not based on the explicit provisions for investigations but rather on a general power, necessitating some form of implicit deduction of powers in order to render this act *intra vires* of the OPCW and specifically the CSP and the Technical Secretariat. Opponents of the decision mainly refuted the notion that the OPCW could have any powers to establish a mechanism that is not directly tied to its conventional powers and therefore require consensus through the ordinary treaty amendment procedure.[67]

65 OPCW (2018) (C-SS-4/Dec.3), preambular clause, 6.

66 Ibid., preambular clause, 8.

67 OPCW (2018), *Statement by Ambassador Bassam Al-Sabbagh, Permanent Representative of the Syrian Arab Republic to the OPCW at the Fourth Special Session of the Conference of the States Parties* (C-SS-4/NAT.19); OPCW (2018), *Statement by Mr. G.V. Kalamanov Head of the Delegation of the Russian Federation on the Results of the Vote on the British Draft Decision at the Fourth Special Session of the Conference of the States Parties* (C-SS-4/NAT.42); OPCW (2018), *Statement by H.E. Ambassador Haifa Aissami Madah Permanent*

Yet, even proponents of the IIT made conflicting statements on which concept of indirect competences, either narrow or wide implied or even inherent powers, the mandate is based on. Indeed, the Director-General Ambassador Üzümcü conveyed in remarks given shortly before the Special Session his belief in an inherent power of the OPCW to attribute responsibility.[68] Similarly, the German delegation used a formulation in their statement at the Special Session that alluded to a belief that the CWC's provisions are to be seen only as external guardrails and that any act not explicitly prohibited would be legal as long as the act relates to a general purpose of the organization.[69] Both these positions align with the very wide interpretation of powers in the *Certain Expenses* and *ERTA* decisions and formulated in Seyersted's inherent power doctrine.

In contrast, statements by some proponents of the IIT rather seem to refer to powers linked to expressed competencies in articles of the CWC: John Walker, then Head of the Arms Control and Disarmament Unit at the UK Foreign and Commonwealth Office, opined in a blog post one week before the decision was passed that the ability of attribution of responsibility is to be found in articles VIII, IX, and XII of the CWC.[70] Similar understandings are

---

Representative of Bolivarian Republic of Venezuela to the OPCW at the Fourth Special Session of the Conference of the States Parties (C-SS-4/NAT. 53); OPCW (2018), *Statement by the Cuban Delegation to the OPCW at the Fourth Special Session of the Conference of the States Parties* (C-SS-4/NAT.32)), OPCW (2018), *Statement by H.E. Dr. Alireza Jahangiri, The Ambassador Extraordinary and Plenipotentiary to the Netherlands and Permanent Representative of the Islamic Republic of Iran to the OPCW at the 4th Special Session of the Conference of the States Parties*, not assigned official document number; OPCW (2018), *Burundi - Statement by H.E. Ambassador Vestine Nahimana, Permanent Representative to the OPCW, 4th Special Session of the Conference of States Parties to the CWC, The Hague, 26–28 June 2018*, not assigned official document number. A bit more cautious but also referring to the requirement to achieve consensus in order to establish attribution mechanism: OPCW (2018), *Statement by H.E. Ambassador Venu Rajamony Permanent Representative of the Republic of India to the OPCW at the Fourth Special Session of the Conference of the States Parties Explanation of Vote* (C-SS-4/NAT.45).

68 The crucial formulation in this context is: *"The notion that the OPCW does not go into attribution needs to be reconsidered. There is nothing in the Convention that precludes such a role for the Organisation."* OPCW (2018), *"Supporting Compliance with and Implementation of the CWC" Remarks by the Director-General of the OPCW Ambassador Ahmet Üzümcü*, Chatham House, 25 May 2018, p. 5.

69 OPCW (2018), *Statement by Niels Annen, Minister of State at the Federal Foreign Office of Germany at the Fourth Special Session of the Conference of the States Parties* (C-SS-4/NAT.9), p. 3.

70 Confusingly, Walker uses the formulation *"An ability to attribute responsibility for non-compliance is inherent in the powers set forth in Articles* […]*"* which might invoke reference to inherent powers. Yet, since the argument here is exactly that the power to

voiced by state party statements with Canada for example referencing article XII CWC as the source for an implied attribution power[71] and several other states holding that conventional provisions, without further specification on the exact articles, provide such competencies.[72] A majority of proponents, at least of those who engaged with the question of competencies at all,[73] seems to align with the concept of implied powers to justify the act of creating an attribution mechanism.

6.2 *Academic Gaps in the Role of Implied Powers*

Unfortunately, the few academic comments on the legality of the IIT do not substantially address the discrepancies in the doctrines claimed to provide the basis for this decision. Orakhelashvili, who concludes that the decision was overall an *ultra vires* act of the Special Session, mainly focusses on the distribution of competencies within the OPCW and in relation to the UNSC.[74] While not explicitly engaging with the question of attributed, implied and inherent powers, his reference to *Certain Expenses* and the fact that the Convention does not prohibit attribution activities may even suggest that he accepts inherent powers as a basis for the decision but rejects its legality due to other factors.[75]

---

attribute is to be found as a link from explicit articles mentioned, this substantively refers to the concept of implied powers. See: John Walker, 'Why the OPCW Should Attribute Responsibility for Chemical Attacks' (*Bulletin of the Atomic Scientists*, 21 June 2018) <https://thebulletin.org/2018/06/why-the-opcw-should-attribute-responsibility-for-chemical-attacks/> (accessed 21 February 2024).

71 OPCW (2018), *Statement by H.E. Ambassador Sabine Nolke Permanent Representative of Canada to the OPCW at the Fourth Special Session of the Conference of the States Parties* ([illegible]).

72 OPCW (2018), *Statement by France to the Conference of the State Parties* (*French*); OPCW (2018), *Statement by H.E. Ambassador Per Holstrom Permanent Representative of the Kingdom of Sweden to the OPCW at the Fourth Special Session of the Conference of the States Parties* (C-SS-4/NAT.23); OPCW (2018), *Statement by H.E. The Honourable Brett Mason Permanent Representative of Australia to the OPCW at the Fourth Special Session of the Conference of the States Parties* (C-SS-4/NAT.29); OPCW (2018), *Bulgaria: Statement on Behalf of the EU Delivered by Ms. Judit Koromi, Chair of the Working Party on Non-Proliferation (CONOP) of the Council of the EU, European External Action Service, at the CSP-SS-4* (C-SS-4/NAT.5).

73 Only a minority of states voting in favor of Decision C-SS-4/Dec.3 issued statement and the vast majority of those statements remain silent on the questions of legal basis and competencies and instead mainly refer to the political necessity to continue the JIM's work.

74 Orakhelashvili (n 5) 672–676.

75 Ibid., 670.

Abe comments critically on Orakhelashvili, arguing convincingly that the mere fact that the UNSC has a primary responsibility to engage questions of peace and security does not *per se* bar the OPCW from also addressing some aspects of the issue through setting up its own mechanisms, even if it lacks the same enforcement powers of the UNSC.[76] Abe acknowledges the issue of implied powers, yet only problematizes the lacking consent of involved states.[77] However, as argued by Orakhelashvili in another contribution, consent is not an imperative requirement for fact-finding to be lawful.[78] Be that as it may, by solely focusing only on the role of consent in relation to the IIT, Abe omits a deeper discussion of the nature of implied powers invoked to justify the mechanism.

Sossai, who does engage the nature of implied powers more thoroughly, concludes that the identification of perpetrators is implied in the explicit articles of the CWC relating to inspections and specifically takes the mention of paragraph 26 (d) Part XI Verification Annex as evidence of this link.[79] While also noting that Ambassador Üzümcü's statement seems to adhere to inherent powers, Sossai does not further examine whether this adherence to a differing doctrine might be a problematic legal basis.[80] Instead he shows support for the idea that the IIT's creation is further legitimized by past UNSC decisions containing the commitment to hold perpetrators accountable.[81] This argument strikingly conflates state's convictions that there should be accountability with the question of whether the OPCW has the appropriate competencies to act as a forum to deliver that and thereby neglects the core of the argument of critics of the IIT. The fact that the UNSC had the appropriate powers to set up the JIM does by no means serve as an argument that the OPCW has the same powers.

The third scholarly evaluation by Haataja, provides more in-depth discussion of the lawfulness of the decision from a procedural perspective. Yet, when engaging the question of implied powers as a legal basis, it falls short to differ-

---

76 Abe (n 43), 62.

77 Ibid., 61.

78 Alexander Orakhelashvili, 'Commissions of Inquiry and Traditional Mechanisms of Dispute Settlement' in Christian Henderson (ed), *Commissions of Inquiry - Problems and Prospects* (Hart Publishing 2017), 131.

79 Sossai (n 5), 221.

80 Indeed, Sossai appears to follow the position that the ICJ's *Certain Expenses* opinion established inherent powers as the applicable doctrine. This, to some extent, does not take into account later reversals by the Court in *Legality of Use of Nuclear Weapons* (*WHO*) and by the CJEU in *ECHR* and *Tobacco Advertising*.

81 Sossai (n 5), 222.

entiate between diverging iterations of the concept and pre-supposes that an act is legal as long as it is rooted in the intention of the drafters.[82] While falling in line with the ICJ's wider conceptions, namely *Effects of Awards* and *Certain Expenses*, this wide definition of implied powers overlooks the narrower positions taken in *Greco-Turkish Agreement, Legality of Use of Nuclear Weapons* (*WHO*), and the CJEU's *ECHR* and *Tobacco Advertising* decisions, that require a direct link to explicit provisions, instead of the general purpose of the convention.

7 The IIT under Different Concepts of Power

In light of the conflicting positions by proponents of the IIT regarding its legal basis, the continued criticism by other states of the lack of clarity thereof, and an academic *lacuna* on the specific issue of the legality of the decision depending on the respective concept of power, the following presents an evaluation of the IIT in light of the differing doctrines.

If one were to follow the doctrine of inherent powers, referred to by Ambassador Üzümcü and the German statement, the OPCW would have a very wide margin of discretion in creating new mechanisms. Indeed, the CWC does not explicitly prohibit the creation of attribution mechanisms. Moreover, attribution can most certainly contribute to the general purpose of prohibiting chemical weapons use by identifying violators and consequently the decision to establish the IIT would be well within the competencies. Nonetheless the inherent powers doctrine, as described above, does not enjoy academic adoption beyond some voices and was arguable abandoned by jurisprudence. Additionally, state positions seeking to link to actual provisions in the Convention as well as vehement opposition to any insinuation of implied powers in a different context by the UK as the main drafter,[83] inevitably lead to the conclusion that inherent powers cannot be an appropriate basis to establish the legality of decision C-SS-4/Dec.3.

Instead, the most appropriate framework would be a narrow reading of implied powers, following the most recent jurisprudence combined with aspects of Judge Hackworth and Judge Quintana's dissenting opinions. For acts to be *intra vires* under this narrow conception, the implied power needs to be directly necessary to attain an explicit objective in the constituent document, link to an attributed power, and do not vary or supplant such express powers.

82 Haataja (n 5), 52.
83 Engström (n 8), 222.

While there may be sufficient link between an attribution mechanism and the objective of ensuring compliance with the CWC, it is highly questionable whether the creation of the IIT is necessary to attain this objective. Direct necessity requires that all less intrusive options have been exhausted and since neither consultation under article IX (3–7) CWC, nor a challenge inspection under article IX (8–25) CWC have taken place,[84] it appears that the creation of the IIT was not necessary, at least at this point in time.[85] Apart from this, the decision does not adequately satisfy the second criterium, the link to an attributed power. The reference to article VIII, which relates to the general powers of different OPCW organs and their role in implementing the Convention stands in contrast with principle of *lex specialis.* Since there already are specific provisions on investigations provided in article IX, the decision refers to the wrong powers by only citing the more general competencies of the organization. Lastly, the decision to establish an attribution mechanism also violates the principle that acts based on implied powers shall not vary or supplant explicit powers. Since article IX CWC and Part XI Verification Annex provide for explicit and detailed procedures to investigate potential non-compliance, subverting these by establishing a new mechanism with differing configurations does supplant the expressed powers to inspect alleged use of chemical weapons. The United States, in a statement at the Special Session, even expressed that the Convention should adapt to remain relevant.[86] Yet, such an adaptation, at least under a narrow conception of implied powers, must not result in the alteration of existing explicit provisions.[87] Decision

84 It is certainly plausible to argue that the Syria's non-compliance made it obvious that consultations would be fruitless; thus, this is not a necessary precondition. However, a challenge inspection would have most certainly provided for a strong measure, less intrusive than the creation of a new mechanism, which has not been explored.

85 This does not preclude the creation of an ad hoc mechanism after the challenge inspection has proven insufficient but requires to at least attempt the conventional measures first. Similar concerns were voiced by Brazil in their national statement. See: OPCW (2018), *Statement by Ambassador Regina Maria Cordeiro Dunlop Representative of Brazil at the Fourth Special Session of the Conference of the States Parties* (C-SS-4/NAT.2).

86 OPCW (2018), *Statement by the Honorable John Sullivan, Deputy Secretary of State of the United States of America, at the Fourth Special Session of the Conference of the States Parties* (C-SS-4/NAT.6), p. 1.

87 Indeed several states opposing the decision argued that the alteration is so fundamental, it requires a treaty amendment under article XV CWC, as discussed further below. See: OPCW (2018), *Statement by Mr. G.V. Kalamanov Head of the Delegation of the Russian Federation on the Results of the Vote on the British Draft Decision at the Fourth Special Session of the Conference of the States Parties* (C-SS-4/NAT.42), p. 1; OPCW (2018), *Statement by Ambassador Fernando Bucheli Permanent Representative of the Republic of Ecuador to the OPCW at the Fourth Special Session of the Conference of the States Parties*

C-SS-4/Dec.3 therefore does not appear necessary to achieve an explicit objective of the Convention, does not sufficiently link to an attributed power, and even supplants existing attributed powers, rendering it *ultra vires* under a narrow reading of implied powers.

Even if one were to accept a wider conception of implied powers, as applied by Sossai and Haataja, the legality of the decision still remains questionable. This wider variant of implied powers builds mainly on the ICJ opinions in *Reparation for Injuries* and *Effect of Awards* as well as the CJEU *Fedechar* decision and *Laying-up Fund* opinion and relies on an *effet utile* conception, only requiring a lose link to attributed powers (in contrast to a direct link under the narrow conception) and a general necessity for the functioning of the organization to achieve a specific object and purpose of the Convention (in contrast to direct necessity under the narrow concept).[88] The link between the implied power to establish an attribution mechanism to an explicit power can be seen in the mention of paragraph 26 Part XI Verification Annex.[89] Through this link to conventional investigations and thus to powers derived from article IX CWC, the decision is justifiably grounded in a necessity to identify perpetrators to achieve the object and purpose of the convention.[90] Yet, the question remains is attribution of responsibility does indeed contribute to a specific object of the Convention – a simple reference to the broad purpose to prohibit chemical weapons use is not sufficient in this context.[91] The specific purpose of article IX CWC and investigations under the CWC in general is to ensure compliance with the Convention.[92] Importantly, this focus on compliance and rebuilding confidence, as contained in the Convention, must be differentiated from attributing responsibility to perpetrators, which was specifically the drafters intention when conceiving the specific object of investigations.[93] In contrast to a compliance-logic, at the core, the IIT follows a logic of achiev-

Explanation of Vote (C-SS-4/NAT.52), p. 1; OPCW (2018), *Statement by H.E. Ambassador Haifa Aissami Madah Permanent Representative of Bolivarian Republic of Venezuela to the OPCW at the Fourth Special Session of the Conference of the States Parties* (C-SS-4/NAT.53), p. 2.

88 This wider conception arguably ignores limitations introduced by later jurisprudence in *Legality of Use of Nuclear Weapons* (*WHO*), *ECHR* and *Tobacco Advertising* and does not sufficiently engage with the logically convincing criteria introduced by Judge Hackworth and Judge Quintana in their dissenting opinions.

89 Sossai (n 5), 221.

90 Haataja (n 5), 52.

91 ECJ (1977), *Laying-up Fund*, paras 3, 4.

92 Art. IX (9) CWC.

93 Marauhn (n 30), 325.

ing accountability by attributing responsibility to specific actors and more importantly by preparing for individual criminal responsibility of perpetrators.[94] Concludingly, attributing responsibility can be seen as a step towards ensuring compliance but there remains an undeniable divergence in focus between Convention's cooperative approach and the IIT's confrontative nature. This is also exemplified by national statements of proponents of the decision expressly referring to attaining individual accountability instead of compliance and trust,[95] as well as in the fact that the decision foresees a cooperation with the *International, Impartial and Independent Mechanism to Assist in the Investigation and Prosecution of Persons Responsible for the Most Serious Crimes under International Law Committed in the Syrian Arab Republic*,[96] a mechanism focused on criminal accountability. Decision C-SS-4/Dec.3 therefore does sufficiently link to an explicit power, i.e. the power to investigate non-compliance, but misses the purpose of this specific part of the Convention and can thus not be regarded as being based on an implied power, even under a wider interpretation of the concept. Frustration over Syria's sustained non-compliance is understandable from a political and moral perspective but should not lead to an unconsensual re-interpretation of the CWC's original spirit.

A comprehensive evaluation of different conceptions of powers is necessary to adequately discuss the legality of Decision C-SS-4/Dec.3 and the subsequent creation of the IIT but has been absent in existing literature. As shown above, the Decision can only be considered *intra vires* if the concept of inherent powers is applied. Since this concept is rejected by states, recent jurisprudence and the majority of scholarly opinion, this cannot serve as a satisfactory basis. Under a narrow conception of implied powers, that takes into account the most recent jurisprudence of the ICJ and CJEU, as well as pertinent dissenting opinions by judges in previous decisions, the decision fails to comply with all three criteria of direct necessity to attain explicit objective, sufficient link to an attributed power, and not varying or supplanting expressed powers. Even under a wider reading of implied powers, the Decision arguably constitutes an act *ultra vires* as it misconstrues the object of investigations under the CWC from re-establishing compliance to achieving accountability.

94 Aloklah (n 63) 556; Sossai (n 5), 212.

95 OPCW (2018), *Statement by H.E. Mr Kevin Kelly Ambassador of Ireland to the Kingdom of the Netherlands at the Fourth Special Session of the Conference of the States Parties* (C-SS-4/NAT.7); OPCW (2018), *Germany* (C-SS-4/NAT.9).

96 OPCW (2018) (C-SS-4/DEC.3), para 12.

8 Looking Back to Look Forward

A bit over five years after the IIT was created and with emerging calls to consider more formalized mechanisms for investigation and attribution, an honest appraisal is necessary. The IIT has undoubtedly provided for immense benefits in conducting professional investigations, presenting convincing evidence of crimes by the Syrian Government and ISIL. However, in order to maintain a system driven by the rule of law, legal scholars must also be critical of the legal basis of any decision, even if the outcome is as helpful in achieving accountability as the IIT certainly is. Decision C-SS-4/DEC.3 was drafted as a reaction to the collapse of the JIM and geopolitical circumstances, such as the UK's desire to show resolve in the wake of chemical weapons use on its territory in Salisbury. This desire to transplant the JIM into the OPCW has resulted in proponents of the decision being ambiguous or even negligent about the legal foundation of such an act.

In hindsight, it there would have been several approaches that would have carried more legitimacy, which are shortly presented in order to close the argument by suggesting some lessons to be drawn when looking forward. A first and most clear option would have been to initiate a challenge inspection of Syria, according to the provisions laid out in the Convention. This would have provided many similar tools to the way of working of the IIT, without raising concerns about necessity and the need to invoke implied powers. In case the challenge inspection would have proven insufficient, then it would have at least shown that all attributed powers have been exhausted and thereby providing a much more convincing case to invoke additional measures under implied powers. Secondly, the CWC contains the possibility to request an Advisory Opinion by the ICJ.[97] The Court could have been requested to opine on whether the OPCW does indeed hold powers to establish an attribution mechanism, providing legal clarity and, in case the Court finds such an act within the powers of the OPCW, once and for all refute the lingering critique of states that oppose the IIT altogether.[98] Lastly, the establishment of an attribution function could have been introduced as a treaty amendment under article XV CWC. This would have unquestionably provided for a future proof the legal basis, not only in the case of Syria but also for potential other cases. However, this avenue was and still is admittedly rather unrealistic, since such an amendment would require consensus, which is unattainable in light

---

97 Art. XIV (5) CWC.

98 A similar suggestion is made by Abe (n 43), 61.

of Syria and Russia's fundamental opposition to ensuring that the prohibition of chemical weapons can be enforced more strongly.

Now looking forward, states sincerely concerned with upholding the CWC, should not make the mistake of seeing the IIT as a precedent that should blindly be followed. Instead, they should use the opportunity to either inquire the ICJ for an assessment of the existing powers to establish an attribution mechanism or just refer back to utilizing the challenge inspection until political realities allow for treaty amendment. An approach that takes seriously the inherent value of a rules based international order should not, even if it is for the sake of a highly preferable step towards accountability, disregard established concepts of powers vested in international organizations.

CHAPTER 10

National Implementation of the Norms against Biological Weapons: An Overview

Barry de Vries

1 Introduction

It is commonly held that the norms against biological weapons are of a customary nature in international law and that these are therefore applicable for every state.[1] However, the fact that states are bound by these norms in the international sphere does not necessarily preclude the possibility of biological weapons being developed or used, especially with regard to non-state actors, as these are not directly bound by the international norms. For these international norms to be of any effect against non-state groups or individuals it is necessary to incorporate them within the national legal system and make them directly applicable to individuals. It has been recognized in international instruments that this is a necessary step in ensuring the protection against biological weapons. This can for example be seen in Art. IV of the Biological Weapons Convention (BWC) or in UN Security Council Resolution 1540.

However, this does not necessarily mean that all states have taken the necessary steps to implement the norms against biological weapons within their national legal system. The issue of implementation has been a recurring discussion point at the BWC Review Conference ([illegible]), for example. An important aspect of this need for implementation is that this necessitates the inclusion of these prohibitions within a state's criminal law, in order to effectively prohibit as well as punish acts related to biological weapons.

Although there has been state-specific research into the issue of implementation and there are processes underway to provide for implementation databases,[2] there is relatively little actual analytical research into the way in which and to what extent states implement the norms against biological weapons.

---

1 Jean-Marie Henckaerts and Louise Doswald-Beck, *Customary International Humanitarian Law Volume I: The Rules* (Cambridge University Press 2012) 256–258.

2 Most notably by UNIDIR and Vertic: Biological Weapons Convention National Implementation Measures Database <https://bwcimplementation.org/>.

 | DOI:10.1163/9789004739192_011

This chapter seeks to at least lessen the gap a little bit by providing a broad overview of some of the more common approaches taken. In order to do this, the chapter will first go over the major international norms against biological weapons and subsequently discuss which international obligations flow from these for states to implement national measures. It will then discuss the most common approaches taken to implement these different international obligations and discuss some of the issues that might exist with such measures. On this basis the chapter will provide an overview of what might be done to improve national implementation as well as pointing out what the main gaps are that should be addressed to ensure an effective network of national prohibitions.

2 The International Norms against Biological Weapons and the Obligation to Implement National Measures

The use of biological agents as a weapon has a long history and examples can be found back into antiquity. Similarly, norms prohibiting their use can also be found referenced throughout history; however, these were generally not strictly legal concepts. It was not until 1925 that an actual international agreement prohibiting the use of biological weapons was adopted within the 1925 Geneva Gas Protocol.[3] This prohibition was restricted to the use of bacteriological agents during war and even in this context was limited due to it only being applicable between the High Contracting Parties as well as many of the states parties making reservations which left the Protocol mainly being a 'no-first-use declaration'.[4] The Protocol did not have any provisions which required states parties to implement this prohibition in their national legal systems.

While the Geneva Gas Protocol prohibited the use of biological weapons in war, it did not address other acts related to biological weapons, leading to the fact that most of the great powers had programmes researching, developing

3 Jean-Pascal Zanders, 'International Norms Against Chemical and Biological Warfare: An Ambiguous Legacy' (2003) 8(2) *Journal of Conflict and Security Law* 396; Dominika Švarc, 'Biological Weapons and Warfare' (Max Planck Encyclopedia of Public International Law 2015) par. 5; William Boothby, *Weapons and the Law of Armed Conflict* (Oxford University Press 2016) 104–105; Bothe (n 10) 251–252.

4 Dan Joyner, *International Law and the Proliferation of Weapons of Mass Destruction* (Oxford University Press 2009)89; Švarc (n 3) par. 12; Boothby (n 3), 111.

and producing biological weapons in subsequent years.[5] This greatly increased the risk of biological weapons actually being used and a broader prohibition was therefore necessary to protect the world from biological weapons. Discussions concerning this broader prohibition ultimately led to the Biological Weapons Convention (BWC) which opened for signature in 1972, which in Article I prohibits States Parties to develop, produce, stockpile or otherwise acquire or retain biological weapons. Although the BWC does not incorporate a prohibition of use and only refers back to the obligations of the Geneva Gas Protocol, the other prohibitions would make it effectively impossible for any state party to use biological weapons. Therefore a later Review Conference held that Art. I BWC is to be interpreted as a comprehensive prohibition, which does include a prohibition of use.[6] The BWC also incorporated an obligation for states parties to implement national measures in Art. IV BWC. This was a first for an international arms control treaty and an acknowledgement that without effective national measures these prohibitions have only limited effectiveness. Art. IV BWC requires states parties to implement 'necessary measures to prohibit and prevent development, production, stockpiling, acquisition or retention of the agents, toxins, weapons, equipment and means of delivery specified in Article I of the Convention, within the territory of such State, under its jurisdiction or under its control anywhere.' The article does not expand on what are considered necessary measures, as this would be too intrusive on the sovereignty of the states parties.[7] The States Parties adopted an expanded interpretation at the Sixth Review Conference of the BWC, which clarified the obligations under Art. IV BWC, which declares that there is a need for adopting these prohibitions within a state parties' penal

5 Una Jakob, 'The Biological Weapons Convention' in Thilo Marauhn & Erik Myjer, *Research Handbook on International Arms Control Law* (Edward Elgar Publishing 2022) 260; Ana Cristina Gallego-Hernández, 'Biological Weapons and Their Incompatibility with IHL' in: Pablo Antonio Fernández-Sánchez, *The Limitations of the Law of Armed Conflict: New Means and Methods of Warfare* (Brill 2022), 60.

6 Final Document – Fourth BWC Review Conference 1996' (BWC/CONF.IV/9), <https://tinyurl.com/bdfjp9n9>, part II, at 15 this has subsequently been consistently reaffirmed. Boothby (n 3) 113; Diego Mauri, 'The Use of CBRN Weapons in Armed Conflict' in: Andrea de Guttry, Micaela Frulli, Frederico Casolari & Ludovica Poli (eds.) *International Law and Chemical, Biological, Radio-Nuclear (CBRN) Events* (Brill 2022), 367.

7 Treasa Dunworth, Robert J. Mathews & Timothy L. H. McCormack, 'National Implementation of the Biological Weapons Convention' (2006) 11 *Journal of Conflict & Security Law* 93, 98; Masahiko Asada, 'Security Council Resolution 1540 to Combat WMD Terrorism: Effectiveness and Legitimacy in International Legislation' (2008) 13 *Journal of Conflict & Security Law* 303, 306–307.

legislation.[8] The scope of the necessary implementing measures is defined by Art. IV BWC, therefore while Art. I BWC has been interpreted by the RevCon to be a comprehensive prohibition, this has not been done for Art IV BWC. Consequently, the national measures only need to address development, production, stockpiling, acquisition or retention and not the use of biological weapons.[9] There have, however, been consistent discussions as to the extent to which states parties actually comply with this obligation and with the BWC not having a compliance mechanism much of the debate is reliant on confidence building measures which states are not legally required to submit.

The next major development with regard to implementing the norms against biological weapons within national legal systems came in 2004, when the UN Security Council adopted Resolution 1540. This resolution came in response to the terrorist threat of the time and information concerning nuclear proliferation by Abdul Qadeer Khan, which underpinned the threat of terrorist WMD proliferation.[10] The most important part of this resolution was its second operative paragraph in which the Security Council decided 'that all States, in accordance with their national procedures, shall adopt and enforce appropriate effective laws which prohibit any non-State actor to manufacture, acquire, possess, develop, transport, transfer or use nuclear, chemical or biological weapons and their means of delivery, in particular for terrorist purposes.' As this resolution was a decision taken by the Security Council under Chapter VII of the UN Charter, all member states are, according to art. 25 UN Charter, legally obligated to implement such measures. While the Resolution clearly has significant overlap with the obligation from Art. IV BWC there are certain ways in which the obligations differ. The scope of Resolution 1540 is in one sense broader, in that it covers some acts that were not included in Art. IV BWC, as it also includes use, financing of activities and transporting. However, the scope of the resolution is significantly narrower with regard to the target of these prohibitions, as it is namely focused on specifically terrorism and therefore requires for these

---

8 'Final Document – Sixth BWC Review Conference 2006' (BWC/CONF.VI/6); Dunworth, Mathews & McCormack (n 7) 99–100.

9 Barry de Vries, 'Recent Developments in the National Implementation of Biological Weapons Convention: What Happened Since Resolution 1540?' 28(3) *JCSL* (2023) 569–592, at 575.

10 Daniel H. Joyner, 'The Security Council as a Legal Hegemon' (2012) 43 *Georgetown Journal of International Law* 225, 227; Ian Andrew Barber, 'U.N. Security Council Resolution 1540: An Exemplary Model for a Framework to Safeguard Dangerous Dams against Sabotage by Nonstate Actors' (2018) 41 *Hastings International & Comparative Law Review* 99, 107.

national measures to be terrorism-focused. As will be shown later the implications of this restrictive scope can clearly be seen in the national measures taken.

The final important international agreement that some states are party to that addresses biological weapons is the recently adopted amendment to the Rome Statute incorporating the use of biological weapons in the list of war crimes of art. 8 ICC Statute. The original Rome Statute did not include biological weapons within the list of war crimes due to the contentious nature of nuclear weapons.[11] At the end of the drafting procedure the compromise was made not to include nuclear weapons but at the same time to also not include chemical and biological weapons. It was, however, immediately recognized by many that this meant that the Rome Statute in some ways was regressive of international customary law and efforts to address this gap were quickly started. While Belgium attempted to have this amendment tabled at the 2010 Kampala Review Conference this was initially unsuccessful. In the period after the Kampala Review Conference Belgium altered their proposed amendment and ultimately a revised amendment was adopted at the 2017 Assembly of States Parties, which defined to be a war crime any act of:

> Employing weapons, which use microbial or other biological agents, or toxins, whatever their origin or method of production.

Identically provisions were included in art. 8(2)(b)(xxvii) and art. 8(2)(e)(xvi) ICC Statute, meaning that this prohibition is applicable in both international and non-international armed conflicts.

Although the Rome Statute does not include an explicit obligation for states parties to implement national measures, the concept of complementarity does provide for a potential indirect obligation. The concept of complementarity means that the ICC cannot exercise its jurisdiction in cases where a state genuinely investigates or prosecutes. Without there being adequate legisla-

11 Philippe Kirsch and John T. Holmes, 'The Rome Conference on an International Criminal Court: The Negotiating Process' 93(1) *The American Journal of International Law* (1999) 2–12, at 4; Mahnoush Arsanjani, 'The Rome Statute of the International Criminal Court' 93 *The American Journal of International Law* (1999) 22–43, at 34; Robert S. Clark, 'Building on Article 8(2)(b)(xx) of the Rome Statute of the International Criminal Court: Weapons and Methods of Warfare' 12(3) *New Criminal Law Review* (2009) 366–389, at 367–368, 371; Annie Golden Bersagel, 'Use of Nuclear Weapons as an International Crime and the Rome Statute of the International Criminal Court' in: Gro Nystuen, Stuart Casey-Maslen & Annie Golden Bersagel (eds.), *Nuclear Weapons under International Law* (Cambridge University Press 2014) 221–244, at 222–223.

tion allowing for the investigation or prosecution a state will be unable to carry these out, therefore if a state wants to preclude the jurisdiction of the ICC it is required to implement the Statute and potential amendments.[12] As will be shown, several states that have ratified this amendment have felt themselves obligated under this concept to implement national measures. While it is likely that more states will ratify this amendment in the near future, at the time of writing only 18 states have done so.[13]

Consequently, there is no direct obligation to prohibit the use of biological weapons within national criminal law, with the exception of specific contexts, such as terrorism or armed conflict, the latter only for those that have ratified the amendment to the Rome Statute.

3 National Implementation

3.1 *Implementation of the BWC*

The longest standing obligation to implement national legislation can be found in Art. IV BWC and although not all states have implemented the BWC in their national legislation, a significant amount of states parties do have legislation addressing some or all of the requirements of Art. IV BWC. There have been a few different main approaches in how states have incorporated penal provisions for the acts mentioned in Art. IV BWC. Some have opted to incorporate the penal provisions within broader legislation implementing the whole of the BWC. In many states this implementing legislation consists mainly of the translation of the BWC into national law, which is then supplemented through inclusion of criminal sanctions for violations of prohibited acts.[14] The fact that this is often an almost literal translation of large sections

12 Ovo Catherine Imoedemhe, *The Complementarity Regime of the International Criminal Court* (Springer 2017) 55–57; Olympia Bekou, 'National Implementation of the ICC Statute to Prosecute International Crimes in Africa' in: Charles Chernor Jalloh & Ilias Bantekas, *The International Criminal Court and Africa* (Oxford University Press 2017) 272; Steven Freeland, 'It's a Good Idea … Isn't It? The Impact of Complementarity at the International Criminal Court on Domestic Law, Politics and Perceptions of Sovereignty' in: Marlene Wind (ed.) *International Courts and Domestic Politics* (Cambridge University Press 2018) 93; Eithne Dowds, *Feminist Engagement with International Criminal Law* (Bloomsbury 2021), 62.

13 United Nations, 'Treaty Series Online' (Treaty Series) <https://tinyurl.com/8s2xx37t> (accessed 12 May 2024). <https://treaties.un.org/Pages/ViewDetails.aspx?src=TREATY&mtdsg_no=XVIII-10-d&chapter=18&clang=_en>.

14 This is, for example, the case in Belgium (Art. 2 Wet houdende goedkeuring van het Verdrag tot verbod van de ontwikkeling, de produktie en de aanleg van voorraden van

of the BWC also ensures that the implementation of criminal sanctions generally comply with the requirements of Art. IV BWC.

A second commonly seen approach to criminalization of the acts mentioned in art. IV BWC is through the inclusion of specific provisions within the existing criminal code specifically addressing the development, production, stockpiling, acquisition and retention of biological weapons specifically,[15] or weapons of mass destruction in a general sense.[16] Other states have similar types of provisions, however, incorporated these in their arms and ammunition legislation instead of their criminal code.[17]

However, there are other manners in which states have addressed this issue as well. Another less common approach is to develop legislation addressing a cluster of weapons, such as for example South Korea having a single legislation

---

bacteriologische (biologische) en toxinewapens en inzake de vernietiging van deze wapens, opgemaakt te Londen, Moskou en Washington op 10 april 1972, 06 July 1979), the Czech Republic (Zákon o některých opatřeních souvisejících se zákazem bakteriologických (biologických) a toxinových zbraní a o změně živnostenského zákona 28.06.2002), Japan (Art. 10 Law on Implementing the Convention on the Prohibition of the Development, Production and Stockpiling of Bacteriological (Biological) and Toxin Weapons and on Their Destruction and the Other Conventions, 8 June 1982 revised 16 December 2001) and Latvia (Section 73 Krimināllikums, Latvijas Vēstnesis, 199/200, 08.07.1998). For other examples see: Section 10 Republic of Trinidad and Tobago, Act No. 4 of 2012 Act to give effect to the Convention on the Prohibition of the Development, Production and Stockpiling of Bacteriological (Biological) and Toxin Weapons and on their Destruction, Act No. 7948, 28 Apr. 2006; Section 2 Ireland, Biological Weapons Act 2011, No. 13 of 2011; Art. 24 Slovakia, 218 ACT of 28 March 2007 on the Prohibition of Biological Weapons and on Amendments and Supplements to Certain Acts; Art. 8–9 Serbia, Law on the ban on the development, production and stockpiling of bacteriological (biological) and toxic weapons and on their destruction "Official Gazette of [illegible]

15 See for example art. 566 of the Spanish Penal Code (Ley Orgánica 10/1995, de 23 de noviembre, del Código Penal, Texto Consolidado 13 de julio de 2022, Boletín Oficial del Estado); Art. 167(3) Turkmenistan Jenaýat Kodeksi; Art. 562 LOI N° 2015–10 du 24 novembre 2015 portant nouveau code penal; Art. 406 Criminal Code of the Kyrgyz Republic, 28 October 2021, no. 127; Article 195 Criminal Code of the Republic of Tajikistan, as amended by Law of the Republic of Tajikistan dated 17.05.2004 and Law No. 35, dated 13.06.2013 No. 966; Art, 282c Albania ligjin nr. 135/2015, date 5.12.2015.

16 This can be seen in for example Russia (Art. 355 The Criminal Code of the Russian Federation No. 63-FZ of June 1996) and Georgia (Art. 406 Criminal Code, LHG, 41(48), 13/08/1999).

17 Examples include: Art. 112, 120 Guatamala Ley de Armas y Municiones, Decreto Número 15–2009; Par. 5 Denmark, Bekendtgørelse af lov om våben og eksplosivstoffer m.v. LBK nr 1736 af 26/08/2021; Art. 90 Cabo Verde, Lei de Armas e Munições Lei No. 31/VIII/2013; Art. 15 Cameroon, Loi No. 2016/015 du 14 Dec. 2016 Portant Regime General des Armes et Munitions au Cameroun.

for both chemical and biological weapons,[18] India's Weapons of Mass Destruction and their Delivery Systems Act[19] and Cambodia's Law on the Prohibition of Chemical, Nuclear, Biological and Radiological Weapons.[20]

In most instances where there has been a deliberate effort to incorporate the BWC within the national legal system the resulting legislation does comply with the requirements of Art. IV BWC and would be able to address any act related to biological weapons, except of use, in any circumstance. However, while many states have done so, this has certainly not been the case for all states parties to the BWC and further progress should still be made to ensure a comprehensive international framework of these national prohibitions to ensure full implementation of the BWC and thereby reduce the threat of biological weapons.

3.2 *Resolution 1540*

Resolution 1540 is binding on all members of the UN and many states have adopted legislation seeking to implement the resolution. As general implementing legislation of Art. IV BWC would not address the whole of the resolution this has even been the case in those states that already had implementing legislation in place for the BWC. At the same time there have also been several states that have implemented this resolution rather than the BWC, which is not sufficient to ensure compliance with Art. IV BWC.

The resolution has been incorporated in most states in one of two ways, either through amending their criminal legislation to include terrorism-related offences[21] or by adopting specific counter-terrorism legislation.[22] As these provisions generally address more than just acts related to biological weapons it should be considered how they incorporate biological weapons. Many states included acts related to biological weapons, such as manufactur-

18 Art. 4–2, 25 Republic of Korea, Act on the Prohibition of Chemical and Biological Weapons and the Control of the Production, Export, and Import of Specific Chemicals and Biological Agents.

19 Section 8, 14 India, The Weapons of Mass Destruction and Their Delivery Systems (Prohibition of Unlawful Activities) Act, Act No. 21 of 2005.

20 Art. 7 Cambodia, Law on the Prohibition of Chemical, Nuclear, Biological and Radiological Weapons, 3 December 2009.

21 See for example: Art. 96 Lesotho Penal Code Act 2010; Art. 328A Malta Criminal Code (Amendment) Act, Act No. VI of 06 June 2005.

22 Such as for example: Art. 16, 20 Tunisia, Loi organique n° 2015–26 du 7 août 2015, relative à la lutte contre le terrorisme et à la répression du blanchiment d'argent; Art. 3 Sri Lanka, Regulations made by the Minister of Foreign Affairs under Section 2 of the United Nations Act, No. 45 of 1968, 4 October 2017; Art. 32(3)(a), 33(1)(a) Romania, LEGE nr. 535 din 25 noiembrie 2004 privind prevenirea și combaterea terorismului.

ing, developing or using, as acts that could fall within the definition of terrorist acts.[23] Other states addressed it through including biological weapons under their definition of 'weapon' or 'lethal device' and prohibit the proliferation of these through prohibiting providing, stockpiling or possessing of weapons in different terroristic contexts.[24]

These forms of legislation generally require acts to be committed with a specific intent for them to fall within the definition of terrorist acts.[25] While terrorist intent is not uniformly defined in all states, the definitions generally revolve around two specific requirements, namely (1) that the acts is done with the intent to incite fear or intimidation and (2) that it is intended to compel a government or international organisations to act or refrain from acting.[26]

---

23 This can be seen in many states, such as: Art. 3 Mauritania Loi n°2010–035 du 21 Juillet 2010 Abrogeant et Remplaçant la loi n°2005–047 du 26 Juillet 2005 relative à la Lutte contre le Terrorisme; Art. 96 Lesotho Penal Code Act 2010; Art. 328A Malta Criminal Code (Amendment) Act, Act No. VI of 06 June 2005; Art. 5 Cyprus O περί της Καταπολέμησης της Τρομοκρατίας και Προστασίας των Θυμάτων Νόμος του 2019, Αριθμός 75(I) του 2019.

24 Art. 2(1) Republic of Kenya, The Prevention of Terrorism Act, No. 30 of 2012; Art. 13, Art. 40 Republic of Ghana, Anti-Terrorism Act 2008, 10 October 2008; Art. 13 Eswatini, Act to provide for the detection, suppression and deterrence of terrorism and for punishment of all forms of terrorist acts and persons engaged in terrorist acts in compliance with the Conventions and Resolutions of the United Nations, Bill No. 5 of 2008.

25 Examples include: Section 10 Vanuatu Counter Terrorism and Transnational Organised Crime Act 29 of 2005, Laws of the Republic of Vanuatu Consolidated Edition 2006 Chapter 313; Section 16 Samoa, Act to Repeal the Prevention and Suppression of Terrorism Act 2002 and to implement United Nations Security Council Resolutions and Conventions dealing with terrorism, 7 April 2014; Art. 328A(2)(f) Malta Criminal Code ([illegible]) [illegible] République du Benin, Loi No. 2018–16 portant code pénal, 4 June 2018; Art. 13, 16 Eswatini, Act to provide for the detection, suppression and deterrence of terrorism and for punishment of all forms of terrorist acts and persons engaged in terrorist acts in compliance with the Conventions and Resolutions of the United Nations, Bill No. 5 of 2008; art. 32(3)(a), 33(1)(a) Romania, LEGE nr. 535 din 25 noiembrie 2004 privind prevenirea şi combaterea terorismului; Art. 96(c)(vi) Lesotho Penal Code Act 2010; Art. 2 Bahrain, law no. 58 of 2006 with respect to protection of the community against terrorist acts; Section 1(2)(c)(iv) Nigeria Terrorism (Prevention) Act, Act. No. 10 2011; Section 13 Republic of Ghana, Anti-Terrorism Act 2008, 10 October 2008; Art. 36, 37, 39 Saudi Arabia, Law of Combating Crimes of Terrorism and its Financing, Royal Decree No. M/21 1 November 2017; art. 12 Seychelles, Prevention of Terrorism Act 2004, Act 7 of 2004.

26 Section 3(1)(ix) Samoa, Act to Repeal the Prevention and Suppression of Terrorism Act 2002 and to implement United Nations Security Council Resolutions and Conventions dealing with terrorism, 7 April 2014; Art. 1 United Arab Emirates Federal Law No. 7 2014/08/20 (government translation); Art. 328A(1) Malta Criminal Code (Amendment) Act,

This need for a specific intent makes these forms of legislation too restrictive to be sufficient for implementation of the BWC, as it only criminalizes these acts in these specific contexts and cannot be used to criminalize such behaviour outside of such contexts.

3.3 *Rome Statute*

There are currently only 23 states that have ratified the amendment to the Rome Statute incorporating the use of biological weapons in art. 8 ICC Statute and while there is not a direct obligation for states to implement the criminal provisions of the Rome Statute in their national legislation, it can be determined whether the amendment did have an influence on domestic criminal law. It must first be stated that for a majority of these states there was no direct influence of the amendment on their national legislation. For most of the states where there was no influence this was due to the fact that these states already had provisions within their criminal law specifically addressing the use of biological weapons in armed conflicts.[27] Several other states have thus far not incorporated the prohibition on using biological weapons in armed conflicts even after ratifying the amendment.[28] However, there were also several states that implemented legislation after the adoption of the amendment and in conjunction with their ratification, where they also indicate that it is their view that they are obligated in light of the ratification to incorporate these provisions in their national legislation.[29] An interesting view can be

---

Act No. VI of 06 June 2005; Art. 161, Republique du Benin, Loi No. 2018–16 portant code pénal, 4 June 2018; Section 2 Eswatini, Act to provide for the detection, suppression and deterrence of terrorism and for punishment of all forms of terrorist acts and persons engaged in terrorist acts in compliance with the Conventions and Resolutions of the United Nations, Bill No. 5 of 2008; Art. 1 Romania, LEGE nr. 535 din 25 noiembrie 2004 privind prevenirea şi combaterea terorismului.

27 Czech Republic (Par. 411 Zákon trestní zákoník); Slovakia (Par. 426(1)(a) Trestný Zákon); Norway (Paragraph 107 Lov om Straff (Straffeloven)); Uruguay (Modificacion Al Codigo Penal. Estatuto De Roma De La Corte Penal Internacional. Genocidio. Crimenes De Lesa Humanidad. Crimenes De Guerra); Switzerland (Bundesgesetz über die Änderung von Bundesgesetzen zur Umsetzung des Römer Statuts des Internationalen Strafgerichtshofs); Sweden (Lag (2014:406) om straff för vissa internationella brott).

28 Mexico and Romania.

29 Netherlands (Wet Internationale Misdrijven); Luxembourg (Loi du 29 mars 2019 portant approbation des amendements à l'article 8 du Statut de Rome de la Cour pénale internationale adoptés le 14 décembre 2017 par l'Assemblée des États Parties au Statut de Rome de la Cour pénale internationale, lors de sa 12ème séance plénière, à New York, et portant modification de l'article 136quater du Code penal); New Zealand (section 4(2) of the International Crimes and International Criminal Court Amendment Act 2020 (2020 No 39)).

seen in the argumentation of Liechtenstein and Germany. Both these states have provisions categorizing the use of biological weapons as a possible war crime, however, did not do so in light of the adopted amendment to the Rome Statute but rather through a reading of the Art. 8(2)(b)(xviii) ICC Statute, arguing that biological weapons already fall within the concept of 'asphyxiating, poisonous or other gases and all analogous liquids, materials or devices'. While this is not the general interpretation of this article, both Liechtenstein and Germany argued that this required them to include the use of biological weapons in armed conflicts as a war crime in their domestic legislation.[30] This development clearly shows the importance of the inclusion of biological weapons in the Rome Statute as a motivator for states to take action on this issue, as can be seen that from the 18 states that have ratified the amendment only two have no adequate legislation addressing the use of biological weapons in armed conflicts.

3.4 *General Prohibitions on Use*

As discussed previously outside of the specific contexts of terrorism, in Resolution 1540, and armed conflicts, for those states that have ratified the amendment to the Rome Statute, there is no obligation for states to implement prohibitions of use within their national legal system. The prohibition against use is, however, commonly recognized as customary international law and is commonly regarded as one of the most important norms against biological weapons.

An aspect that becomes very clear is how in most states there is a clear distinction between the prohibition of use and other prohibitions. Although there is a small minority of states that address use and other acts similarly,[31] the vast majority of states separates the prohibitions of use from proliferation-centred acts.[32]

The way in which states do prohibit use is not uniform among all states; however, there are certain specific approaches that are seen more commonly

30 Bericht und Antrag der Regierung an den Landtag des Fürstentums Liechtenstein Betreffend Die Abänderung des Strafgesetzbuches, Der Strafprozessordnung, des Gesetzes Über die Zusammenarbeit mit dem Internationalen Strafgerichtshof und Anderen Internationalen Gerichten sowie des Naturschutzgesetzes Nr. 90/2018, 257; Gesetzentwurf der Bundesregierung, Entwurf eines Gesetzes zur Einführung des Völkerstrafgesetzbuches, Deutscher Bundestag Drucksache 14/8524, 35.

31 Examples include Namibia, South Africa, Sri Lanka.

32 Most of the examples fall within this, among them are, for example: Armenia, Belgium, Benin, Cameroon, Canada, Dominican Republic, Luxembourg, Malta, Monaco the Netherlands, New Zealand, Russia, the United Kingdom, the United States.

than others. The first of the more common approaches is through specific provisions within a state's penal code prohibiting the use of weapons. These can be formulated in different ways, one common approach is by referring to weapons prohibited either by international law[33] or a treaty to which the State is party.[34] Another way is the explicit mention of biological weapons, or through prohibiting the use of weapons of mass destruction.[35]

Outside of these types of provisions the most commonly found way in which the use of biological agents can be prosecuted is through the inclusion of a provision in the criminal code regarding the intentional or negligent spreading of disease. These provisions are generally older provisions and were not originally intended to address biological weapons, it is therefore often the case that while these provisions can address some potential uses of biological weapons, they do not cover the whole range of biological weapons. This can especially be seen in the fact that these provisions are commonly restricted to a specific set of targets. Many of these provisions are specifically focused on spreading diseases to humans[36] or have specific pro-

33 Such as Bosnia and Herzegovina (Art. 193a Krivični Zakon Federacije Bosne i Hercegovine) Poland (Art. 120 Poland Kodeks karny, 6 czerwca 1997 as amended).

34 Such provisions can be found for example in Belarus (Art. 134 Уголовный Кодекс Республики Беларусь 9 июля 1999 г. № 275-З), Kyrgyzstan (Art. 406 Criminal Code of the Kyrgyz Republic dated October 28, 2021 No. 127), Russia (Art. 356 Russian Criminal Code No. 63-FZ of 13 June 1996 as amended) Ukraine (Art. 439 Criminal Code of Ukraine 5 April 2001 as amended) Spain (Art. 566(2) Spain Código Penal Ley Orgánica 10/1995) Hungary (Art. 155 and art. 326 Hungary 2012. évi C. törvény a Büntető Törvénykönyvről) and Moldova (Art. 140 Republic of Moldova Codului Penal, Nr. 872-III 6 septembrie 2002 as amended).

35 This is for example the case in Rwanda (Art. 680 Rwanda Organic Law Instituting the Penal Code No. 01/2012/OL), Andorra (Article 266, Andorra, Llei 9/2005, del 21 de febrer qualificada del Codi Penal) Tajikistan (Art. 399 Criminal Code of the Republic of Tajikistan, as amended) Colombia (Art. 367 Codigo Penal Colobiano, Ley 599 de 25 juli 2000, as amended), Norway (Art. 142 Norway Lov om straff, Lov-2005-20-28 as amended) San Marino (Art. 337 quater san Marino, Legge 25 febbraio 1974 nr 17 Emanazione del Nuovo Codice Penale as amended) Uzbekistan (Art. 255 Uzbekistan Jinoyat Kodeksi as amended) Panama (Art. 7 Panama Ley 14 de 30 de octubre de 1990 Por la cual se desarrolla el Artículo 307 de la Constitución Política, se modifican algunos Artículos del Código Fiscal y se dictan otras disposiciones).

36 Such as Austria (Art. 178 Österreich Strafgesetzbuch, Fassung vom 19.06.2022), Cook Islands (Art. 223 Cook Islands Crimes Act 1969), Brunei (Art. 270–271, Penal Code Chapter 22 Consolidated Laws of Brunei 216 Revised Edition), Pakistan (Art. 270 The Pakistan penal Code 1860 as amended), Nepal (Art. 104 Nepal The National Penal (Code) Act 2017).

visions for animals and humans.[37] It is far less common for states to have provisions specifically addressing or even including the spreading of diseases or pests to plant life.[38] Consequently, it would be impossible in most states that rely on spreading of disease provisions to address all potential biological weapons use, as the common definition of biological weapons includes all biological weapons, regardless of intended targets.

These are the most common approaches; however, there are many other approaches that have been taken, such as for example classifying the use of biological weapons as releasing dangerous materials[39] or incorporating it within legislation setting up authorization regimes for the use of biological agents.[40] However, while these are the most common even within these there is large divergence on the exact way in which they are implemented.

Overall, it can clearly be seen that there is significantly more divergence in the approaches taken to prohibiting the use of biological weapons than can be found with regard to legislation criminalizing acts in Art. IV BWC, UN SC Resolution 1540 and the amendment to the Rome Statute. However, it is also clear that there appears to be a majority of states that have provisions that criminalize at least aspects of biological weapons use regardless of whether there is an international obligation to do so. This shows that the taboo against

---

37 Examples of these include: Kenya (Art. 186 and 341 Kenya Penal Code Revised Edition 2012), Sao Tome and Principe (Art. 337, 338 São Tomé E Príncipe Código Penal Lei 6/2012), Seychelles (Art. 176 and 327 Seychelles The Penal Code 1 February 1955 as amended), Malawi (art. 192 and 346 Malawi Penal Code as amended), Tanzania (Art. 179 and 328 United Republic of Tanzania Penal Code 28 September 1945 as amended), Uganda (Art. 171, 337 Uganda Penal Code Act 15 June 1950 as amended).

38 These include Angola (Art. 284 Angola, Lei No 38/20 de 11 de Novembro 2020), Chile (Art. 289 Chile Codigo Penal Versión – 12-OCT-2022), Eritrea (Art. 264 2015 Penal Code of the [illegible] Brottsbalken) Ethiopia (Art. 517–518 Criminal Code of the Federal Democratic Republic of Ethiopia May 2005), Mongolia (Art. 19.6 Mongolia Criminal Law 3 December 2015 as amended), Libya (Art. 362 Libya Penal Code 1953 as amended), Somalia (Art. 388 Somali Xeerka Ciqaabta, Legislative Decree No. 5 of 1962 as amended).

39 Such as China (Art. 114–115 Criminal Law of the People's Republic of China), Azerbaijan (Art. 248 Azərbaycan Respublikasinin cinayət məcəlləsi), Costa Rica (Art. 1(2)(c) Ley de Fortalecimiento de la Legislación contra el Terrorismo, No. 8719 de 4 de marzo de 2009) and the Netherlands (Art. 173, 173a Nederlands Wetboek van Strafrecht 3 Maart 1881 as amended).

40 These include Canada (Human Pathogens and Toxins Act) Thailand (Pathogens and Animal Toxins Act BE 2258(2015)) Denmark (Lov om sikring af visse biologiske stoffer, fremføringsmidler og relateret materiale, LOV nr 474 af 17/06/2008; Bekendtgørelse om ændring af bekendtgørelse om sikring af visse biologiske stoffer, fremføringsmidler og relateret materiale BEK nr 1159 af 22/11/2019) Singapore (Biological Agents and Toxins Act 2005 (No. 36 of 2005)).

biological weapons is strong and that there is a clear commonly held understanding that biological weapons are an issue and should be addressed. This indicates that the lack of implementation of the other instruments is not due to an objection to the general norm against biological weapons or potentially even towards disagreeing with the standards set in the international obligation. It appears as though the lack of implementation could far more likely be caused by a lack of expertise, ability or resources to implement the international standards effectively and adequately. This understanding can be used to develop strategies and approaches to assist and further progress the national implementation.

4 Conclusions

As shown, many states have developed provisions to incorporate criminal offences for acts related to biological weapons; however, a large segment of states do not address all aspects. While many states have implemented penal sanctions compliant with Art. IV BWC, there are also states that have not done so but have instead only implemented legislation in the context of other obligations, such as UN Security Council Resolution 1540 or the amendment of the Rome Statute. This obviously means that there is still significant work to be done to ensure a comprehensive international framework of national legislation implementing the BWC, because without such national legislation it is more difficult to ensure compliance within a state with obligations from the BWC. Although the implementation of these other obligations is a step in the right direction, they do not address the whole of the scope of Article IV, which can be seen in the fact that multiple states that have implemented terrorism-related legislation, which does not cover the full scope of the BWC.[41] Such particular implementation only addresses the obligations included in resolution 1540 specifically and focus on terrorism in this form of legislation runs counter to a comprehensive implementation of the BWC.

This obviously raises the question as to why states implement some norms more readily than other norms. It might be easy to assume that the lack of a compliance mechanism in the BWC and the lack of a legal obligation to participate in the confidence building mechanisms is the reason why states do not implement their obligations under Article IV BWC; however, this is likely not the only or even the most pressing reason. The reason why this might be

41 De Vries (n 9) 580–586.

assumed not to be the sole factor is that the majority of states do have criminal provisions addressing the use of biological weapons and while in many states this might not be entirely comprehensive and might not be specifically developed for use in the context of biological weapons, it is noteworthy that the majority of states do have these provisions even though there is not an international obligation to incorporate this through national measures. This is, first of all, a clear indication that the taboo against the use of biological weapons is very widely shared and that even in the absence of such an international obligation there is a common understanding that any such acts are prohibited. But what is more, it also seems to indicate that a hesitation to implement measures against biological weapons, as those required by the BWC, might not be due to a lack of agreement on the underlying taboo but is more likely due to other factors.

There are different factors that need to be considered in this regard. It is noticeable that the majority of states that do not have any adequate legislation can be found in the Global South, which is likely due to two major factors. The first of these is that in many of these states there is a potential lack of resources and expertise to develop the necessary legislation. Over time it has become clear that through support several states have developed relevant legislation, especially within the context of Resolution 1540. The other major factor is that many of the states that do not have relevant legislation lack a significant bio-industry. This leads to the notion in some of these states that legislation specifically addressing these aspects is less necessary. This can also further exacerbate the lack of resources on the matter, as this will create a situation where a government is unwilling to expend resources on an effort to develop adequate legislation, as it is seen as less important.

This has a consequence that since the likely most important factors in determining whether there is adequate legislation is the existence of a bio-industry and especially whether a state has the resources and expertise to develop the necessary legislation, a focus needs to be put on supporting developing states in developing adequate legislation. This has long already been recognized by the ISU and the 1540 Committee; however, there is still limited resources and active support. If states are serious about ensuring an universal framework preventing biological weapons proliferation and use, more significant support needs to be offered. A beneficial development that is currently underway is the UNIDIR and VERTIC database of national legislation, which can form a significant resource for states seeking to develop legislation, as it will allow for a consideration of best practices. It is very important that such efforts are expanded upon and more support is provided if there is a desire to ensure a full implementation of the BWC.

CHAPTER 11

The Biological Weapons Convention's Article V Dispute Resolution Mechanism

Robert Lawless

1 Introduction

In June 2022, Russia initiated a Formal Consultative Meeting pursuant to Article V of the Biological Weapons Convention (BWC). According to Russia, the purpose of the Meeting was to address unanswered questions about the collaboration between the United States and Ukraine on the alleged development of biological weapons in Ukrainian scientific laboratories in violation of the BWC. The United States and Ukraine responded that Russia's allegations were unsubstantiated and merely were an attempt to spread false claims as part of a broader Russian disinformation campaign, as well as to distract the international community from Russia's unlawful aggressive war in Ukraine.

In this article, I examine the Article V Formal Consultative Meeting process. In the next section, I provide an overview of the BWC. In Section 3, I explore the dispute resolution mechanism established in Article V of the Convention. I explain the historical development of the Article V process, including the single pre-2022 example of the mechanism's employment (involving Cuba's allegations against the United States). In Section 4, I discuss the 2022 Formal Consultative Meeting in Geneva as an example of the Article V process in action. In Section 5, I conclude by highlighting the role of the Article V process in the larger context of efforts to prevent biological warfare. I especially note the importance of the distinction between 'hard law' and 'soft law', the Convention as an example of both kinds in action.

2 The Prohibition of Biological Weapons

2.1 *Overview of the BWC*

The BWC, completed in 1971, was the result of a three-year negotiation among states at the Conference of the Committee on Disarmament.[1] Currently, the

1 Convention on the Prohibition of the Development, Production and Stockpiling of Bacteriological (Biological) and Toxin Weapons and on Their Destruction [1972] United Nations

 | DOI:10.1163/9789004739192_012

Convention has 183 states parties, including the United States, Ukraine, and Russia, as well as four state signatories.[2] States parties to the Convention have four main obligations. First, states are prohibited from developing, producing, stockpiling, acquiring, or retaining biological weapons.[3] Second, for those states that had biological weapons programs, the Convention requires their destruction, or else the diversion of such programs to peaceful purposes.[4] Third, states are prohibited from transferring biological weapons to others, or assisting or encouraging the development or acquisition of biological weapons.[5] Finally, obligates states to facilitate the furtherance of peaceful biological materials and information to ensure international cooperation toward discoveries in the biological sciences.[6]

In addition to these obligations, the BWC established a basic control and dispute resolution structure. Within this structure, states 'undertake to consult one another and to cooperate in solving any problems which may arise' under the Convention.[7] Establishing what has become known as the Formal Consultative Meeting, this mechanism constitutes the Convention's only internal dispute resolution procedure. As I discuss further below, during periodic Review Conferences and through subsequent practice, states have

---

Treaty Series, Vol. 1015, page 163 [hereinafter BWC]. The Convention was opened for signature on April 10, 1972 and entered into force on March 26, 1975. United Nations Office for Disarmament Affairs, 'Biological Weapons Convention', <https://disarmament.unoda.org/biological-weapons> (accessed 4 April 2024).

2 International Committee of the Red Cross, 'Treaties and States Parties: Biological Weapons Convention' <https://ihl-databases.icrc.org/en/ihl-treaties/bwc-1972/state-parties?activeTab=default> (accessed 4 April 2024). The BWC is not the only international law governing biological weapons. In 1925, a League of Nations convention concluded the Geneva Gas Protocol, which expressly prohibits the use of 'bacteriological methods of warfare'. Protocol for the Prohibition of the Use of Asphyxiating, Poisonous or Other Gases, and of Bacteriological Methods of Warfare, [1925] League of Nations Treaty Series, Vol. 94, page 65.

3 BWC (n 3), art. I. I will return to Article I to examine it more closely. It does not refer expressly to 'biological weapons', but rather to 'biological agents', 'toxins', and weapons and other equipment designed to use such agents or toxins in hostile ways or in war. Ibid.

4 Ibid., art. II.

5 Ibid., art. III.

6 Ibid., art. X. This provision was designed 'to avoid hampering the economic and technological development of States Parties to the Convention or international cooperation in the field of peaceful bacteriological (biological) activities, including the international exchange of bacteriological (biological) agents and toxins and equipment for the processing, use or production of bacteriological (biological) agents and toxins for peaceful purposes in accordance with the provisions of the Convention.' Ibid.

7 BWC (n 3), art. V.

developed procedures for carrying out cooperative meetings under Article V of the Convention.

2.2 *The Article I Prohibition*

Article I prohibits 'microbial or other biological agents', as well as 'toxins whatever their origin or method of production'.[8] The prohibition is limited to types and quantities of such agents and toxins having 'no justification for prophylactic, protective or other peaceful purposes'.[9] Beyond the agents and toxins themselves, Article I also prohibits 'weapons, equipment [and] means of delivery designed to use such agents or toxins' in war or other hostile ways.[10]

The Convention does not define 'microbial agents' or 'other biological agents'.[11] The standard approach to treaty interpretation instructs the reader to consult the ordinary meaning of the term in question 'in their context and in the light of [the treaty's] object and purpose'.[12] Thus, the preambular references to biological 'weapons' suggests that Article I refers to agents designed to cause direct harm to an identified or known target.[13] Moreover, the Convention's apparent inclusion of biological weapons within the broader category of 'weapons of mass destruction' signifies the intention to address a class of weapons that are particularly dangerous and capable of causing widespread and indiscriminately harmful effects.[14]

Throughout the negotiation of the Convention, states regularly referred to a 1969 report produced by the United Nations Secretary General on 'chemical

---

8 Ibid., art. I. The Convention does not expressly prohibit the 'use' of such agents or toxins, but only their development, production, stockpiling, acquisition, and retention. Ibid., The 1925 Geneva Gas Protocol prohibits 'the use of bacteriological methods of warfare'.

9 BWC (n 3), art. I.

10 Ibid.

11 This paper concerns the prohibition against biological weapons and therefore will largely set aside questions related to prohibited toxins.

12 Vienna Convention on the Law of Treaties (1969), art. 31(1), United Nations Treaty Series, vol. 1155, page 331. I will forego trying to ascertain the ordinary meaning of 'microbial agents' or 'other biological agents' without regard to contextual factors or the treaty's object and purpose. Even if it were possible to do so, Article 31(1) of the Vienna Convention does not demand this approach. Indeed, it seems to reject this approach. Richard K. Gardiner, *Treaty Interpretation* 10 (Oxford University Press, 2nd ed., 2015) (finding that the Vienna Convention calls for a 'crucible' approach that rejects a hierarchy of interpretive elements).

13 Vienna Convention (n 31), art. 31(2) ('The context for the purpose of the interpretation of a treaty shall comprise, in addition to the text, *including its preamble* and annexes ...'.) (emphasis added). Neither international law.

14 See BWC (n 3), preamble.

and bacteriological (biological) weapons and the effects of their possible use'.[15] The report, which was clearly influential in negotiators' thinking,[16] defined 'bacteriological (biological) agents of warfare' as 'living organisms, whatever their nature, or infective material derived from them, which are intended to cause disease or death in man, animals or plants, and which depend for their effects on their ability to multiply in the person, animal or plant attacked'.[17]

The negotiators of the BWC also frequently references and relied upon a 1970 report by the World Health Organization on chemical and biological weapons.[18] In the report, 'biological agents' are defined as 'those that depend for their effects on multiplication within the target organism, and are intended for use in war to cause disease or death in man, animals or plants'.[19] As was the case with the 1969 Secretary General report, this definition centers the weaponized use of bacteriological agents and other biological agents against living objects under the BWC.

3 Article V Mechanism

Article V of the BWC provides a means for states parties to consult and cooperate in resolving disputes that arise under the Convention.[20] The Convention does not clarify the form and procedures of such consultations. Over time, states parties have developed the Article V mechanism through discussions at the review conferences of states parties to the convention, which have

15 United Nations Secretary General, Report of the Secretary General on Chemical and Bacteriological (Biological) Weapons and the Effects of Their Possible Use, UN Doc. S/9292 (UN Security Council, 1 July 1969).

16 For example, see Remarks of Canadian Delegate, Verbatim Record of the Four Hundred and Ninety-Sixth Meeting of the Conference of the Committee on Disarmament, UN Doc. CCD/PV.496, para. 46 (25 February 1971).

17 Secretary General's Report (n 36), 6.

18 World Health Organization, Health Aspects of Chemical and Biological Weapons (World Health Organization, Geneva, 1970). For an example of reliance upon the WHO Report during the treaty negotiation, see Remarks of Italian Delegate, Verbatim Record of the Five Hundred and Twelfth Meeting of the Conference of the Committee on Disarmament, UN Doc. CCD/PV.512, para. 12 (29 April 1971).

19 WHO Report (n 39), 12.

20 Article V also allows for states parties to resolve disputes 'through appropriate international procedures within the framework of the United Nations and in accordance with its Charter'. BWC (n 3), art. V. In this article, I focus on the former and set aside the possibility of the latter.

been convened roughly every five years since the Convention entered into force.

At the Second Review Conference of 1986, states parties agreed that the Article v consultation mechanism conferred a 'right' upon any state party to request 'a consultative meeting … at the expert level'.[21] Furthermore, states determined that any state requesting an Article v consultative meeting was entitled to have one convened[22] and asserted that other states parties were required to cooperate with any such meeting.[23] States also clarified the ends to which a consultative meeting may be put. In addition to resolving problems arising under the Convention, such ends may include determining 'ways and means for further clarifying, *inter alia*, with assistance of technical experts, any matter considered ambiguous or unresolved' under the Convention.[24]

States further developed the Article v consultation mechanism at the Third Review Conference of 1991. States parties asserted that a consultative meeting 'could be preceded by bilateral or other consultations by agreement among those states parties involved in the problems which had arisen'.[25] Any request for a consultative meeting under Article v would have to be 'addressed to the Depositaries' established in the Convention.[26] The latter would then 'immediately inform all states parties of the request' and 'convene within 30 days an informal meeting of interested states parties to discuss the arrangements for the formal consultative meeting'.[27] The formal consultative meeting would have to be 'convened within 60 days of receipt of the request'.[28] Furthermore, states determined that an Article v consultative meeting would 'proceed in accordance with rule 28 of the rules of procedure of the Review Conference'.[29]

States may meet bilaterally to resolve disputes or disagreements about the application of the Convention. For example, prior to Russia's multilateral Formal Consultative Meeting, in June 2022 Russia informally consulted the

21 Final Declaration of the Second Review Conference of the Parties to the BWC 5, BWC/CONF.II/13/II, in Final Document of the Second Review Conference of the Parties to the BWC, BWC/CONF/II/13 (30 September 1986).

22 Ibid.

23 Ibid., 6.

24 Ibid., 5.

25 Final Declaration of the Third Review Conference of the Parties to the BWC 15, in Final Document to the Third Review Conference of the Parties to the BWC, BWC/CONF.III/23 (1992).

26 Ibid.

27 Ibid.

28 Ibid.

29 Ibid., 16. Rule 28 is set out on pages 237–238 of the Third Review Conference's Final Document.

United States and Ukraine – each bilaterally – to raise concerns about their biological research activities in Ukraine.[30] As with cooperative meetings, such consultations aimed at dispute resolution fall under Article v, which may be marshaled toward 'solving any problems' that arise under the Convention.[31] Given the informal nature of bilateral consultations under Article v, it is difficult to determine how often states resort to such meetings.[32]

States may also resort to the Article v mechanism as a multilateral Formal Consultative Meeting. Prior to 2022, states had used the formal mechanism only once. On April 29, 1997, Cuba's representative at the United Nations presented to the U.N. Secretary-General a note verbale in which it accused the United States of releasing *thrips palmi*, an insect that targets crops, on Cuban territory.[33] Subsequently, Cuba requested a Formal Consultative Meeting under Article v to address its allegation against the United States.[34] In August 1997, states parties convened to discuss the allegations.[35]

The note verbale detailed the Cuban investigation and concluded that Cuba had 'once again been the target of biological aggression'. The United States 'categorically denie[d]' Cuba's allegation, which it called 'outrageous'.[36] Referring to Cuba's charge as 'deliberate disinformation', a US. State Depart-

---

30 Filippa Lentzos and Tancredi Francese, 'Biological Weapons Convention: In the Crosshairs of Geopolitical Tensions, Part 1' (*Georgetown Journal of International Affairs* 17 May 2023) <https://gjia.georgetown.edu/2023/05/17/biological-weapons-convention-in-the-crosshairs-of-geopolitical-tensions-part-1>

31 BWC (n 3), art. v. Notably, such informal, bilateral consultations need not precede a request for a Formal Consultative Meeting under Article v. Final Document of the Third Review Conference (n 47) 15 (asserting that a Formal Consultative Meeting '*could be* preceded by bilateral or other consultations') (emphasis added).

32 As an example of informal, bilateral consultation under Article v, one study notes a meeting between the United States and the Union of Soviet Socialist Republics in which the two states discussed a 1979 outbreak of anthrax in Sverdlovsk. James Revill, 'The Past, Present and Future of BWC Article v Consultations, United Nations Institute for Disarmament Research' (*UNIDIR*, 27 July 2022) <https://unidir.org/the-past-present-and-future-of-bwc-article-v-consultations>.

33 Note Verbale Dated 28 April 1997 from the Permanent Mission of Cuba to the United Nations Addressed to the Secretary-General, UN Doc. A/52/128 (29 April 1997).

34 Declan Butler, 'U.S.-Cuba Row Over Insects Goes to Weapons Meeting' (1997) 388 *Nature* 705, 705.

35 Report of the Formal Consultative Meeting of States Parties to the Convention on the Prohibition of the Development, Production and Stockpiling of Bacteriological (Biological) and Toxin Weapons and on Their Destruction, para. 1, Doc. No. BWC/CONS/1 (29 August 1997).

36 John Dinger, 'Press Statement: Cuba: No Use of Biological Weapons' (US. Department of State, 6 May 1997) <https://1997-2001.state.gov/briefings/statements/970506c.html>.

ment spokesperson asserted that the 'United States has not engaged in any act which would be in violation of [its] obligations under' the BWC.[37]

Eighty-one states parties, including the United States and Cuba, attended the Meeting,[38] which was chaired by a representative of the United Kingdom and vice-chaired by six elected representatives of states parties in attendance.[39] Over the course of three days, delegations from Cuba and the United State each delivered formal statements to the group of participating states.[40] Following these statements, a plenary discussion was held in which states parties 'welcomed the fact that the delegations of Cuba and the United States had sought to clarify their positions'.[41] At the conclusion of the meeting, although the group was split as to the correct factual conclusions to draw from the discussion, it was concluded that 'there ha[d] been general agreement throughout the process that the requirements of Article V of the Convention and of the consultative process … [were] fulfilled in an impartial and transparent manner'[42] and 'lacking in objectivity', Cuba declared that the concerns it expressed had not been dispelled.[43] Following Cuba's response, the chair met in person with Cuba's Deputy Minister of Foreign Affairs, at which meeting the Deputy Minister 'reiterated that her Government continued to adhere to the suspicions which had given rise to the original complaint'.[44] The chair and vice chairs then met to consider the additional filings. The group was split, with some sharing the US. view that 'no causal link' had been established between the United States and the alleged infestation, and others stating that the 'technical complexity of the issue and the lack of further detailed information made it impossible to draw any definitive conclusions'.[45]

4 The 2022 Formal Consultative Meeting in Geneva

In March 2022, still in the initial phase of its invasion of Ukraine, Russia claimed to have found evidence that the United States and Ukraine developed

37 Ibid.

38 Ibid., para. 2. Three additional signatory states also participated in the Meeting. Ibid.

39 Ibid., para. 1. The elected vice chairs were representatives from Brazil, Canada, Iran, the Netherlands, Nigeria, and Russia. Ibid.

40 Ibid., para. 3.

41 Ibid., para. 4.

42 Ibid.

43 Ibid.

44 Ibid.

45 Ibid.

biological weapons in violation of international law. Russia publicly asserted it found 'evidence of an emergency clean-up performed by the Kiev regime', which was 'aimed at eradicating traces of the military-biological program, in Ukraine, financed by' the US. Department of Defense.[46] A spokeswoman for the US. White House called the Russian claims 'preposterous' and responded that it 'does not develop or possess [biological] weapons anywhere'.[47]

On June 13, 2022, Russia submitted diplomatic notes to the United States and Ukraine detailing concerns about their compliance with the BWC.[48] On June 29, asserting it had not received the 'necessary explanations', Russia requested a formal consultative meeting under Article V of the BWC.[49] The meeting would aim at 'resolving the issues with the United States and Ukraine regarding their compliance' with the Convention 'in the context of operation of biological laboratories in the Ukrainian territory'.[50] The Formal Consultative Meeting requested by Russia took place in Geneva over the course of five days in August and September 2022.[51] Attendance was limited to states parties and signatory states to the BWC.[52] The meeting was attended by more than eighty states, including, Russia, the United States, and Ukraine.[53]

As detailed in documents submitted to the United States and Ukraine, Russia claimed to have uncovered evidence in Ukraine of US. 'military biological activities' that violate the Convention.[54] Russia alleged to have found evidence of laboratory research on an 'assortment and accumulated volumes of bio-

---

46 Ministry of Foreign Affairs, Russian Federation (*Twitter*, 6 March 2022) <https://twitter.com/mfa_russia/status/1500539810418671626?s=20&t=ky-wlRryBCakXi8Y62UiOg>.

47 Edward Wong, 'US. Fights Bioweapons Disinformation Pushed by Russia and China' (*N.Y. Times*, 10 March 2022) <https://www.nytimes.com/2022/03/10/us/politics/russia-ukraine-china-bioweapons.html>.

48 Bilateral Diplomatic Exchanges between the United States and the Russian Federation Preceding the Russian Federation's Request for an Article V Consultative Meeting 5, Formal Consultative Meeting of the States Parties to the BWC, BWC/CONS/2022/WP.51 (9 September 2022).

49 Bilateral Diplomatic Exchanges (n 87), 41.

50 Ibid.

51 Letter from the BWC Implementation Support Unit to the Permanent Representatives of the States Parties and Signatory States to the BWC, BWC – Formal Consultative Meeting Database (5 August 2022) <https://meetings.unoda.org/meeting/65052/documents> (accessed 4 April 2024).

52 Ibid.

53 List of Participants, Formal Consultative Meeting of the States Parties to the BWC, BWC/CONS/2022/INF.1 (13 September 2022).

54 Statement by the Head of the Delegation of the Russian Federation, Formal Consultative Meeting of the States Parties to the BWC, para. 3, BWC/CONS/2022/WP.6 (6 September 2022).

logical agents' which 'cast doubt as to their intended use for preventive, protective or other peaceful purposes'.[55] These agents include anthrax, brucellosis, tularemia, cholera,[56] tick-borne encephalitis viruses, and unidentified arthroviruses.[57]

Russia was particularly forceful in arguing that biological warfare research activities in Ukraine were done at the bequest of the United States. Russia alleged that Ukrainian research focused on 'only those infections considered a priority' by the US. Defense Threat Reduction Agency,[58] which 'implie[d] a situation where the objects of research [were] pathogens that [were] of interest to the Pentagon's DTRA, but, in fact, [were] not current threats to Ukrainian health care'.[59] Russia directed certain allegations directly at the United States. For example, it assailed US. interest in the study of 'rickettsiae and tick-borne encephalitis virus in arthropods in northwestern Ukraine'.[60]

Claiming to have found evidence of these activities during its 'special military operation in Ukraine', Russia summarized its allegations by noting its general concerns regarding US. 'military biological activities' outside US. territory, including 'in laboratories in the territories of the former Soviet Union Republics in the vicinity of Russian borders, with direct assistance and participation of military agencies and affiliated organizations'.[61] Russia asserted that such activities by the United States and, in this case, Ukraine constituted violations of their obligations under the BWC.[62]

---

55 Russian Federation, Questions to Ukraine Regarding Compliance with Obligations Under Party 1 of Article I of the BWC in the Context of Activities of Biological Laboratories, Formal Consultative Meeting of the States Parties to the BWC, para. 12, BWC/CONS/2022/WP.7 (6 September 2022).

56 Ibid., para. 8.

57 Ibid., para. 9.

58 Russian Federation, Questions to Ukraine, BWC/CONS/2022/WP.7 (n 98), para. 20.

59 Ibid., para. 21. Russia argued that a 2018 agreement between the United States and Ukraine created the 'basis for direct interaction in the biological sphere between the US. and Ukrainian defense agencies' and provided funding from the Defense Threat Research Agency for Ukrainian research facilities. Russian Federation, Questions for the United States Regarding Compliance with Obligations Under Article IV of the BWC in the Context of Activities of Biological Laboratories in Ukrainian Territory, para. 8, BWC/CONS/2022/WP.11 (6 September 2022). According to Russia, under the 2018 agreement, the US. Department of Defense was 'tasked with setting objectives' for Ukrainian research projects and 'determining lists of necessary equipment'. Ibid., para. 11.

60 Russian Federation, Questions for the United States, BWC/CONS/2022/WP.11 (n 109), para. 14.

61 Statement by the Head of the Delegation of the Russian Federation (n. 97), para. 3.

62 Ibid., para. 6.

The heart of the US. and Ukrainian response to Russian allegations was to deny any effort to research and develop biological weapons and instead assert the existence of a collaborative research effort to address international health risks. For its part, Ukraine described the relevant US.-Ukraine agreements as concerned with providing a 'framework for cooperation'[63] directed at 'countering biological threats', specifically 'consolidation of strains and their management in secure centralized laboratories'.[64] Ukraine rejected the allegation that any of its research and US. collaboration was 'indicative of malign intent' and asserted that the Russia 'concocted' these allegations 'during the unjustified and unprovoked full-scale war of aggression' against Ukraine as part of a 'powerful disinformation' campaign.[65]

Similarly, the United States asserted it was in full compliance with obligations under the BWC, declaring unconditionally that the US. 'Department of Defense does not engage in, support, or condone the development of biological weapons. Not in the United States, not in Ukraine, and not anywhere else in the world'.[66] The United States justified its activities in Ukraine – and elsewhere – as in conformity with Article X of the Convention.[67] The DoD-supported initiatives 'play a critical role in improving human and animal health in Ukraine'.[68] It rejected Russia's claim that 'any public health assistance by the Department of Defense is suspicious'[69] and 'must inherently be for some secretive purpose'.[70]

In sum, the United States admonished Russia for 'mischaracterizing' US. biological research activities and for drawing 'little or no connection' between its factual assertions and legal compliance issues related to the BWC.[71] As one

63 Ukraine, Presentation on Biological and Toxin Weapons Convention Article V Consulta-[illegible] Meeting of the States Parties to the BWC 6, BWC/CONS/2022/WP.24 6 September 2022).

64 Ibid., 7.

65 Statement of Ambassador Yurri Klymenko, Head of Delegation of Ukraine, Formal Consultative Meeting of the States Parties to the BWC, para. 4, BWC/CONS/2022/WP.21 (6 September 2022).

66 Kingston Reif, Statement to the Article V Consultative Meeting under the BWC, paras, 3, 4, BWC/CONS/2022/WP.23 6 September 2022).

67 Ibid., para. 37.

68 Ibid., para. 5.

69 Ibid., para. 7.

70 Ibid., para. 8.

71 United States of America, Response by the United States of America to the Request by the Russian Federation for a Consultative Meeting under Article V of the BWC, Formal Consultative Meeting of the States Parties to the BWC, para. 2, BWC/CONS/2022/WP.4 (5 September 2022).

example, the United States explained that personnel in Ukraine that Russia referred to as 'biological weapons experts' were in fact diplomatic and project management personnel performing duties under publicly available agreements to ensure biological clinical samples were safely collected, stored, and transported.

As noted previously, more than eighty states attended the Geneva Meeting. The international politics of the moment are inescapably present in states' submissions, virtually all of which suggest a predetermined posture toward the US.-Russia dispute based less on the merits of the arguments than on politics, international relations, and the context of Russia's war in Ukraine. For example, in its national statement submitted to the Meeting, Australia accused Russia of 'blatant disinformation' to, *inter alia*, 'distract from [its] own illegal, immoral aggression against the people of Ukraine'.[72] Likewise, Iran found space in its national statement to suggest that the United States allowed 'politics' to intrude into 'humanitarian' efforts, accusing the United States during the COVID pandemic of disguising within public health policy certain 'Unilateral Coercive Measures against targeted nations'.[73]

Political discourse on tangential issues notwithstanding, at the Geneva Meeting states were eager to express their strong support of non-proliferation policies, in particular those related to the prohibition of biological warfare. States asserted their commitment to 'full and universal implementation of the provisions of the BWC'.[74] For example, calling for robust international support for the Convention, Ireland asserted that the 'use of biological agents or toxins as instruments of war is abhorrent and there can be no impunity for those who would seek to use them'.[75] Likewise, Poland called the Convention 'one of the most important disarmament agreements',[76] emphasizing that 'absolute compliance with its provisions is crucial to international peace and security'.[77]

72 National Statement of Australia, Formal Consultative Meeting of the States Parties to the BWC, para. 6, BWC/CONS/2022/WP.29 (7 September 2022).

73 Mehdi Aliabadi, Statement of the Islamic Republic of Iran to the United Nations and Other International Organizations in Geneva, Formal Consultative Meeting of the States Parties to the BWC, para. 10, BWC/CONS/2022/WP.65 (12 September 2022).

74 Henrik Yeritsyan, National Statement of Armenia, Formal Consultative Meeting of the States Parties to the BWC, para. 2, BWC/CONS/2022/WP.40 (7 September 2022).

75 Jamie Walsh, National Statement of Ireland, Formal Consultative Meeting of the States Parties to the BWC, para. 3, BWC/CONS/2022/WP.33 (7 September 2022).

76 National Statement of Poland, Formal Consultative Meeting of the States Parties to the BWC, para. 2, BWC/CONS/2022/WP.49 (9 September 2022).

77 Ibid., para. 3.

5 Key Takeaways from the Article v Meeting

While the political moment was evidently reflected in the Geneva Meeting records, the Meeting nonetheless also embodied a significant normative dimension. In this section, I will highlight a few aspects of how the Meeting fits within the broader context of efforts to prevent biological warfare.

First, the Meeting records clearly embody states' commitment to the BWC as a general legal prohibition against biological warfare. Throughout the discussion, despite their deep-seated differences regarding the facts, Russia, the United States, Ukraine, and the other attending states returned to their concerns about the development of biological weapons. Likewise, other states, despite their political affiliations, were insistent on condemning any recourse by states or other to biological warfare.

Of course, any argument that the Geneva Meeting reinforced the norms against biological warfare must grapple with the undeniable questions it raises about the participants' bad faith engagement with the Meeting discussion's factual predicate. Clearly, it is a vast factual gulf between Russia's allegations, on the one hand, and the United States' and Ukraine's, on the other. Sceptics no doubt will point toward the Meeting's factual gap as strong evidence that at least one side of the debate – most would likely say Russia – was not employing the Article v Formal Consultative Meeting process in good faith. Indeed, several states argued during the meeting that misuse or abuse of the BWC procedures could undermine its normative integrity. As Norway said in its national statement, Russia's 'abuse' of 'one of the [Convention's] few essential mechanisms' risks damaging the Convention's 'integrity'.[78]

No doubt states, especially powerful ones, routinely instrumentalize international law. However, notwithstanding such misuses and abuses of international law, the 2022 Article v Meeting in Geneva [illegible] effort of all participant states to confirm a normative commitment against biological weapons and warfare.

Additionally, the Geneva Meeting discussions highlight the distinction between states' use of 'hard law' and 'soft law. It is uncontroversial that treaties establishing review mechanisms and dispute resolution procedures rely on both 'hard law' (for example, substantive prohibitions contained within the treaty) as well as 'soft law' (for example, procedural rules established in meetings of states parties) in carrying out their activities. As an example of the use of 'soft law' during the Geneva Meeting, Russia challenged Ukraine's alleged

78 National Statement of Norway, Formal Consultative Meeting of the States Parties to the BWC, para. 11, BWC/CONS/2022/WP.55 (12 September 2022).

failure to disclose data related to research and funding by noting the BWC's 'confidence-building measures developed by states parties in order to prevent or reduce the occurrence of ambiguities, doubts and suspicions' about biological research activity.[79] Furthermore, the mere fact of robust attendance at the Geneva Meeting – more than eighty states participated – indicates a certain level of commitment to the 'soft law' procedural elements rounding out the Convention. We must not overlook the multi-normative character of this interaction between hard and soft law in the context of the Geneva Meeting and the Convention more broadly.

It is worth dwelling for a few moments further on this distinction between 'hard law' and 'soft law.' The distinction itself it sometimes problematic and leads to questions about meaning. For example, the term 'soft law' is used to mean different things.[80] Some simply refer to it as anything that does not constitute 'hard law'.[81] Others use it to refer to non-law, such as agreements governed by political or moral norms.[82] Additionally, questions arise as to whether and how far the distinction between 'hard law' and 'soft law' may be maintained.[83] Such a distinction, for example, suggests that states may intentionally and purposefully engage with one or the other form of law, and that such engagement has real-world or practical consequences regarding compliance, breach, and responsibility. These questions are difficult and remain open to debate.[84]

Nevertheless, the distinction between 'hard law' and 'soft law' is frequently made and reinforced and serves the purpose of highlighting the informal ways

79 Russian Federation, Questions to Ukraine Regarding Compliance with Obligations Under the BWC in the Context of the Activities of Biological Laboratories, para. 16, BWC/CONS/2022/WP.3 (15 September 2022). Russia continued, 'This raises the question of a violation of political obligations regarding the submission of data on confidence building measures adopted by the States Parties to the BTWC'. Ibid., para. 16.

80 Jan Klabbers, 'The Redundancy of Soft Law', 1996 Nordic Journal of International Law, vol. 65, 167–182.

81 Ibid., at 168.

82 Ibid.

83 Ibid., at 169.

84 See, for example, Jerzy Sztucki, 'Reflections on International 'Soft Law'', in Jan Ramberg et al. (eds.), Festskrift till Lars Hjerner: Studies in International Law, 549575 (Norstedts, Stockholm, 1990); Tadeusz Gruchalla-Wesierski, 'A Framework for Understanding "Soft Law"', McGill Law Journal, vol. 30, 37–88 (1984); Ignaz Seidl-Hohenveldern, 'International Economic "Soft Law"', Recuile des Cours de l'Academie de Droit International, vol. 163, 165–246 (1979); Alan Boyle, 'Soft Law in International Law-Making', in Malcolm David Evans (ed.), International Law, 118–136 (2010); C. M. Chinkin, 'The challenge of Soft Law: Development and Change in International Law', International & Comparative Law Quarterly, Vol. 38:4, 850–866 (1989).

in which international disputes are resolved in practice. Disputes about biological weapons and warfare, including the 2022 Formal Consultative Meeting, are a prime example of such efforts to resolve disputes. The Geneva meetings, as already discussed previously, incorporate several 'soft law' aspects, such as references to the Biological Threat Reduction Program and other global partnership initiatives. Although these programs and partnerships may qualify only as 'soft law', they are an important aspect of states' arguments about addressing disputes about and challenges regarding biological weapons.

Additionally, 'soft law' plays an important role in the larger context of biological disarmament and prevention of biological warfare. For example, states have developed Confidence Building Measures through the review conference meetings to develop voluntary commitments by states parties aimed at increasing transparency and reducing suspicions about biological weapons programs. States achieve this by committing to report on their research and funding for biological technology development efforts. Additionally, states rely on the efforts of non-state actors to contribute to developing the norms against biological weapons and warfare. These organizations include the International Committee of the Red Cross, which has repeatedly published guidance on strengthening preventive measures regarding biological weapons.[85] Finally, the scientific community has played a significant role in regulating and setting norms for biological weapons research. For example, the American Society for Microbiology urges members to comply with a 'Code of Ethics' to avoid research that could risk contributing to biological weapons proliferation.[86] The 2022 Geneva meetings included references to such scientific bodies and their role in controlling biological research and risks regarding dual-use technology.

Third, and by way of conclusion, it is worth examining the Geneva Meeting through the lens of the future of the BWC's normativity. The combination of states' recommitment to the Convention's core prohibition, along with emerging advances in biological technology, especially those technologies with potential military applications, raises the possibility of fragmentation in the law of biological warfare. One possible (although far from certain) future involves a divergence between states' normative approaches to core cases of biological warfare and penumbral cases. In such a scenario, states may continue to view

85 See, for example, 'Biological Weapons: Efforts Needed to Strengthen Preventive Measures Meeting of States Parties, 2013' (12 December 2013).

86 American Society for Microbiology, ASM Code of Ethics and Conduct, 13 December 2021 <https://asm.org/articles/ethics/coes/asm-code-of-ethics-and-conduct> (last visited 13 September 2024).

core cases as prohibited by the Convention, while taking a more permissive posture toward some military applications of emerging biological technology, which may potentially offer a much broader range of military effects than what is available today. Furthermore, such technologies may be employable militarily with fewer concerns about the widespread, indiscriminate, and massive scales of direct human harm involved in core cases of germ warfare.[87] The precise implications about potential fragmentation of the international law of biological warfare is beyond the scope of this paper. It is sufficient for present purposes to note the potential of such fragmentation. Furthermore, we must evaluate the risks of such fragmentation occurring against the desirability of what the Geneva Meeting reveals – a firm commitment by states to ensure a strong prohibitive norm against core cases of biological warfare.

---

87 Examples of potential military applications of emerging biological technologies include bio-sensors, bio-deception, and anti-materiel weapons designed to degrade military vehicles and equipment. For example, see Patrick Tucker, 'The US. Army Is Making Synthetic Biology a Priority' (*Defense One*, 1 July 2019) <https://www.defenseone.com/technology/2019/07/us-army-making-synthetic-biology-priority/158129>.

Index

www.ingramcontent.com/pod-product-compliance
Lightning Source LLC
Chambersburg PA
CBHW051358240926
51852CB00001B/59
9789004739185